ERRANS

Cultural Inquiry

EDITED BY CHRISTOPH F. E. HOLZHEY
AND MANUELE GRAGNOLATI

The series 'Cultural Inquiry' is dedicated to exploring how diverse cultures can be brought into fruitful rather than pernicious confrontation. Taking culture in a deliberately broad sense that also includes different discourses and disciplines, it aims to open up spaces of inquiry, experimentation, and intervention. Its emphasis lies in critical reflection and in identifying and highlighting contemporary issues and concerns, even in publications with a historical orientation. Following a decidedly cross-disciplinary approach, it seeks to enact and provoke transfers among the humanities, the natural and social sciences, and the arts. The series includes a plurality of methodologies and approaches, binding them through the tension of mutual confrontation and negotiation rather than through homogenization or exclusion.

Christoph F. E. Holzhey is the Founding Director of the ICI Berlin Institute for Cultural Inquiry. Manuele Gragnolati is Professor of Italian Literature at the Sorbonne Université in Paris and Associate Director of the ICI Berlin.

ERRANS
Going Astray, Being Adrift, Coming to Nothing

EDITED BY
CHRISTOPH F. E. HOLZHEY
ARND WEDEMEYER

ISBN (Hardcover): 978-3-96558-035-0
ISBN (Paperback): 978-3-96558-036-7
ISBN (PDF): 978-3-96558-037-4
ISBN (EPUB): 978-3-96558-038-1

Cultural Inquiry, 24
ISSN (Print): 2627-728X
ISSN (Online): 2627-731X

Bibliographical Information of the German National Library
The German National Library lists this publication in the Deutsche Nationalbibliografie (German National Bibliography); detailed bibliographic information is available online at http://dnb.d-nb.de.

© 2022 ICI Berlin Press

Cover design: Studio Bens

Except for images or otherwise noted, this publication is licensed under a Creative Commons Attribution-ShareAlike 4.0 International License. To view a copy of this license, visit: http://creativecommons.org/licenses/by-sa/4.0/.

In Europe, the paperback edition is printed by Lightning Source UK Ltd., Milton Keynes, UK. See the final page for further details.

The digital edition can be downloaded freely at: https://doi.org/10.37050/ci-24.

ICI Berlin Press is an imprint of
ICI gemeinnütziges Institut für Cultural Inquiry Berlin GmbH
Christinenstr. 18/19, Haus 8
D-10119 Berlin
publishing@ici-berlin.org
www.ici-berlin.org

Contents

'Submit Your References': Introduction
ARND WEDEMEYER   1

The Punakawans Make an Untimely Appearance:
In Praise of Caves, Shadows, and Fire (or A Response
to Plato's Doctrine of Truth)
PRECIOSA DE JOYA 19

The Animal That Laughs at Itself: False False Alarms
about the End of 'Man'
JAMES BURTON 49

Not Yet: Duration as Detour in
Emmanuelle Demoris's *Mafrouza* Cycle
ROSA BAROTSI 75

Incomplete and Self-Dismantling Structures:
The Built Space, the Text, the Body
ANTONIO CASTORE   93

Camera Fog; or, The Pendulum of Austerity
in Contemporary Portugal
MARIA JOSÉ DE ABREU 113

Rinko Kawauchi: Imperfect Photographs
CLARA MASNATTA 141

Inbuilt Errans: What Is and Is Not 'Radical Indifference'
ZAIRONG XIANG 159

Errant Counterpublics: 'Solidarność'
and the Politics of the Weak
EWA MAJEWSKA 177

'The Exile from the Law': Keeping and
Transgressing the Limits in Jewish Law
FEDERICO DAL BO 201

References 235
Notes on the Contributors 253
Index 257

'Submit Your References'
Introduction
ARND WEDEMEYER

We are constantly told to get lost — and not just in the unfriendly way. And we are very much celebrating our having gone astray with a new research interest, letting it take us far afield, its vagaries requiring many a detour, and in any case, the search itself is already marked by a necessary surrender to the inexhaustible intractabilities of our 'archive'. Exhortations of errancy, vindications of failure abound in a variety of critical discourses today — but they also do in self-help manuals, career-advice columns, and business mantras. The taste for a departure from progress and other teleologies, the fascination with disorder, unfocused modes of attention, or improvisational performances cuts across wide swaths of scholarly and activist discourses, practices in the arts, but also business, warfare, and politics. Is there a clear line, a fixed measure or threshold of 'negativity', that sets apart Samuel Beckett's notorious 'Fail again. Fail better' from the slightly menacing adage being handed around management tracts and leadership manuals: 'Failure itself may not be a catastrophe, but failure to learn from failure definitely is'?[1] And conversely one might ask whether radical

---

[1] On the memeification of the Beckett quote from *Worstward Ho* (New York: Grove, 1983), p. 7, see Mark O'Conell, 'The Stunning Success of "Fail Better": How Samuel Beckett Became Silicon Valley's Life Coach', *Slate*, 29 January 2014 <https://slate.com/culture/2014/01/samuel-becketts-quote-fail-better-becomes-the-mantra-of-silicon-valley.html> [accessed 31 May 2022].

critiques of ideals of productivity, success, and determination can ultimately amount to something other than the 'I would prefer not to' of Bartleby the scrivener,[2] 'the most implacable vindication of th[e] Nothing as pure, absolute potentiality'.[3] The crucial touchstone for this search proved to be Lauren Berlant's reflections on attachment's cruel time warps and the syntactically cooled distance she takes from Bartleby:

> Cruel optimism is [...] a concept pointing toward a mode of lived immanence, one that grows from a perception about the reasons people are not Bartleby, do not prefer to interfere with varieties of immiseration, but choose to ride the wave of the system of attachment that they are used to, to syncopate with it, or to be held in a relation of reciprocity, reconciliation, or resignation that does not mean defeat by it.[4]

~

In the fall of 2014, the ICI Berlin convened a group of scholars from a wide variety of disciplines and backgrounds to explore these questions over the course of two years. The starting assumption of their collective research project was, on the one hand, that many of the above-mentioned critical concerns of the day could be bundled and brought into focus using the Latin word *errāre*, its derivations, formations, and transmutations in several modern languages, but also, on the other, that this very rich word-field and its heterogenous history would provide the resources for a new and multiplicitous rethinking of phenomena and modalities of erring, of errors, errantries, and errancies across discourses, disciplines, and demarcations. The project, hence, was placed under the name 'ERRANS'.[5]

---

2   Herman Melville, 'Bartleby, the Scrivener', in Melville, *The Piazza Tales, and Other Prose Pieces, 1839–1860*, ed. by Harrison Hayford, Alma A. MacDougall, G. Thomas Tanselle, and others (Evanston, IL: Northwestern University Press, 1987), pp. 13–45.

3   Giorgio Agamben, 'Bartleby, or On Contingency', in Agamben, *Potentialities: Collected Essays in Philosophy*, ed. & trans. by Daniel Heller-Roazen (Stanford, CA: Stanford University Press, 1999), pp. 243–71 (pp. 253–54).

4   Lauren Berlant, *Cruel Optimism* (Durham, NC: Duke University Press, 2011), p. 28.

5   For a description of the project, related documentation of its activities, and an extensive video archive of its lecture series, see 'ERRANS, ICI Focus 2014-16', website of the ICI Berlin <https://www.ici-berlin.org/projects/errans-2014-16/> [accessed 2 May 2022].

The present volume features some of the work resulting from the varied activities of the research group, from weekly colloquia, reading groups, film screenings to intimate workshops and public conferences, but of course also reflects the individual research and commitments of its authors. It presents it in a form that will appear familiar if not trivial to some, a form that upon closer inspection invites a reflection on its entanglements with errancies and ambivalences — the form of what is commonly called an edited collection, something between a genre of scholarship and a publishing format, and one that has acquired a particularly bad reputation. A quick flashback to understand its discomfited situatedness within scholarly communication: Roughly with the beginning of the millennium, talk of a crisis in academic publishing had intensified. Complaints about this crisis certainly took note of the larger technological changes in book publishing — affecting commercial and academic, trade and university presses alike. Yet while the digital transformation challenged the existing formats of publishing at large, including those of newspapers and magazines, scholarly publishing was affected by new media and technologies in particular ways and was arguably facing more profound changes on several fronts — articulated and attenuated in the desperate pleas, presidential letters, reports, and special commissions of the professional associations of scholars across many disciplines of the humanities and social sciences (in particular those not entirely relying on journal publications),[6] but also registered

---

[6] In 2002, Stephen Greenblatt, in his capacity as president of the MLA (Modern Language Association) wrote an alarmist letter to his society's members, pointing out the economic underpinnings, but also the uneven ways in which different disciplines were affected by the crisis in academic publishing: 'Call for Action on Problems in Scholarly Book Publishing: A Special Letter from Stephen Greenblatt', 28 May 2002 <https://www.mla.org/Resources/Guidelines-and-Data/Reports-and-Professional-Guidelines/Publishing-and-Scholarship/Call-for-Action-on-Problems-in-Scholarly-Book-Publishing/A-Special-Letter-from-Stephen-Greenblatt> [accessed 20 April 2022]. The MLA formed an Ad Hoc Committee on the Future of Scholarly Publishing, which shortly thereafter published its report: 'The Future of Scholarly Publishing', *Profession 2002* (New York: MLA, 2002), pp. 172–86 <https://www.mla.org/Resources/Guidelines-and-Data/Reports-and-Professional-Guidelines/Publishing-and-Scholarship/The-Future-of-Scholarly-Publishing> [accessed 21 April 2022]. The AHA (American Historical Association) followed suit: James McPherson, 'From the President: A Crisis in Scholarly Publishing' and Robert B. Townsend, 'History and the Future of Scholarly Publishing', *Perspectives on History*, 41.7 (October 2003) <https://www.historians.org/publications-and-directories/perspectives-on-history/october-2003-x43317>

by academic librarians.⁷ The crisis was primarily understood as the result of a massive privatization and commercialization of scholarly communication, with dramatic price increases of institutional journal subscriptions eating into university library budgets — between 1982 and 2002, the prices of scientific and medical journals rose by 600% —,⁸ and an equally dramatic loss of profitability for book publications across the board, but in particular in smaller academic disciplines.⁹ These economic difficulties reflected a large-scale transformation of, as of today, still uncertain outcome.¹⁰ Modern scholarly communication has of course always been a commercialized (albeit generally subsidized) interaction between scholars, publishers, and libraries that at best amounted to a fragile equilibrium. In some privileged parts of the globe, the academic 'marketplace of ideas' could seem to constitute a short circuit or, to put it more politely, an 'ecology', inasmuch as larger universities would operate university presses publishing scholarly work to be sold to university libraries and assigned in university courses. Yet the large-scale defunding of higher education — arguably motivated politically more than economically — threatened the closed circuits of non-profit academic publishing. At the same time, universities were pressured to institute evaluative controls in their operations, mimicking the tools of financialization becoming ever more prevalent in corporate and political governance. These controls would consist in tracking the acquisition of research funds (with respect to the humanities, this was more decisive within European university systems),

---

and <https://www.historians.org/publications-and-directories/perspectives-on-history/october-2003/history-and-the-future-of-scholarly-publishing> [accessed 3 May 2022].

7 'Principles and Strategies for the Reform of Scholarly Communication 1', American Library Association, 1 September 2006 <https://www.ala.org/acrl/publications/whitepapers/principlesstrategies> [accessed 15 April 2022], which makes the crucial point that traditional arrangements of library access and intellectual property rights are being obviated by the digitization of scholarly communication, which submits access to contract rather than copyright law.

8 Townsend, 'History and the Future of Scholarly Publishing'.

9 Greenblatt, 'Call for Action'.

10 Lindsay Waters, executive editor of the Humanities at Harvard University Press, would register the collapse of the system despite appearances (i.e., the steady increase of academic publications): 'It is a paradoxical moment that is very hard to read, just like the last days predicted in the Bible.' Waters, *Enemies of Promise: Publishing, Perishing, and the Eclipse of Scholarship* (Chicago, IL: Prickly Paradigm Press, 2004), p. 3.

but also shaped the universities' hiring and promotion practices, relying on the quantification of 'output', efficiency, quality of teaching, etc., which in turn led to a dramatic overvaluation and fetishization of 'double blind peer-review' practices, which previously had largely been a way to manage publication decisions in large-scale, field-dominating journal publishing. As a result, the edited collection became marked as doubly undesirable: It is generally assumed to not have been peer-reviewed (blindly) and it comes as a *book* — and an undesirable one at that, with a severe disadvantage over monographs.[11] One might add that its loose boundaries also seemed to make it particularly vulnerable to the challenges of digitization, with the introduction of electronic reserves and made-to-order course packs making it increasingly unlikely for collections to serve as course material.

The denigration of the edited collection primarily registers in two areas: In the general unwillingness of university presses to publish them[12] and in the advice literature geared towards emerging scholars warning against them.[13] Any rehabilitation of the edited collection, thus, has to assuage young academics fearful that their publications only 'count' in peer-review journals or as monograph. Most commen-

---

11 Much of this seems strictly based on hearsay: 'Edited volumes are a curious hybrid. They are neither journal articles (although some may have chapters that have been recycled as journal articles), nor exclusively conference proceedings (although some may be), nor always representing original works. Long the stepsister of monographs, conventional wisdom had it that the printed edited volume sold less well than single-authored monographs.' Frances Pinter and Laura White, 'Development of Book Publishing Business Models and Financing', in *Academic and Professional Publishing*, ed. by Robert Campbell, Ed Pentz, and Ian Borthwick (Oxford: Chandos, 2012), pp. 171–93 (p. 187).

12 Two pick but two examples: Columbia University Press: '[W]e do not consider edited collections unless they are specifically designed for course use.' 'Manuscript Submissions', publisher's website <https://cup.columbia.edu/manuscript-submissions> [accessed 7 May 2022]; Harvard University Press: 'We do not publish original fiction, original poetry, religious inspiration or revelation, cookbooks, guidebooks, children's books, art and photography books, *Festschriften*, conference volumes, unrevised dissertations, or autobiographies.' 'Proposal Guidelines', publisher's website <https://www.hup.harvard.edu/resources/authors/proposal.html> [accessed 7 May 2022].

13 In particular junior faculty is routinely warned against getting involved in editing a collection in the strongest terms possible. To quote two bestsellers of the genre: Karen L. Kelsky, 'Should I Do an Edited Collection?', *The Professor Is In*, 24 July 2012 <https://theprofessorisin.com/2012/07/24/should-i-do-an-edited-collection/> [accessed 7 May 2022]. William Germano, 'Ten Reasons Why You Shouldn't', in Germano, *Getting It Published: A Guide for Scholars and Anyone Else Serious about Serious Books* (Chicago: University of Chicago Press, 2001), p. 123.

tators remark the absence of reliable studies of either the economic or scholarly value of edited collections, hence most defences rely on anecdotal evidence, marshalling the successes of exemplary edited collections that came to define a new discipline, paradigm, or a new generation of scholarship, though these 'successes' might well, in the long run, undermine themselves, inasmuch as the contributors of successful, that is, paradigm-shifting collections are more likely to reuse their contributions in single-author monographs that, in the long run, tend to become more canonical than the collection that might have functioned as an incubator of sorts.[14]

The occasional defences of the edited collection therefore have had to resort to other measures: For William Germano, former editor-in-chief at Columbia University Press and former publishing director at Routledge, the edited collection simply needs 'clear focus' and 'star power' to succeed.[15] For less cynical defenders the 'collection' is supposed to be justified by the genuine accumulation of knowledge it projects: 'Edited volumes tend to include reports on original research or they are commissioned instead of a single-author work because there is no one who knows enough in both breadth and depth to cover all the topics pulled together in the volume.'[16] In reality, however, this simple accumulation — or 'coverage' — is at issue in and guides the selection of contributors to only a few select subgenres of the edited collection: 'handbooks', 'companions', 'guide books', and similar enterprises that purport to exhaustively treat an author, a period, field, work, etc. As a weak criterion, of course, it should hold for any edited collection of research papers: It is indeed hard to imagine that an edited collection has ever been published that could have also been authored by a single person. These radically divergent spatial metaphors — the 'clear focus' guided by 'stars' against the 'breadth and depth' of a quilt of specialization— already signal the fundamental errantry of the col-

---

14   Edited collections have played a crucial role, for example, in Queer Theory. To pick but two relatively early examples filled with a disproportionate amount of material that would later become part of discipline-defining monographs: *Displacing Homophobia*, ed. by Ronald R. Butters, John M. Clum, and Michael Moon (Durham, NC: Duke University Press, 1990); *Fear of a Queer Planet: Queer Politics and Social Theory*, ed. by Michael Warner (Minneapolis: University of Minnesota Press, 1993).
15   Germano, *Getting It Published*, p. 146.
16   Pinter and White, 'Development of Book Publishing Business Models', p. 186.

lection. In most cases, contributions are 'collected' only in the weak sense that they are not assigned, and anyone with any familiarity with the process knows that a metaphor more suitable than 'coverage', let alone 'focus', would be that of scattering or dispersion. Why, then, is it so hard, even for the few who don't wish to dismiss edited collections in book form as a significant part of scholarly communication, to acknowledge their inherently unruly, errant, unpredictable nature? When William Germano refers to the fact that Italian title pages identify editors with the phrase 'a cura di ...', he quips about the phrase's 'overtones of medical assistance', which to him aptly describe the difficulties of compiling academic work.[17] But one might also take it as a hint that edited collections are shaped not by muscular research programmes, resolute marching orders for scientific avantgardes, but rather by a curatorial logic curiously disavowed among scholars.[18] Their construction principles are decidedly exogenous, their parts are not organized to amount to an integral whole but relate to one another according to varied contextual parameters or networked tangents.

The more ambitious defence of the edited collection Peter Webster has recently provided proceeds from the rather surprising fact that really all the scorn, all the dismissals directed at the format are based on absolutely no hard evidence whatsoever.[19] Indeed, many of the claims made can easily be refuted: there is no reason to assume that collections involve less peer review than journals; it is simply not the case that a publication in a collection is any less visible or less widely available as the same contribution would have been in a journal; and in terms of quantifiable evidence, citation indices are not showing any

---

17   Germano, *Getting It Published*, p. 141.
18   It is important to note, in this connection, that the focus on the disintegration of an alleged unity ('mono') of the book ('graph') — electronically or otherwise — has distracted from the perhaps much more consequential transformation, that of the library, that is, the spatial scatter of books responding to 'call numbers', into an algorithmically sequenced and mined blend of information streams. Curatorial operations in other practices have sought to very much define themselves in opposition to these transformations.
19   Peter Webster, *The Edited Collection: Pasts, Present, and Futures* (Cambridge: Cambridge University Press, 2020). See also the forum discussion, Peter Webster, Pat Thomson, and Mark Carrigan, 'Edited Collections May Still Have Much to Offer Academics in the Humanities and Social Sciences', *LSE Impact Blog*, London School of Economics, 23 July 2013 <https://blogs.lse.ac.uk/impactofsocialsciences/2013/07/23/in-defence-of-edited-collections/> [accessed 2 May 2022].

disadvantage of collected essays as opposed to those fed through journal pipelines.[20]

Yet in his considerations of the virtues of edited collections, Webster seems to acknowledge that it is impossible to justify the format by any reflection on its immanent form. He would rather we understand collections as representing and materializing scholarly communities and argues that it can foster a more collaborative enterprise, counteracting the competitiveness and hierarchization of the contemporary university, cultivating mutual obligation and extending, rather than merely reproducing, existing networks.[21] But for this 'communitarian' revaluation of a publishing format, Webster, too, needs to insist on a compactness of purpose, the coherence of contributions, the collaborative closure of the form. He therefore does not register the fact that perhaps the most puzzling aspect of the vilification of the edited collection — what Webster calls the 'meme complex' of unfounded prejudices — is the close correspondence of the format to the generally appreciated if not cherished forms of ad-hoc interdisciplinarity increasingly dominating the humanities and social sciences. Even more than the traditional (disciplinary) conference proceedings, the edited collection has become the go-to format for interdisciplinary work pursued in ever changing constellations within the universities and in their orbits. The conventional idea of interdisciplinarity, according to which scientific disciplines explore their shared border regions in order to ultimately establish a new discipline out of this multidisciplinary encounter, typically generates new journals as flag posts marking territorial gains. But the much more unpredictable, confusing, errant exchanges in the 'curated' encounters of many transdisciplinary networks, topic-based cohorts in societies of fellows, thematically bounded research centres, etc. tend to pool into edited collections.

---

20   These ideas ('the meme complex') are debunked at length in Webster, *The Edited Collection*, pp. 38–54.

21   Webster, *The Edited Collection*, p. 47. Webster's conception has decidedly more evidence-based substance than many of metaphorical associations of collections and sociability à la 'Academic communication is often likened to an ongoing conversation. The edited volume is an excellent forum where scholars can conduct such a conversation on a specific topic.' Andrea Hacker, 'In Defense of the Edited Book', *A Hacker's View*, blog, 3 December 2013 <http://www.andreahacker.com/in-defense-of-the-edited-book/> [accessed 2 May 2022].

Their fascination does not primarily result from collaborative exertion and mutual aide, but more often from the frictions or misalignments part and parcel of a non-territorial understanding of extra-disciplinary exploration. The 'success' of many edited collections might very well depend on its capacity not to survey or claim new fields, but to till the ground, to aerate rather than solidify, to suspend disciplinary intelligibilities, allowing itself to scatter.[22]

But Webster's insistence holds true: The exogenous nature of the edited collection refers to its reliance on and active transformation of scholarly sociabilities, whether they are institutionally fostered, based on solidarities, or threaded by affect.

This present volume, from 'within' which this reflection on the errancy of its form is undertaken, is, as indicated already, based on the temporally limited scholarly community of a group of twelve postdoctoral fellows who convened at the ICI Berlin to pursue their own research in collaboration, confrontation, corroboration, and conflict with one another and a collective question. It is based, hence, on a particularly intense form of scholarly community, compared, say, to academic conferences or even geographical dispersed research networks. And yet, the 'communal' aspect of the work gathered here will not be evident to the outsider. There is no 'division of labour', no relay, no platform. The notoriously errant question of influence rarely imposes itself, or one could say that mutual influence in this case is best thought of according to a model of marination.

This quite lengthy consideration of the scholarly genre of the collected edition was meant to sketch, on the one hand, how the project was understood to also always reflect on our own practices, including those configuring the institutional setting of the research project, and on the other hand, it also demonstrates that ERRANS has a way of practically peeling itself out of the most innocuous assumptions and everyday actions. This is to be blamed less on the fact that any lengthy pursuit ultimately tends to recognize its topic everywhere, then on the inherited (although often genealogically obscured) errantries of a

---

22 This insistence on a radical passivity of dispersion ought to credit Geoffrey Bennington's attempt to refine familiar critiques of teleology by following the word(s) 'scatter': *Scatter 1: The Politics of Politics in Foucault, Heidegger, and Derrida* (New York: Fordham University Press, 2016), in particular pp. 243–49.

certain kind of 'endeavouring' research. Michel Serres has tried to reconstruct a wider frame of this errancy in his *Troubadour of Knowledge*:

> [T]he philosopher who seeks [...] has chosen to wander [a choisi d'errer]. Wandering includes the risk of error and distraction. [L'errance comporte des risques d'erreur et d'égarement.] Where are you going? I don't know. Where are you coming from? I try not to remember. Through where do you pass? Everywhere and through as many places as possible, encyclopedically, but I try to forget. Refuse to recognize your references. [Décline tes références.]²³

ERRANS had started, as mentioned before, from the observation that the word-field surrounding the Latin *errāre* had generated a multiplicity of meanings strained by ever diverging valuations. Errors seem to call for correction. Even scientific vindications of the category of error and falsification nonetheless hold that errors are to be and over time have a good chance to be eliminated. And yet the historical epistemology of Georges Canguilhem has invited a more radical understanding of the ineluctability of error.²⁴ The medieval institutions of knight-errantry (alongside the troubadour's *trouver*), defining crucial conceptions of the epic still in play today, might seem foreign in a world in which the territorial enclosure of nation-states and the notion of 'real estate' largely go unquestioned, yet in decidedly less heroic registers, talk of nomadic errancies — of its strategic necessity, indisputable joys, and entanglement with fantasy — have proliferated.²⁵

---

23   Michel Serres, *Le Tiers-Instruit* (Paris: François Bourin, 1991), p. 155; English as Serres, *The Troubadour of Knowledge*, trans. by Sheila Faria Glaser and William Paulson (Ann Arbor: University of Michigan Press, 1997), p. 98. The translation, quite wonderfully, renders errantly: The quote's last sentence should also — or primarily — be translated simply as 'Submit your references.'

24   Samuel Talcott surveys the importance of error for Canguilhem: *Georges Canguilhem and the Problem of Error* (Cham: Palgrave Macmillan, 2019). The origin of the category in Canguilhem's engagement with French philosopher Alain's (Émile-August Chartier) subversion of Cartesianism is explored further in Michele Cammelli, *Canguilhem philosophe. Le Sujet et l'erreur*, preface by Etienne Balibar (Paris: PUF, 2022). On the surprising proximities of Donna J. Haraway's far-reaching work on the sciences and their histories to Canguilhem, see *Situiertes Wissen und regionale Epistemologie. Zur Aktualität Georges Canguilhems und Donna J. Haraways*, ed. by Astrid Deuber-Mankowsky and Christoph F. E. Holzhey (Vienna: Turia + Kant, 2013) <https://doi.org/10.37050/ci-07>.

25   This enthusiasm for the nomad was generated by the extraordinary revival of interest in the work Gilles Deleuze, which peaked, according to the Google N-Gram Viewer,

But idioms of failure, errancy, interruption, serendipity, metanoia have also entered common parlance in human resource departments, sugarcoating the systematic proliferation and instrumentalization of precarity and the circumvention of labour laws and protections. This corporate glorification of errantry has been filtered through the shifting discursive machinations of management and organization theory, leadership studies, military science, and self-improvement manuals, only to take on an even more threatening dimension in recent years. The end of the fellowship period, and with it the end of the ICI's first focus on ERRANS, in the summer of 2016 would coincide, with Clayton Christensen's concept of 'disruptive innovation',[26] having echoed through Silicon Valley for several years, being transposed into the realm of US-American presidential politics.[27] The very fact that the celebrations of 'heroic disruptors' frequently forget the technical specificities of Christensen's conception (and increasingly run counter to his own political inclinations, marked by his devout Mormonism), can be attributed to a widespread fascination with the destructive aspects of capitalism, which hears in 'disruptive innovations' vague resonances of Joseph Schumpeter's 'creative destruction' and the attendant hope that this destructive dynamic would ultimately dismantle the exist-

---

in 2013 (in English-language books, earlier in other European languages). See, in particular, Gilles Deleuze and Félix Guattari, *Mille plateaux. Capitalisme et schizophrénie* (Paris: Minuit, 1980), but notably also Rosi Braidotti, *Nomadic Theory: The Portable Rosi Braidotti* (New York: Columbia University Press, 2012) and, resituating errancy in the Carribean and other archipelagos in ways that have become wonderfully generative, Édouard Glissant, *Poetics of Relation*, trans. by Betsy Wing (Ann Arbor: University of Michigan Press, 1997).

26 Clayton M. Christensen and Joseph L. Bower, 'Disruptive Technologies: Catching the Wave', *Harvard Business Review*, 73.1 (January 1995), pp. 43–53 <https://hbr.org/1995/01/disruptive-technologies-catching-the-wave> [accessed 4 May 2022].

27 Sheldon Filger made this observation in September 2015 already: 'Donald Trump, Presidential Politics and the Art of Disruptive Innovation', *Huffpost*, blog, 23 September 2015 <https://www.huffpost.com/entry/donald-trump-presidential_b_8183138> [accessed April 27 2022]. At the same time, Christensen felt compelled to protest the misuse of his theories: Clayton M. Christensen, Michael E. Raynor, and Rory McDonald, 'What Is Disruptive Innovation?', *Harvard Business Review*, 93.12 (December 2015), pp. 44–53 <https://hbr.org/2015/12/what-is-disruptive-innovation> [accessed 10 May 2022], presumably also because, in the year prior, he had been prominently mocked by historian Jill Lepore, 'The Disruption Machine: What the Gospel of Innovation Gets Wrong', *The New Yorker*, 23 June 2014 <https://www.newyorker.com/magazine/2014/06/23/the-disruption-machine> [accessed 10 May 2022].

ing economic order.[28] Yet while 'disruption' — as it is used today — can also be seen as a camouflaged theory of market domination (and, under certain circumstances, an attack on democratic processes and the rule of law),[29] other mobilizations of errancy in management literature have included talk of a 'VUCA world' (volatility, uncertainty, complexity, ambiguity), a conception of somewhat uncertain origin. The approach or 'practical code' was, inasmuch as it can still be reconstructed today,[30] inspired by the post-Weberian reconfigurations of the sociology of organizations introduced by Warren Bennis and Burt Nanus in the 1980s in what came to be called 'New Leadership Studies' — emphasizing 'leadership' against the prevalent functionalism of management studies while committing to a post-hierarchical, 'democratic' fluidity of the concept of 'authority'.[31] Bennis and Nanus explicitly attacked the command-and-control approaches dominant in corporate management and other organizational structures. The four dimensions of VUCA were supposed to cast doubt on the reliance of traditional governance on rigid and determinable mechanisms of cause and effect. What is more remarkable, however, is the particularly errant trajectory of the conception: From the theoretical labs of

---

28   Joseph A. Schumpeter, *Capitalism, Socialism, and Democracy* (New York: Harper & Brothers, 1942). The resonance is noted in the magisterial Thomas McCraw, *Prophet of Innovation: Joseph Schumpeter and Creative Destruction* (Cambridge, MA: Harvard University Press, 2007), pp. 689–90, ftn. 10. The most recent, politically volatile standard bearers of these expectations have branded themselves 'accelerationists'.

29   For a glimpse of the Silicon climate created by such discussions, of considerable political consequence, see Drake Baer, 'Billionaire VC Peter Thiel Says Silicon Valley's "Obsession" with Disruption Is Totally Misguided', Business Insider, 18 September 2014 <https://www.businessinsider.com/peter-thiel-disruption-is-stupid-2014-9> [accessed 15 June 2022]. But these omnipresent obsessions are perhaps more efficiently reflected in popular culture's more recent archeologies, such as the TV series *WeCrashed*, created by Drew Crevello and Lee Eisenberg (Apple TV+, 2022–) or *Super Pumped*, created by Brian Koppelman and David Levien (Showtime, 2022–), reconstructing the rise (and fall) of the supposed disruptors WeWork and Uber, respectively.

30   'Q. Who First Originated the Term VUCA (Volatility, Uncertainty, Complexity and Ambiguity)?', website of the U.S. Army Heritage and Education Center at the U.S. Army War College, 22 November 2021 <https://usawc.libanswers.com/faq/84869> [accessed 23 January 2022].

31   Warren Bennis and Burt Nanus, *Leaders: The Strategies for Taking Charge* (New York: Harper & Row, 1985). Bennis had been considered a radical throughout the 1960s and 1970s, advocating for 'participatory management' and outright corporate 'democracy' in, for example, Warren Bennis and Philip Slater, 'Democracy Is Inevitable', *Harvard Business Review*, 42.2 (March–April 1964), pp. 51–59.

sociologically inspired organizational studies at MIT to the explosion of management literature in the 1980s, on to the US Army War College curriculum. The superior talent of the US military to create memorable acronyms seems responsible for enshrining the fourfold 'VUCA', but its career really took off with the loss of Cold War certainties at the end of the decade and the emergence of the so-called 'new wars' thereafter. Firing on the fuel of geostrategic uncertainties, VUCA reentered business guru stratospheres and has been spreading beyond warfare and management into higher education, philanthropy, environmental policy, linking up with newer buzzwords such as sustainability and resilience.[32]

In their 1999 *Le Nouvel Esprit du capitalisme*, Luc Boltanski and Ève Chiapello proceed from a discussion of corpora of management literature not unlike the ones invoked above. The book has been enormously influential, far beyond the confines of its discipline (sociology), dominating many discussions of the new century relating to, for example, contemporary art under capitalist regimes or structures of urbanization and gentrification. For Boltanski and Chiapello, their object of study, the tracts on management, serve as 'main vehicles for the diffusion and popularization of normative models in the world of enterprise', unburdened, they argue, by 'realism' and quintessentially hybrid, advising how to profit but also justifying profiting itself: 'In the manner of edifying books or manuals of moral instruction, they practice the *exemplum*.'[33] They compare two corpora, one from the 1960s, the other from the 1990s, in order to argue that even the most radically anti-capitalist impulses of the 1960s rebellion in both polit-

---

32 US military strategists were quick to credit the surprising successes of the Ukrainian military response to the Russian invasion of February 2022 to their having received, in the aftermath of the 2014 defeat, US military training, in particular with respect to 'battlefield decision-making', that is lower-ranked junior leadership making unauthorized decisions in what is considered in the Army's leadership courses extreme VUCA environments. By contrast, Russian difficulties were blamed on its continued reliance on command-and-control mechanisms, with logistical failures in particular attesting to what could be considered a non-VUCA-readiness of the Russian military. David Hersenhorn and Paul McLeary, 'Ukraine's "Iron General" is a Hero, But He's No Star', *Politico*, 8 April 2022 <https://www.politico.com/news/2022/04/08/ukraines-iron-general-zaluzhnyy-00023901> [accessed 9 May 2022].

33 Luc Boltanski and Ève Chiapello, *The New Spirit of Capitalism*, trans. by Gregory Elliott (London: Verso, 2005), p. 58.

ics ('social critique') and bohemian counterculture ('artistic critque') have been absorbed into what they synthesize as the 'new spirit' of capitalism.[34] This 'new spirit', for Boltanski and Chiapello, is marked by the eclipse of 'old' family structures, but also by a rhetoric flexibilization, a favouring of networks over hierarchies, creativity against bureaucracy. While this might seem to include, upon first inspection, the celebration of errancy in Christensen, Bennis, and Nanus, a focus on the idioms of 'innovative disruption' and 'VUCA worlds' might also call the overall construction of Boltanski and Chiapello into question: Their very framing clearly is designed to limit or even eliminate any errancy. This is accomplished by insisting that the literature in question has a clearly circumscribed, sociologically defined audience, the cadres or managerial class, that the change in question pivots around a singular unquestioned historical marker— May 1968 — that can be naturalized as a generational divide, and, perhaps the most fraught aspect of the project, results in a synthesis of a unified, singular 'spirit', attesting to a integrative, stabilizing power — in stark contrast to all post-Schumpeterian accounts — of capitalism. Seen in the light of the question of errancy, Boltanski's and Chiapello's account, however, appears not only as preoccupied with insulating itself from its 'ideological' object of study, not only as invested in a rigid homogenization, but as constituting an almost apotropaic ritual warding off the very errancy they seek to relegate to bohemian lifestyles, 'artistic critiques', the 'projective city'. This magical construction is supported by the totemic use of the ancestral founders of sociology (Max Weber, Émile Durkheim, et al.) throughout the book. To clarify: The critique here does not disagree with Boltanski's and Chiapello's skepticism concerning Bohemian critiques of capitalism — who could argue with that? —, but reflects on their inability or unwillingness to consider issues of errancy within a sociological research logic. Their confinement of erring is at issue, not their distaste for it.

These two reflections on errancy — an errancy hidden in edited collections such as this one, and another exhibited in a discourse ut-

---

[34] The reference here is, of course, to Max Weber, *The Protestant Ethic and the Spirit of Capitalism*, trans. by Talcott Parsons, foreword by R. H. Tawney (London: Allen & Unwin, 1930).

terly foreign to most scholars — are not only showing just how pervasive and far-reaching idioms of errancy have become or how confusing their genealogies can be. They also serve as signposts of the expansive reflections undertaken as part of the ICI project ERRANS and exemplified in the contributions to the present volume. One might seem embarrassingly intimate: the reflection on the difficult 'care work' part and parcel of scholarly communities and communications; the other threateningly alien: the sloganeering prophets of neoliberal labour or technologically determined posthumanism with their uncanny ability to err into view in many unsuspecting moments. Yet in one way or another, the contributions to this volume are marked by similar attempts to think radically different aspects of erring, errantry, errancy in conjunction, most crucially with an awareness of one's own implication in ERRANS, however partial that awareness will have to remain.

The first contribution of the book begins with a consideration of Javanese shadow puppet theatre, its extensive plotlines, exhaustive performances, its interludes and their unruly characters showing an exuberant disrespect bound to lodge the traditional cultural form in complicatedly resistant configurations. Preciosa de Joya follows these mobilizations of the grotesque off-stage and into political history, but she also mobilizes the ambling, loitering, explosive puppeteering to shuffle Western assumptions about the relationship between philosophy and theatre. If Plato's own shadow play has drawn the familiar frontlines in the West, other modes of theatre and theatricality allow the philosopher to reemerge on stage, as a trickster, a buffoon, androgynous, flatulent, and resolutely unassimilable.

Much like de Joya, James Burton is interested in the irreverent stakes of laughter. But in reviewing prominent modern theories of laughter, which are always also theories of indirection, he shows them to be haunted by extremely volatile moral-political valuations: Is laughter inherently cruel or liberating; is its function to destabilize unbearable orders or to exclude from them? Burton focuses the anthropological reflections inherent in theories of laughter on the universalizing camouflage they promote and calls into question these Eurocentric conceptions inasmuch as they rely on the dubious generality of 'Western Man' and his genealogies.

If the problem humour poses is that of the intractable ambivalence of deliberate misdirection, the emergence of what has frequently been called 'slow cinema' also deviates purposefully from traditional theatrical ideas of plot, drama, catharsis, or suspense. Rosa Barotsi considers the strategy of slowness and durational extremes as a detouring device, studying, in particular, the exemplary case of Emmanuelle Demoris's *Mafrouza* cycle (2007–2010), a sequence of five documentary films with a running of time of altogether twelve hours. Set in Mafrouza, a shanty town on the periphery of Alexandria built on or in an ancient cemetery, the films initially follow the lure of a cohabitation with the dead, but by giving room to the routines of Mafrouza's inhabitants, allow the temporal stasis of everyday life invade the screen and question the very preconditions of 'documentary' work.

Franz Kafka's late story 'The Burrow' — reflections on the life of a burrowing animal, its fears and tribulations, perhaps despair — famously presents a scenario of self-entrapment and paralysis, yet it also constitutes a vertiginous form of self-reflexive errancy and disorientation. Antonio Castore argues that the story and the subterranean labyrinth it describes needs to be seen within the context of classical modern reflections on architectural wholeness. In an astonishingly revealing comparison, Castore reads Kafka alongside Georg Simmel's sociological conception and Paul Valéry's poetics of architecture, presented in the polylogue *Eupalinos or the Architect*, carefully preparing an account of non-closure that doesn't not amount to openness.

The global turmoil of the financial markets in 2008 left Portugal, like several other European countries, in the chokehold of 'punishing' austerity measures, policies that treated massive hardships and precarities as collateral damage of 'necessary' economic 'reforms'. Maria José de Abreu presents a series of diverse individual fates in reported conversations, stressing the particular way in which the Portuguese case is lodged within history by tracking the economic legacies of the authoritarian, corporatist Salazarismo. Starting from the insight that neoliberal austerity can never be tallied as a simple contradiction, let alone a subtraction of the state, Abreu develops a complex toplogical model that seeks to account not only for the position of the state within the neoliberal crisis, but for the way in which these crises shape, twist, and transform the space of politics itself. This requires an attention, as well, to the cultural imagineries in which these deformations take hold. In a series of stunning photographs of Portuguese youth in fog-filled spaces, Inês d'Orey has mobilized the messianic dimension of Sebastianism — the expectation that the sixteenth-century Portuguese king Sebastian, who went missing during his Moroccan campaign, would return from the fog of Portugal's coastline.

In a not altogether dissimilar use of photography to question the conditions of visibility and legibility, the Japanese photographer Rinko Kawauchi has created an oeuvre in which photos are collected, yet not ordered, in large series, exhibited in parallel projections, but ultimately presented in book form. Clara Masnatta shows how these cloud-like assemblages question many of the commonplaces of the theory of photography, instead exploring the constitutive role of blurs, glitches, mistakes, and aleatoric processes for the medium itself, not understood according to a strictly modernist stylization of its specificity, but its frequently frayed and errant contours. As Masnatta shows, in Kawauchi's work, imperfection offers a different reflection on the photographic medium but also of the aesthetic and affective valences of the beholder's engagements with it.

Within the semantic complexities of the word fields spawned by the Latin *errāre*, Zairong Xiang considers those aspects that obstruct, in intricate and subtle ways, considerations and mobilizations of fluidity, flexibility, or elasticity in queer theory and other contexts. Xiang connects these locally observable obstacles or rigidities that often also manifest themselves as willfulness or stubbornness, to the body — not as a phenomenological grounding, but through Traditional Chinese Medicine and the I Ching, with their cosmological and speculative expansiveness. Assembling its own obstacle course out of personal encounters, meme videos, and ethnographic notes, Xiang's essay derives notions of radical indifference and weak resistance from his conception of a tension within Errans.

Ewa Majewska considers the particular counterpublic that manifested itself in the Solidarność labour union in Poland not as a self-contained historical episode, let alone as contributing to a 'victory' of Western liberalism, but as a much larger and more profound political-theoretical problem. To this end she is revisiting the conflictual construction of the very notion of a 'counterpublic', and proceeds to connect it to questions of the periphery, postcolonial theory, and feminist activism to resituate Solidarność in ways that renders it urgently relevant for contemporary questions, including that of locally instantiated resistant formations and their universal potentials in globalized contexts.

The final contribution also comes to bear on burning political questions, albeit via a considerable, radically innovative detour: Federico Dal Bo tackles the monumental question of the relationship between Halakhic law and the predominantly exilic and diasporic conditions of Jewish life and history. In a radical rereading of Talmudic sources, Dal Bo short-circuits the question of the possibility of an 'exilic law' with fundamental questions of interpretation inherent in Talmudic textual strategies, on the one hand tethered to a conception of the literal, but on the other thematizing deviance, deviation, and heretical errancies as genuine interpretive possibilities. In a final 'displacement', Dal Bo reconsiders the questions posed by the binding of Isaac.

The Punakawans Make an Untimely Appearance
In Praise of Caves, Shadows, and Fire
(or A Response to Plato's Doctrine of Truth)
PRECIOSA DE JOYA

> Wayang is good to think with.
>
> A. L. Becker

It is way past midnight, and the dhalang *(puppeteer) takes the* kayon, *the leaf-shaped puppet symbolizing the tree of life. To the quickening drumbeat and agitated sound of metallophones and gongs, he vigorously shakes the* kayon *as it swoops back and forth across the screen. Against the light of the* blencong *(lamp), the movements of the* kayon *project quivering shadows, as though the shadows themselves were caught on fire.*

This marks the beginning of the scene known in Javanese shadow puppet theatre or *wayang kulit* as *gara-gara*, a time when the world, plagued by disease, earthquakes, and volcanic eruptions, is 'as dark as a dust-clouded night'.[1] Fortunately, the turmoil eventually subsides, and in its place appears the androgynous clown, Semar, known not

---

1   *On Thrones of Gold: Three Javanese Shadow Plays*, ed. by James R. Brandon (Honolulu: University of Hawaii Press, 1993), p. 115.

only as the servant and wise counsel to the Pandhawa hero, Arjuna, but also the ancient god, Ismaya, descended on earth as the protector of Java.[2] *Gara-gara* is therefore not merely a time of chaos but also the *punakawan* (clown) scene, the moment when Semar, along with his wacky sons, Gareng, Petruk, and Bagong, enter the stage and delight the audience with a repertoire of social critique, slapstick, and obscene jokes. But while their humour has never failed to win the hearts of spectators, the importance of these clowns to people's lives extends far beyond the time and place of the performance. As the shadows (bayang-bayang) give way to the everyday and fade into the morning light, the *punakawan* lose their material form and sink deep into the mind, as a way to imagine (mbayangke) an errant and erring life.

Entering the world at the brink of complete annihilation, the clowns dance their way into the stage at the most inappropriate time. They are the untimely ones, the antithesis to the climax because they interrupt the plot and mock the seriousness of what is deemed eventful or historical. They exist at the margins of history, not only because they are of no concern — in most *wayang* plays, their actions have no significance at all in the development of the plot — but also because they lack concern by being seemingly oblivious to the crisis of the times. Hence, the lightness of their gait and their propensity for laughter, banter, and carefree dance. And so as the brave hero Arjuna meditates in the forest to gather strength for an impending battle, we find his entourage of clowns at close distance, trying to outwit each other as they happily fool around. Unlike their masters, who are endowed with spiritual and mental acuity and often depicted with graceful movements and sexy, slim bodies, the clowns are shamelessly corrupt and materialistic, extorting and begging for money whenever they can. They are offensively obscene as they brag about their sexual adventures and act out their perverse fantasies. Though they may sometimes appear dullwitted, they often defeat their enemies in battle, either by throwing fecal matter or gassing them with their smelly farts. And as their beautifully eccentric shapes reveal, they are the perfect embodiments of the inappropriate form and the uncontainable and unrestrainable spirit of

---

2   Ibid., p. 120.

the grotesque, dramatized in body parts that either bulge out, droop, or elongate to exaggerated lengths.

By evoking the idea of the untimely, I am proposing a way to understand the temporal structure of *wayang*, particularly of the *garagara* scene. In this regard, one must take into account the excellent analyses done by A. L. Becker and René Lysloff.[3] Juxtaposing the *wayang* plot to Aristotle's notion of the narrative, Becker explains that while the latter is constructed on causality and a series of linear sequences, the former allows, from time to time, the possibility for coincidences (i.e., events that *just* happen, for no causal reason). Thus, for example, there is no causal explanation for why Arjuna meets the demon Cakil in the forest. It just happens, and 'because they are who they are, they fight and Cakil dies'. This chance meeting, however, is not just a physical encounter, but the clash of two different epistemologies, of two different conceptual worlds. While Arjuna attacks Cakil because he recognizes him as a demon and is compelled by his duty (dharma) to defeat evil, Cakil attacks Arjuna who, having raised the heat of the forest through his meditation and thus causing thermal pollution, has made his life uncomfortable. Neither can really claim a higher moral ground; for while Arjuna kills Cakil dispassionately out of *dharma*, Cakil is only passionately 'defending his forest home against the intruder'.[4] René Lysloff takes Becker's idea and claims that the *garagara* is one of the scenes where such coincidence happens, when the epistemology of heroes exists side by side with the epistemology of the clowns. He describes it as a 'wrinkle in time' that brings about 'a peculiarly sustained moment of timelessness' in the middle of the *wayang* performance.[5]

With the idea of the untimely, however, I would like to emphasize not how everything comes together but the interruption, the disturbance, the distortion, the disjointedness of time, which arises from the phenomenon of the grotesque. Lysloff takes Mikhail Bakhtin's idea of

---

3   See A. L. Becker 'Text-Building, Epistemology, and Aesthetics in Javanese Shadow Theatre', *Dispositio* 5.13–14 (1980), pp. 137–68 and René Lysloff 'A Wrinkle in Time: The Shadow Puppet Theatre of Banyumas (West Central Java)', *Asian Theatre Journal*, 10.1 (1993), pp. 49–80.
4   Becker, 'Text-Building', p. 146.
5   Lysloff, 'Wrinkle in Time', p. 49.

chronotopes, which literally means time-space, describing it as time that 'thickens, takes on flesh, becomes artistically visible'.[6] But what I am proposing here is slightly different: it relates not just to how time informs or makes itself visible in space but to how it takes particular spatial qualities, in this case, the grotesque, the 'grandiose, exaggerated, immeasurable' growth of the material form.[7] This is time that is constantly othering, generating multiples of itself, and in doing so, what sometimes emerges as exaggeration, as monstrosity, a distortion, a gross interruption, a time out of joint.

Through monstrous distortions and absurd proportions, the grotesque celebrates the bodily element: capturing what Mikhail Bakhtin describes as the ongoing, transmogrifying, 'grandiose, exaggerated, immeasurable' growth of the material form.[8] From this arises what he calls a carnival, festive laughter — a laughter that is, in its ambivalence, both joyful and mocking, destructive as it gives life. It is laughter that temporarily suspends hierarchic distinctions, social norms and prohibitions by degrading and dragging back to the 'lower stratum of the body, the life of the belly and the reproductive organs' everything perceived as 'high, spiritual, ideal, abstract'.[9] Deprived of status, and completely lacking a sense of propriety, the *punakawan* speak and behave irreverently towards authority, exposing the foolishness and hypocrisy of heroes and gods. But it is precisely through comic relief, the interruption to both the drama of *wayang* and the seriousness of a social order and its prevailing 'truths' that the clowns offer their spectators a 'second life', a fleeting moment when 'time enter[s] the utopian realm of community, freedom, equality, and abundance'.[10]

The grotesque, however, manifests itself not only through physical malformations. It resurfaces with greater threat when we least expect it or when it appears at the most inopportune time as the expression of the *id* — that 'alien, inhuman power' to which a certain madness

---

6 Ibid., p. 52.
7 Mikhail Bakhtin, *Rabelais and his World*, trans. by Helene Iswolsky (Bloomington: Indiana University Press, 1984) p. 19.
8 Ibid.
9 Ibid., p. 20.
10 Ibid., p. 9.

governing people's behaviour is sometimes attributed.[11] This loss of control over one's own faculties is one of the things the Javanese fear the most; and they believe that the lack of consciousness makes one susceptible to the possession of spirits. Thus, defying the temptation of sleep (often more in theory than in practice) becomes key to enacting one's ability for ultimate self-control and consequently to achieving concentration and great spiritual power. In staying awake and delivering an eight-hour performance without interruption, the *dhalang* displays such prowess and transforms *wayang* from a mere theatre space in which stories are told to a theatrical spectacle in itself.

At a performance held at the Art Institute in Solo, the dhalang Ki Tristuti Rachmadi Suryasaputra makes a parody of the ascetic practice of wakefulness. It is one of the last scenes towards the end of Ramayana, and the demon Indrajit had cast a sleeping spell on King Rama's entire kingdom. No one is spared, everyone falls prey to the seduction of sleep; not even the great monkey hero Hanuman can resist, despite the desperate measure he takes at propping his eyes open with matchsticks. Deep in the forest, Semar, the wise one, slumbers almost throughout the whole scene, occasionally rousing from his sleep only to yawn and complain that staying awake is too great a feat for an old man like him. Gareng, Petruk, and Bagong keep themselves busy with games and puns, but eventually, one by one, succumb to the world of dreams. Only Petruk manages to keep awake, at least for a while, although not out of ascetic calmness, but due to the grotesquerie of his uncontrollably errant and troubled mind as he worries about tuition fees for his children's schooling and the enormous debts he will inevitably incur. Meanwhile, the king of the monkeys, Sugriwa, shouts at his army (and at the audience as well) that a thief is on the loose and that everyone should stay vigilant and awake. But even he proves no match against Indrajit's spell. As he yells at everyone, his words gradually grow faint and garbled, until he finally dozes off mid-sentence. He jolts back into wakefulness, but only to realize that it is a lost cause. As he feels himself slipping back into deep slumber, he makes a final, heroic gesture to take full control of the twilight moments of his consciousness: through lucid (self-)observation, he declares that his eyes are about to close, and reasons that his failing can only be due to the fact that he never performs. At

---

11 Ibid., p. 49.

Figure 1. Petruk, Gareng, and Bagong (a and b), and Semar (c) in stills from Enthus Susmono, *Dewa Ruci* [The Resplendent God], Contemporary Wayang Archive, Singapore <http://cwa-web.org/en/DewaRuci> [accessed 4 July 2021].

Figure 2. Installation at Sonobudoyo Museum, Yogyakarta, 2017.
Image credit: Miguel Escobar Varela.

that moment, the audience bursts out laughing, realizing that Sugriwa had suddenly become the alter-ego of the dhalang Tristuti *who, after decades of being banned from performing by President Suharto (1967–98), is himself struggling to stay awake as he delivers an eight-hour long show.*[12]

---

12   This scene is taken from a recording of a performance by the puppeteer Ki Tristuti Rachmadi Suryasaputra, entitled *Brubuh Ngalengko*, at the Art Institute in Solo, Indonesia. While the exact date of the performance is unknown, it most likely happened in the late 1990s when Tristuti would again perform after fourteen years of exile on Buru island and twenty more years of being banned from the stage despite the amnesty that proclaimed him a 'free' man. His associations with the cultural organization *Lembaga Kebudayaan Rakyat* (LEKRA) had linked him to the Communist party (*Partai Komunis Indonesia* or PKI), whose members and sympathizers became political targets during Suharto's 'New Order' regime (1965–1999). In light of the massive killings and disappearances that were happening at that time, Tristuti was one of the luckier ones who, after prison, only had to suffer the stigma of having the words E.T. on his identity card (E.T., not for extra-terrestrial — and here, one cannot but think of the *id* — but ex-*tawanan*, which literally means ex-prisoner). Nevertheless, the stigma caused him serious financial troubles as he could barely make a living from ghost-writing for well-known *dhalangs* such as Ki Anom Suroto, Ki Manteb Sudarsono, Ki Purbo Asmoro, and the like. Ki Tristuti Rachmadi, 'My Life as a Shadow Master under Suharto', in *Beginning to Remember: The Past in the Indonesian Present*, ed. by Mary S. Zurbuchen (Singapore: Singapore University Press, 2005), pp. 38–46 (pp. 42–43).

Carnival laughter is the laughter of the people that, unlike satirical humour, does not place anyone at a higher moral ground. No one is spared, everyone becomes the object of derision. But while the *punakawan* may be constantly testing the limits of the current order, and always come across, beyond what is tolerated or tolerable, as gross, rude, obscene, and stupid, they do not champion the cause of the marginalized, at least not in the radical way that some people would like. Often, we think of marginality as an alternative discourse, a combative position, which could erupt (at least we hope) into a serious social revolution. But with the clowns, one gets the impression that at every moment they strike, they retreat. They poke, criticize, turn things upside down, get a good laugh, but in the end reaffirm Javanese values, calling for the need to respect one's elders, for egalitarianism and mutual helping of each other (gotong royong), and the necessity of social propriety encoded in Javanese etiquette (tata krama). As Ward Keeler argues, the *punakawan* may be 'non-structural', but it does not mean that they reject the structure altogether.

> They do not affirm pan-human or pan-social values in conflict with heroic ideals and strictures. They simply present a contrast with them, an alternative rendering that does not put the normatively dominant one into question.[13]

The *punakawan* are therefore the non-heroic characters who will never make history. While they offer humour that wreaks havoc, laughter is the turmoil that always eventually subsides.

Caught in a self-perpetuating feudal structure, *wayang* reeks of the ahistorical. Renowned Javanese novelist Pramoedya Ananta Toer condemns his own culture, claiming that Javanism is a form of fascism that generates an 'unthinking loyalty and obedience to superiors' and 'tolerates no opposition'.[14] Indeed, when one sees how the Javanese love to rehearse and reduce everything to their philosophical formula of *manunggaling kawula gusti* (the union of servant and lord, of human and God), one realizes that it not only begins to sound like a broken record; from the constant repetition of this mantra-idea arises a cultural monster that forces everything to fit into a harmonious order. This was the

---

13   Ward Keeler, *Javanese Shadow Play, Javanese Selves* (Princeton, NJ: Princeton University Press, 1987), p. 210.
14   Pramoedya Ananta Toer, *Exile: Pramoedya Ananta Toer in Conversation with Andre Vltchek and Rossie Indira* (Chicago: Haymarket Books, 2006), pp. 85–86.

reason why, according to John Pemberton, former Indonesian President Suharto was able to ingeniously create an uncanny 'appearance of order', 'political stillness', and a lack of public demonstration despite the tumultuous events of the peasant movements and politicized killings that accompanied the establishment of his New Order government in 1966.[15] And this political indifference, this 'ideal absence in which nothing, as it were, happens', could have only been possible by reaffirming Javanese core values, such as 'the mutual adjustment of interdependent wills, the self-restraint of emotional expression, and the careful regulation of outward behaviour'[16] all of which are expressions of the kind of refinement that the Javanese love.

Wayang was, of course, very much part of Suharto's political propaganda, as it had been and will always be for a society where language and behaviour are profoundly imbued with theatricality. But while *wayang* is deeply feudal and the *punakawan* complicit in the constant renewal and affirmation of this world, censorship and control were still necessary to ensure that both *dhalang* and the clowns did not overstep their bounds.

In her essay on the 'Portrayal of National Leaders as Clown-Servants', Helen Pausacker explains how Suharto associated himself with Semar in the early days of the New Order, as well as in the last decade of his regime, in his desperate attempt to hold on to power. On 21 January 1995, Suharto invited several *dhalang* 'to rediscover the Javanese values of "individualism, mysticism, and social-pragmatism"' by creating a new *lakon* (story) with Semar as the central character. The aim of the story, entitled *Semar mbabar jati diri* (Semar discloses his true self), was to show the clown not merely 'as faithful servant but someone who was critical and represented the voice of the *rakyat* [people]'.[17] And the point was to represent Suharto as the 'super version of Semar, the *dhanyang*[18] of Java and protector of the people'.[19]

---

15   John Pemberton, *On the Subject of 'Java'* (Ithaca, NY: Cornell University Press, 1994), p. 4.
16   Clifford Geertz, *The Religion of Java* (London: The Free Press, 1960), p. 29.
17   Helen Pausacker, 'Presidents as Punakawan: Portrayal of National Leaders as Clown-Servants in Central Javanese Wayang', *Journal of Southeast Asian Studies*, 35.2 (2004), pp. 213–33 (p. 220).
18   A spirit that protects a particular locality.
19   Pausacker, 'Presidents as Punakawan', p. 219.

In the mid to the late 1990s, writers of the New Order sought to transform and rework *wayang* narratives and wrest them from the clutches of Suharto's political propaganda by challenging the *kawula-gusti* ethos. As Marshall Clark explains, this was achieved not only by modernizing and humanizing the heroes, depicting them as '"ordinary" Indonesians who performed their tasks in a routine manner';[20] in his study of Emha Ainun Nadjib's *Gerakan punakawan atawa arus bawah* (The clown-servant movement or the undertow, 1994), for instance, Clark further shows how the *punakawan* take a more radical role in 'reject[ing] the Javanese court culture's traditional hierarchical principles and promot[ing] a more democratic social and political system.'[21] Marshall cites a scene where Gareng starts to complain that he has been 'Gareng-ing' for too many centuries only to find 'the same old things: the viciousness of power, exploitation, slavery, oppression, stupidity, lack of foresight and ignorance'.[22]

Another interesting analysis with regard to the reworking of *wayang* narratives is the redefinition of Semar's character, which writers have done as a critical response to Suharto's appropriation of the clown. Pausacker cites Nano Riantiarno's *Semar gugat* (Semar accuses), a performance staged by Teater Koma in December 1995, where Arjuna steals the forelock of Semar, which possesses not only magical powers but the child-like qualities of honesty and lack of prejudice. Here, Semar is no longer depicted as a symbol of Suharto 'but rather of the people, who suffer because of the elite's actions', referring to the corruption of Suharto who here is represented by Arjuna.[23] In another story, in Sindhunata's *Semar mencari raga* (Semar in search of a body, 1996), Semar disappears in search of his identity and mistakenly believes that the solution would be to return to his pure spiritual form

---

20 Marshall Clark, 'Shadow Boxing: Indonesian Writers and the Ramayana in the New Order', *Indonesia*, 72 (2001), pp. 159–87 (p. 161).
21 Marshall Clark, '"Smells of Something like Postmodernism": Emha Ainun Nadjib's Rewriting of the Mahabharata', in *Clearing a Space: Postcolonial Readings of Modern Indonesian Literature*, ed. by Keith Foulcher and Tony Day (Leiden: KITLV Press, 2002), pp. 273–92 (p. 274).
22 Emha Ainun Nadjib, *Gerakan Punakawan Atawa Arus Bawah* (Yogyakarta: Yayasan Bentang Budaya, 1994), p. 28, quoted in Clark, 'Smells of Something like Postmodernism', p. 275.
23 Pausacker, 'Presidents as Punakawan', p. 222.

and abandon his earthly suffering and grotesque body. But Sang Hyang Tunggal, the supreme *wayang* deity explains to Semar that he must remain *samar*, and that once he abandons his suffering, he gives up his *samar* quality for clarity and certainty: 'Suffering never gives you clarity and certainty. But suffering gives you hope [...] and only if you courageously endure suffering, Semar, then you can live in *samar*, which brings happiness.'[24]

Clark ingeniously connects this passage from Sindhunata to an essay by Goenawan Mohamad, where the latter explains *kesamaran*, the state of having the quality of *samar*, as a refusal to be homogenized, defined, or explained.[25] But in his entire discussion, Clark consistently translates *samar* as formlessness, which is problematic and misleading, given that the word means 'dim, vague, indistinct'. This (mis)translation surreptitiously enforces a stock assumption that being 'dim, vague, indistinct' has no form, and that form can only be clear, certain, and well-defined. But then one remembers that it is precisely for an earthly body that Semar gives up the idea of existing as a pure, spiritual form. Thus, to think of this slippage of meaning, of Semar as *samar*, one might have to reflect further on how these qualities of dimness, vagueness, and indistinctness have their own materiality (a slippery quality both in actuality and in the mind), how they are enfleshed in specific operations and how they impinge on our senses with a certain force.

When one reads the literature on Semar and sees how people have reflected on his character in a philosophical manner, we find *samar*, this quality of obscurity, invoked repeatedly. It is sculpted into the very name of Semar and consequently what allows for the capacity for disguise (menyamar), as well as what gives the clown his spherical

---

24 Sindhunata, *Semar Mencari Raga* (Yogyakarta: Kanisius, 1996), pp. 49–50, quoted in Clark, 'Smells of Something like Postmodernism', p. 280.

25 Ibid. The word *samar* may be, for some, uncannily similar to Édouard Glissant's idea of 'opacity', for example in 'For Opacity', in Glissant, *Poetics of Relation*, trans. by Betsy Wing (Ann Arbor: University of Michigan Press, 1997), pp. 189–94. But while it is curious to see where these ideas converge, I would also alert the reader to think where they differ. In resisting the tendency of a certain humanism to disembody, homogenize, and universalize ideas, I am hoping here to present the idea of *samar* as something that arises from its own historical context, exploring how it has been used, developed, and problematized within its own culture and politics.

shape (semat). Despite the semantic playfulness, these explanations depict Semar in all his seriousness and essentialize him as an enigma, a profound vagueness which does not come from confusion or chaos but from being able to embody all contradictions. He is spherical in shape, both male and female, because he is complete, which according to Sri Mulyono is the reason why anyone who Semar assists is ensured victory and success.[26] This emphasis on a spiritual or mystical interpretation of Semar can also be seen in the work of Sumastuti Sumukti, who criticizes foreign scholars for being 'superficial and fragmentary' in their analysis of Semar as a trickster. In presenting Semar 'as understood by Javanese', she insists that we focus on the power of his wisdom, which includes 'the quality of unselfishness and the conviction of the necessity of justice'. Similar to Siddharta and Christ, Semar rejects the life of a god-king and transforms himself into a servant. This, according to Sumukti, is Semar's way of restoring social and natural order and that, by exhibiting a life of humility, he demonstrates 'that even those who are humble should be respected'.[27]

There is, however, something to be said about this propensity to mysticize as an obsession to impute a spiritual meaning to everything. Historically, one could say that it was partly the result of an important collaboration between the conservative *priyayi* (Javanese nobility/intellectual class) and 'sympathetic Dutch Javanologists' to codify and 'purify' Javanese culture in an attempt to inculcate the values of *adiluhung* (the beautiful sublime) and *halus* (refinement). The result was the creation of 'Java' as a 'cultural spectacle', which some scholars claim was part of the reaction and resistance of the Javanese to a colonial power that had made them politically impotent. Vis-à-vis their Western colonizers, the Javanese felt the need to assert cultural superiority. By exoticizing the Javanese soul, it presented itself as what could never be fully subjugated or comprehended.[28]

---

26   Sri Mulyono, *Apa dan Siapa Semar* (Jakarta: CV Haji Masagung, 1989), pp. 29–30.
27   Sumastuti Sumukti, 'An Analysis of Semar Through Selected Javanese Shadow Play Stories' (unpublished doctoral thesis, University of Hawaii, 1990), p. 1.
28   To know more about *halus*-ination, or the hallucinating emphasis on refinement in Javanese culture, see Pemberton, *On the Subject of 'Java'* and Nancy K. Florida, 'Reading the Unread in Traditional Javanese Literature', *Indonesia*, 44 (October 1987), pp. 1–15. See also Mangkunegara VII, *On the Wayang Kulit (Purwa) and its Symbolic and Mystical Elements*, trans. by Claire Holt (Southeast Asia Program, Dept. of Far Eastern

But not only scholars speak like this. In one of my visits to Yogyakarta, I invited my host's driver, Pak Ego,[29] and his friends to a conversation about the *punakawan*. Over black tea and cigarettes, I coaxed them into telling me what they loved about the clowns and in what ways they thought they were funny. Curiously, none of the grotesque, obscene, and rude nature of the clowns, as one sees them on stage, was ever raised. They insisted, despite my stubborn attempts, to speak 'philosophically' or to analyse (*mengupas*, to remove or strip off the peel of something, to get rid of the outer covering), the spiritual significance of the clowns. *Itu ada filsafatnya* (This has its [own] philosophy) — the Javanese love to say this about everything, whether it be the way a dancer walks with bended knees on stage or how a small dagger (kris) is kept under the pillow to establish some spiritual connection with its owner. And so that evening, Pak Ego and his friends would proudly teach me how the clowns were representations of the stages of one's spiritual journey: Bagong, born from the shadow of Semar, being the dumbest and therefore the opposite of his wise father, is supposedly a reminder of the ugliness that co-exists with the goodness in the human soul. Petruk is known to have a gaping hole on his side, which signifies a stage of emptiness that drives one to search for God. And finally, in the end, is Gareng, whose deformed feet are a sign not of physical defect but of long hours sitting in meditation. The longer we talked, the further I felt I was from the *wayang* of their childhood.

Seeing Semar on stage, with his grotesque figure and shadowy texture, I wondered if there was something missing in these conversations that too easily took leave of the body and expedited the clown to the lofty realm of the spirit. But was I, by simply doing away or underestimating the Javanese's love for mystical interpretations, equally obscuring or denying understanding? Here, I began to realize that the way they keep returning and bringing everything back to the

---

Studies, Cornell University, 1957) on how mysticization affirms a certain opacity of the Javanese as other. Here, Mangkunegara proudly explains in his analysis of *wayang* how he is merely lifting a tip of the veil in revealing the secret of Javanese knowledge 'concerning the deepest significance of life'.

29 Ego is the shortened version of Bagong, which was the nickname given to him for being plump when he was young.

idea of *manunggaling kawula gusti* may not be so much a way to explain a truth as to rehearse what needs to be remembered (kudu eling), which in this case, as Keeler points out, relates to a constant mindfulness of God. To be mindful would be to have a kind of wakefulness that is only possible through 'emotional invulnerability' and self-control, the capacity to remain 'calm, untroubled, unmoved', in the midst of great adversities.[30]

Like sleep, laughter for the Javanese is something that one should try to avoid (again, at least in theory). In moments of boisterous laughter, it is common practice, Keeler observes, for the audience to let out a 'stylized hoot'. Such stylization 'puts a stop to the humor's effects' enabling spectators to regain their self-control.[31] To understand further this ambiguous relation that the Javanese have with laughter, we turn to the *wayang* story, *Murwakala* (Birth of Kala), where we find the blood-thirsty ogre Batara Kala struck by the beauty of the *dhalang's* words (kena ing sabda). Kala, which is the allegorical representation of time, arises from the seed of Batara Guru, which was accidentally spilled into the sea as a result of the god's uncontrollable passion for his wife and an untimely ejaculation. Kala, not knowing his father, grows up to become destructive, having an insatiable appetite for children. Vishnu is sent to earth to manage the crisis and incarnates himself as a *dhalang*. It is said that only he can read the writing on Kala's body, which is the only way to effectively subdue (for one can never vanquish completely) the demon. Vishnu stages a *wayang* performance as Kala is passing by, and the latter is irresistibly drawn to the *dhalang's* storytelling. He finds himself bursting into peals of uncontrollable laughter that he gives up his weapon in exchange for the *dhalang's* promise to keep the show going. Here, the *Murwakala* narrates not only the myth of human ill-fortune as the condition of being devoured by time, but also the origin of *wayang* itself, and how, through the seductive power of speech and laughter, it causes a forgetfulness that suspends time and puts it momentarily off track.[32]

---

30   Keeler, *Javanese Shadow Play*, pp. 219–220.
31   Ibid., p. 218.
32   Jan Mrázek, *Phenomenology of a Puppet Theatre: Contemplations on the Art of Javanese Wayang Kulit* (Leiden: KITLV Press, 2005), p. 354.

However, to complicate further the relation between laughter and forgetting, one must keep in mind that the Javanese also regard the comical (lucu) as *aneh* (odd).[33] One encounters the *aneh* not only in the odd faces and bodies of the clowns but in language as well. In an essay by Hildred Geertz, we learn about the phenomenon of *latah*, which she describes as follows:

> An involuntary blurting of obscene words or phrases, compulsive imitation of the words or actions of others, and compulsive unquestioning obedience when ordered to perform actions which may be ridiculous, improper, or even dangerous. The stimulus to such behaviour is any sudden loud sound, a tickling prod in the ribs, or an abrupt gesture.[34]

Thus, for instance, a Javanese woman would be forced to respond 'in, out, in, out, in, out' when someone utters the word 'penis'.[35] Such a phenomenon, according to James Siegel, arises because of the constraints of High Javanese (Kromo) on Low Javanese (Ngoko). Contrary to the 'quick, abbreviated, abrupt, and usually harsh' *Ngoko*, *Kromo* is a manner of speaking whereby a person uses 'slow, soft, long sentences and full of archaism'.[36] It is a skill where one is able to create 'a pleasing vacuity', that is, to 'speak for so long and say nothing'.[37] While *Ngoko* is spoken among friends and to children, *Kromo* is a way of deference towards people whose status demands recognition, and in doing so, the speaker replaces the words he ordinarily uses for words deemed appropriate and respectful. To have this ability is to have refinement or *halus*, which is the very essence of *being* Javanese. From time to time, however, *latah* occurs, and in that moment when the speaker briefly loses control, the rude and crude *Ngoko* appears causing him great embarrassment. *Ngoko* is therefore sometimes the language spoken when one loses control, either by being excited or

---

33 James Siegel, *Solo in the New Order: Language and Hierarchy in an Indonesian City* (Princeton, NJ: Princeton University Press, 1986), p. 98.
34 Hildred Geertz, 'Latah in Java: A Theoretical Paradox', *Indonesia*, 5 (April 1968), pp. 93–104 (p. 94).
35 Siegel, *Solo*, p. 28.
36 Ibid., p. 18.
37 Ibid., p. 17.

when one talks in one's sleep, which makes the *ngoko* speaker into 'the perpetrator of errors' due to an untimely appearance.[38]

One could perhaps easily interpret the relation between *Kromo* and *Ngoko* as a form of subjugation, where the former becomes a second language that inhibits or suppresses the speaker's 'own' tongue. But as Siegel points out, such deference 'lacks all sense of subservience'. In language that is seemingly affirming a feudal, hierarchical structure, the use of *Kromo* is in fact a kind of self-protection: that in consciously replacing the words one ordinarily uses, one practices an emotional detachment, which in turn frees the speaker from having to experience a feeling of embarrassment and inferiority.[39]

Sugriwa finally manages to wake up and runs to the forest, where he happens to find the sleeping punakawan. *A thief is on the loose; he needs all the help he can get to catch the perpetrator, so he tries to wake up the clowns. As he feels his way through the darkness, however, he touches Gareng's 'stick', which is proudly erect, as the* punakawan *lies on his back. Sugriwa, who all this time had been shouting, falters and in that awkward moment, mutters, 'Saru' ('Obscene'). Gareng is woken up, and unaware that it is Sugriwa, snaps angrily: 'Leave me alone, I can do whatever I like!' He suddenly realizes it is the king of the monkeys and apologizes, but immediately after, he again falls back to sleep.*

Becker would interpret a scene like this as a coincidence, something that just happens, an event without causal explanation. It is a moment when the world of kings/heroes and clowns briefly coincide, which I would say not only brings different epistemologies together but causes an 'error' in time, an interruption to the progressive, dramatic narrative of dharma as part of a temporal, grotesque transmogrification, enacted by the sudden appearance of the *ngoko* speaker, the untimely one.

As I contemplate the shadow of Semar and see this philosopher clown with his sons, causing a riot on stage, I am reminded of Socrates who was condemned to death by hemlock, the buffoon who they say got himself taken too seriously. But would Socrates have wanted anything less and deprive the philosopher of the NOBLE *sacrifice of his own life in the name of truth?*

---

38   Ibid., p. 25.
39   Ibid., p. 27.

Nietzsche says that a physiognomist once revealed that Socrates, beneath his Apollonian guise, was 'a cave of [...] evil passions', which leads me to believe that the wise philosopher himself may have actually belonged to the ranks of the grotesque (a word which comes from grottesca, or cave paintings). But the fear of being completely ruined by decadence had forced him to take the drastic measure of making a tyrant out of reason. Virtuous reason, the crowning glory of humanity, was therefore never a creation of free choice, but the 'last expedient' in a very desperate situation. By putting 'a permanent daylight' to his obscure desires, Nietzsche claims that Socrates had wanted nothing more than 'to be rational, clear, and distinct, at any price', believing that 'yielding to the instincts, to the unconscious' could only lead downwards.[40]

In discussing the problematic relation between 'Western' thought and the medium of theatre and theatricality, Samuel Weber explains that the antagonism can be traced back to Plato, who 'exchang[ed] the cave, its fire and shadows, for the bright sunlight and its direct, if dazzling illumination'. In his myth, the cave is depicted as a theatre stage where shadow images and phantasmagoria appear, like a narcotic that causes the dwellers to forget that the real is elsewhere. But the enslaved condition of the cave dwellers is the result not so much of oppression as it is a consent and their 'desire to remain the *same*, [...] in the same place'. Thus, the cave for Plato is 'a place not just of dissimulation and delusion but, worse, self-dissimulation and self-delusion'.[41] The escape from this cavernous hell is dramatized in the myth as 'the liberating if painful ascent into the open and natural light of the sun'. This world of ideas and truth, Weber claims, is a space that 'need no longer be localized'.

> For what counts is never a particular place but rather the ubiquity of daylight itself. No shadows or obscurities, no echoes, projections, or simulacra: only light as it is and things as they are, in and of themselves: such is the dream of a liberation that would leave behind the cavernous nightmare of theatre in which enslavement appears as freedom.[42]

---

40   Friedrich Nietzsche, 'The Twilight of the Idols', in *The Works of Nietzsche*, trans. by Thomas Common (London: T. Fisher Unwin, 1899), p. 11.
41   Samuel Weber, *Theatricality as Medium* (New York: Fordham University Press, 2004), p. 8.
42   Ibid.

In the course of his discussion, Weber makes an insightful reference to *wayang*, showing how it poses an alternative, perhaps even an objection, to Plato's allegory of the cave.[43] While the cave dwellers in Plato's myth are chained in one place and depicted with a certain fixity and lack of freedom, the spectators of *wayang* are free to move from one side of the screen to the other, to witness either the puppets themselves or their shadows. And to add to Weber's observation, the Javanese, as I've explained above, are in fact quite aware of the seduction of the *dhalang's* speech and make efforts to resist its power.

What seems to be at stake here is a notion of truth that Plato asserts in exchanging cave, fire, and shadows for the illuminating light of the sun. In his essay 'Plato's Doctrine of Truth', Martin Heidegger explicitly sets his aim, not without a tinge of irony, 'to learn and henceforth know what [Plato] has left unsaid':[44] to *grasp* the real significance of Plato's allegory of the cave, to *exhaust* its content and *make visible* the essential aspect.[45] To achieve this, one must realize that the allegory 'does not just report on the abodes and situations of man inside or outside the cave', but narrates a series of incidents, transitions, movements 'from the cave out into the light of day and back again from the latter into the cave'.[46] It is therefore a story of a 'constant overcoming' of ignorance, of being uneducated, and that this movement is the underlying operation that leads one from 'the standardly unhidden' (i.e., shadows), to the 'most unhidden'. Given that the unhidden is not only what makes something shine, visible and accessible, but what *overcomes* the 'hiddenness of the hidden', truth (aletheia) therefore becomes a way of uncovering what Heidegger describes as 'a perpetual wrenching-away',[47] i.e., wrenching something from its hiding.

For Heidegger, the unhidden refers to what Plato calls the Idea. The Idea, which is the emerging that makes an outward appearance (eidos) visible, is

---

43 Ibid., p. 6.
44 Martin Heidegger, 'Plato's Doctrine of Truth', in *Philosophy of the Twentieth Century: An Anthology*, ed. by William Barrett and Henry D. Aiken, 4 vols (New York: Random House, 1962), III: pp. 251–70 (p. 251).
45 Ibid., p. 255 and p. 260 (my emphasis).
46 Ibid., p. 255.
47 Ibid., p. 260.

pure shining in the sense of the phrase 'the sun shines'. The 'idea' does not just let something else (behind it) 'make an appearance', it itself is what appears, and it depends upon itself alone for its appearing. The ιδέα is the apparent. The essence of the idea lies in the qualities of being apparent and visible. The idea achieves presence, namely the presence of every being as what it is. Each being is continuously present in the What of beings. Presence however is really the essence of Being. Being, then, for Plato, has its real essence in its What.[48]

Heidegger then alerts us to a subtle movement, a change in orientation, a transition that 'the inquiry into unhiddenness is shifted to the way outward appearance manifests itself and with that to the associated ability to see: to what is right and the correctness of seeing'.[49] With the emphasis on the recognition of beings, Idea becomes the master of *aletheia*, and correctness, not unhiddenness, becomes the basic feature of Being.

Elsewhere, Jacques Derrida presents a similar critique of Plato, this time by reflecting on the myth of Theuth in the *Phaedrus*. In the story, the inventor, Theuth, presents to the king, Thamus, the gift of writing (grammata), claiming it as a remedy that induces remembering and increases knowledge. But the king, the father of *logos*, will deprecate and reject this gift, condemning it as poison that causes people to forget, by discouraging them from knowing things by heart. But the *pharmakon*, Derrida explains, is also what refers to *mythos*, to the *logoi en biblios*, 'words that are deferred, reserved, enveloped, rolled up, words that force one to wait for them in the form and under cover of a solid object, letting themselves be desired for the space of a walk'. Contrary to speech that is 'purely present, unveiled, naked', it is *logos* that lends itself to mystery or to the unknown, making it powerfully seductive and causing one to be led astray.[50]

In presenting writing as this movement of deferral, Derrida critiques Plato's notion of truth as self-presence and offers in its place the 'ambiguity or duplicity of the presence of the present' as both

---

48   Ibid., pp. 261–62.
49   Ibid., p. 265.
50   Jacques Derrida, *Dissemination*, trans. by Barbara Johnson (London: Athlone Press, 1981), p. 71.

'that which appears *and* its appearing',[51] i.e., a present that does not completely coincide with itself. Taking the notion of the present participle, Weber argues that the present is always 'after' itself, 'in hopeless self-pursuit', and its '*appearing* [...] is the grammatical index of those disjunctive "goings-on" that make the "present" into a "tense" in the most intense sense: "coming before" (*devançant*) or anticipating (the future) by "remembering" (the past).'[52]

As I think of the myth of Theuth, I am reminded of how wayang is also an invention, granted by Batara Guru and enacted by Vishnu, in order to subdue the blood-thirsty demon, Kala. But unlike in Plato's story, wayang is a pharmakon that regards itself not so much as a cure but as a narcotic, a temporary fix in the form of a seduction that causes one to forget and lose control. But in this moment of forgetting, this momentary suspension of time, does remembering not also occur? And if so, does remembering necessarily make one wiser?

I am again thinking of Socrates, the philosopher par excellence, whom the oracle proclaimed not so much the wisest as the measure against whom no one can be wiser. As god-fearing, he was compelled by a divine call to remind everyone of their ignorance. But following Nietzsche's cynical assessment of the philosopher, I wonder if Socrates's noble and humbling affirmation of our epistemological human condition was not merely a device to rule out every possibility of an erroneous assumption, either that one knows something or that one knows anything at all. To be fool-proof, to be completely immune to one's own foolishness so that one would never have to make a fool of oneself — this indeed forces a permanent daylight of sense and reason to cast upon one's every act. But how different everything is when one looks at Semar! He is the wise clown who we can never take too seriously. Because despite efforts to 'clean-up' his act, Semar's grotesque, disfigured physique will always remind us of his greed, of how he once swallowed up a mountain to prove to his brother Togog that he was the rightful heir to their father's throne. And we can definitely be certain that his folly, which profoundly marks his body, anticipates future bunglings, an ongoing testimony to the stupidity that 'continues to haunt and heckle, creeping up as the other work in progress'.[53]

---

51   Ibid., p. 192.
52   Weber, *Theatricality*, p. 15.
53   Avital Ronell, *Stupidity* (Champaign: University of Illinois Press, 2002), p. 28.

Semar, therefore, is the 'grammatical index of those disjunctive goings-on', an allegory of the gerund or present participle, of a present constantly overshadowed by the past and foreshadowing the future. But as a shadow image, he is also the present that never stays still. He is what 'take[s] place', what exists in a particular place, and what 'simultaneously also *pass[es] away* — not simply to disappear but to happen somewhere *else*'.[54]

I would like to go back to Plato's cave, and return to Heidegger's reflections on how the allegory is essentially a series of transitions and movements, a story of overcoming. I am struck by the violence required to wrench oneself from the cavernous pit of 'false' beliefs, and the decisive action that one must take to suffer a turning towards the light. This, according to Heidegger, is the task one must undertake to arrive at the place of the unhidden. But while he criticizes the notion of *eidos*, of being as presence, and tries to return to the idea of unhiddenness in *aletheia*, giving priority not to sight but to attunement, his thought is still very much centred on truth and on a profound concern for its veiling and unveiling.

But what, then, of those 'cave dwellers' who refuse to abandon the cave, fire, and shadows for the blinding light and decide to stay the same and in the same place? Say, for example, the clowns and everyone else who continue to subscribe 'Javanism' to a feudal relation of master and slave? Are we to think of them, in light of the heroic gesture of those who stepped out of the cave into the light as weak for as long as they dwell in their non-truth?

Maurice Blanchot tries to get beyond the notion of truth as revelation, 'seeking a way, without getting there', seeking 'a speech such that to speak would no longer be to unveil with light'. Further, he says:

> We would want to arrive at a mode of 'manifestation', but a manifestation that would not be one of unveiling-veiling. Here what reveals itself does not give itself up to sight, just as it does not take refuge in simple invisibility.[55]

---

54 Weber, *Theatricality*, p. 7.
55 Maurice Blanchot, 'Speaking Is Not Seeing', in Blanchot, *The Infinite Conversation*, trans. by Susan Hanson (Minneapolis: University of Minnesota Press, 1993), pp. 25–32 (p. 29).

'To reveal, to remove the veil, to expose directly to view' — Blanchot finds these movements unsuitable. And because revelation is implicated in the notion of *aletheia*, what seems to be closest to what he is seeking is non-truth.

In trying to arrive at a mode of manifestation that forces neither an unveiling nor veiling, I reflect on the notion of mimesis. While constant doubling enacts the present participle and allows for the ambiguity of presence as what appears and what is appearing in the production of variants, I would argue that mimesis is not a function of truth, a moment in the life of its ongoing revelation. Rather, mimesis is the staging of non-truth; it does not aim to reveal and make us wiser or understand reality better. Rather, it is the macabre ritual of endless repetition, a rehearsal that prepares one for the hearse.

The reason perhaps why we might think of mimesis and the movement of deferral as a function of life is that we regard such operations as the overproduction or the result of an abundance. The grotesque, as I have said earlier, in its playful distortions and absurd manifestations, is for Bakhtin the result of (quoting him and myself) 'the ongoing, transmogrifying, "grandiose, exaggerated, immeasurable" growth of the material form'. But the grotesque, again from the word *grottesca*, are fanciful projections of images in the cave, and is therefore also related to a certain mania, which Derrida argues is the result of the abuse of drugs, of the *pharmakon*.[56]

Furthermore, when Derrida speaks of writing as *pharmakon*, he describes it as half-living. The *pharmakon* is a

> weakened speech, something not completely dead: a living-dead, a reprieved corpse, a deferred life, a semblance of breath. The phantom, the phantasm, the simulacrum [...] of living discourse is not inanimate; it is not insignificant; it simply signifies little, and always the same thing. This signifier of little, this discourse that doesn't amount too much, is like all ghosts: errant. It rolls (*kulindeitai*) this way and that like someone who has lost his way, who doesn't know where he is going, having strayed from the correct path, the right direction, the rule of rectitude, the norm; but also like someone who has lost his rights, an outlaw, a pervert, a bad seed, a vagrant, an adventurer,

---

56 Derrida, *Dissemination*, p. 72.

a bum. Wandering in the streets, he doesn't even know who he is, what his identity — if he has one — might be, what his name is, what his father's name is. He repeats the same thing every time he is questioned on the street corner, but he can no longer repeat his origin.[57]

Writing is therefore the shadow of living speech, a mere duplication, one that is itself in the habit, in the business of self-duplication, of repetition *ad infinitum*. But the *pharmakon* is also associated with the ceremonial rite. In this sense, Thamus may have had reason to reject Theuth's invention as a device for remembering insofar as one takes the written *logos* not so much as a function of *anamnesis* but as a reminder of what one already knows. It is therefore not knowledge, 'a repetition of truth (*alētheia*) which presents and exposes the *eidos*' but '*nonknowledge as rememoration*', where one 're-presents a presentation, repeats a repetition'.[58]

Deep in the forest, Semar and his sons accompany their master who is deep in meditation. Semar had just woken up, and Gareng complains that their father had been asleep for two hours. Semar tries to defend himself: 'Aku wong tuwa ora kuwat (I'm an old man, I'm not strong enough). And later you might need to take me to the hospital.' Petruk laughs and says that their father is asking for donations again. Semar ignores him and instructs his sons to stay awake and watch the pendapa *(the pavilion), and soon after, announces that he will go rest. Bagong makes fun of Semar: 'Look at this old man, he cannot even stay awake. And he drools.' He goes closer to the sleeping Semar and hears a sound coming out of his father's lips: 'Poh, poh.' Bagong turns to Petruk, 'Truk, what is poh?' Petruk laughs, and mocks Bagong: 'This person really does not understand anything.' He then explains: 'Gong, old people, when they sleep, are like that. Because they no longer have teeth. So when they breathe, and air comes out of their mouth, and passes through their lips, it sounds like "poh".' Bagong is more curious than ever, and decides to examine Semar more closely. But as soon as he approaches, Semar lets out a huge fart into Bagong's face. Bagong is in momentary shock: 'Tak tilik, kebos! (I check him out, he blows!) Semar awakens momentarily, again to defend himself: "It's* masuk

---

57 Ibid., pp. 143–44.
58 Ibid., p. 135 (emphasis is mine).

angin'."[59] *Bagong retorts, 'Ora masuk angin, ngebrak!' (That's not* masuk angin. *Ngebrak!)*

Bagong is particularly interesting because he is known to be born out of the shadow of Semar. With his impenetrable stupidity, his consistent mishearing and misunderstanding of what his fellow *punakawan* tell him, he is the grotesque distortion of the wise philosopher, a simulacrum turned bad. But is it not the fate of the mimetic double to be so? In the internal division that happens within *mimesis* as the *ad infinitum* 'self-duplication of repetition itself', Derrida notes that the copy is what interrupts or *supervenes*, 'the strange mirror that reflects but also displaces and distorts one *mimēsis* into the other, as though it were itself destined to mime or mask *itself*.[60]

In *wayang*, Semar is usually the didactic element, the endless repetition and over-production of wise adages. Bagong, in his stupidity, will never grasp sense or understand the meaning of words. Rather, he is the interruption that supervenes upon *logos*, upon living speech, which for as long as it hinges on truth, will always be an unveiling of the unhidden; an interruption because, for Bagong, words are no longer about sense but about their physicality, their materiality. Onomatopeia is his playing field, the place where language no longer is about veiling or unveiling, but what hinges on the non-truth: it is the death mask of the word. It does not explain to make us understand better, but it is the stage that allows language to perform itself, to rehearse and repeat itself in its own death ritual. *Kebos*, it is the sound of an explosion; *Ngebrak*, the sound of 'ripping action', of 'splitting wood', or 'slapping sound', the sound of a fart, of hot air tearing out.

~

---

59   *Masuk angin* is an illness the Javanese believe is caused by cold wind entering one's belly.
60   Derrida, *Dissemination*, p. 191.

> And the Dreamer, ready for the sacrifice, replies: 'Here I am! Envelop me in rivers of burning lava, clasp me in your arms of fire as a lover clasps his bride.'
>
> Gaston Bachelard, *Psychoanalysis of Fire*

Between wakefulness and sleep, between remembering and forgetting, there exists the realm of the in-between. In his analysis of fire, Bachelard speaks of how we are drawn to the comfort and warmth of the flame, and how it invites us to repose, lulling us to contemplation, to a state of reverie. In its contemplation, reverie, Bachelard explains, 'works in a star pattern', return[ing] 'to its center to shoot out new beams'.[61] And in this movement of an errant mind, I hear the echo of Blanchot who also spoke of a going astray that 'moves steadily ahead and stays at the same point'.[62]

When I reflect on the shadow image of Semar, and on Bagong who in turn reflects (on) Semar, do I really stay at the same point? Do I not know better, and move, even a tiny bit, towards overcoming ignorance and unveiling the unhidden? Because of his impenetrable stupidity, Bagong will always misunderstand, mishear, and will always stay in the same place, having no option of an overcoming. Perhaps he will never be able to explain the sense or meaning of things; or wrench the unhidden from its hiding; or peel off the outer covering. But it is he, the copy as a grotesque distortion, who comes closest and hears the breath of the god.[63]

I keep thinking of Descartes meditating by the fireplace. In his reveries, he conjured the image of an evil genius, but only in the end taking it as a device to get to the most unhidden, to the cogito that shines forth as clear and distinct, as what can never ever be doubted. Watching wayang, *I feel myself detached from the world, and in suspended animation, I remain the same, and in the same place. From night till dawn, there exists no destination, no urge/urgency to get to the place where the unhidden may*

---

61   Gaston Bachelard, *The Psychoanalysis of Fire*, trans. by Alan Ross (London: Routledge and Kegan Paul, 1964), p. 14.
62   Blanchot, 'Speaking Is Not Seeing', p. 26.
63   I am indebted to Prof. Dr. Hans Jürgen Scheuer for this wonderful insight.

reveal itself; just this lull where time is interrupted, briefly stopping in its tracks. The wayang had ended, and everyone was slowly going home to prepare for the new day. I hitched a ride with the sleepy pesindhen (female singers) and took a bus back to town from the dhalang's house. On the way, I saw the roads covered in white, as though it had snowed. I realized later that it was ash; people had told me that the sacred mountain, Merapi, had begun to 'cough up' (Merapi batuk lagi, the Javanese would say) and that scientists were predicting an eruption in a matter of days. Anxious, I begged Pak Ego, who agreed to be my translator, to take me to the mountain the next day. I had plans to speak to the juru kunci, the guardian of the mountain, Mbah Maridjan, who I heard was a powerful mystic and was known for notoriously refusing to speak Indonesian, adamantly insisting on the use of Javanese — a curious conviction at a time when the educated ones are trying so hard to disassociate themselves from their feudal culture. The next morning, however, it was too late. The town of Mbah Maridjan, Kinahrejo, was closed and pronounced a disaster zone.

While the fire gives us comfort and warmth, and invites us to a state of reverie, it is also what 'speeds up the passage of time, brings all of life to its conclusion, to its hereafter'.[64] The fire that projects shadows is also the hearth that reminds us of the volcano, and the desire for 'death on the funeral pyre' — 'to disappear, to be swallowed up, to leave no trace!'[65]

On 20 May 2012, an article was published in the newspaper, *Merdeka*, reporting the sighting of a cloud in the shape of Semar, hanging over the summit of Mount Sumbing in Temanggung, Central Java. Residents were alarmed because it reminded them of a previous incident, of a hot cloud, appearing in the shape of Petruk, a day before Merapi erupted in 2010.[66]

Days before the eruption in 2010, I remember how Mbah Maridjan had caused a controversy by refusing to leave the mountain despite warnings of an imminent eruption and Sultan Hamengkubuwana X's appeal for a mandatory evacuation. The *juru kunci* had pulled the same

---

64 Bachelard, *Psychoanalysis*, p. 16.
65 Ibid., p. 19.
66 Anwar Khumaini, 'Dulu Mbah Petruk, sekarang Mbah Emar', *Merdeka.com*, 20 May 2012 <http://www.merdeka.com/peristiwa/dulu-mbah-petruk-sekarang-mbah-semar.html> [accessed 4 July 2021].

stunt in 2006, and this was in fact the reason for his fame as he urged hundreds of families to remain in their homes, convincing them that the mountain meant them no harm. Aside from a few burns, Mbah Maridjan and his followers survived the volcanic blasts and pyroclastic flow. The *juru kunci* was then hailed as a hero and was believed to possess great spiritual power, which afforded him a real connection with the spirit of the sacred mountain. Later, he would reveal in an interview that it was through a dream that the mountain spoke, assuring him that while an eruption was bound to take place, no one would get hurt.

In *Merapi omahku* (Merapi my home), a book published by the French journalist Elizabeth Inandiak, we find Mbah Maridjan's own account of a dream he had in 1994, predicting the eruption that would take place that year. In that dream, he recounts how he was visited by tall people (orang-orang tinggi), who were good (orang bagus), clean (bersih), and of yellow skin (berkulit kuning).

> And the people spoke in this way: '*kami punya uang, silakan dibagi*' [we have money, please share it]. In Javanese language [Bahasa Jawa], this means: '*aku duwe dhuwit dum na*.' But its [real] meaning is not this. What is meant by *dhuwit* is '*arta*' [money], the word used in Bahasa Jawa *halus*. I take '*arta*' to mean '*warta*', '*kabar*' [news]. And thus I was told to spread the news that Merapi would become dangerous. Next morning, at 10 am, indeed came a continuous eruption.[67]

Here, we see that Kromo or Bahasa Jawa halus does not only offer the Javanese protection from a feeling of embarrassment and inferiority; it is also the key to understanding esoteric signs. And curiously, mishearing, the blunder for which Bagong's impenetrable stupidity is known, is here intentionally employed as the device that deciphers the message of the spirits.

In humbling himself, Mbah Maridjan would often say, *Saya ini orang bodoh* (I'm a stupid person). For the Javanese, the statement itself is a philosophical dictum, one that I've often heard uttered not just by the *juru kunci* himself but also by others, including Pak Ego. But here, stupidity is not at all what we think it is. In speaking further

---

67   Elizabeth D. Inandiak, *Merapi Omahku* (Yogyakarta: Babad Alas Elizabeth D. Inandiak/Heri Dono, 2010), p. 69 (my translation, P.d.J.).

about this, Mbah Maridjan does not try to explain or shed light on its meaning but gestures towards stupidity's mode of manifesting: *'Kalau orang pinter, diberi satu akan minta dua. Tapi kalua orang bodoh, diberi satu akan disyukuri.'* (For a smart person, given one he will ask for two. But for a stupid person, given one he will be thankful.)[68] For Inandiak, however, such stupidity and gratitude can only be possible for one who leads a life of simplicity. Thus, what immediately follows Mbah Maridjan's statement is Inandiak's description of his humble home, which consists of only a few basic things: a grounded mat, a cabinet, a Javanese-Islamic calendar and several photos, including one of Sultan Hamengkubuwona X, of Merapi erupting, and of the Javanese ancestor, Semar.[69]

On 26 October 2010, Mbah Maridjan and a few others who refused to leave Merapi, perished in a cloud of gas and ash with a temperature of a thousand degree Celsius. A few days later, the *juru kunci's* incinerated body was found in a prostrated position. Some people speak of this tragedy as Mbah Maridjan's own failure, a gross error in calculation — he miscalculated the danger, believing that the mountain would spare them all. But did he? Was it not more the certainty of death, rather than survival, which urged him to stay?

Mbah Maridjan often said that 'he would guard Merapi until his death'.[70] On several occasions, he also explained that his refusal to follow Sultan Hamengkubuwana X's order was not due to stubbornness or arrogance, but because the mandate that declared him the guardian of Merapi was authorized not by the current sultan but by the previous one, Sultan Hamengkubuwana IX.[71] It would therefore be only

---

68 Ibid., pp. 42–43.
69 Ibid., p. 43.
70 This phrase, 'dia akan menunggu Merapi hingga ajal menjemputnya' (he will guard Merapi until his death), was taken from 'Duka Bencana Merapi. Mbah Maridjan meninggal sujud', news clip video, <https://www.youtube.com/watch?v=UVGKtatChK8> [accessed 1 November 2015; the video can no longer be accessed]. See also Rimawan Prasetiyo, 'Pesan Terakhir Mbah Maridjan dan Kisahnya Tepat Ramalkan Letusan Merapi Gara-gara Burung', *Tribunwow*, 28 July 2017, <https://wow.tribunnews.com/2017/07/28/pesan-terakhir-mbah-maridjan-dan-kisahnya-tepat-ramalkan-letusan-merapi-gara-gara-burung> [accessed 4 July 2021]. Here, again, Mbah Maridjan is quoted: 'Saya akan tinggal di sini akan menunggu Merapi sesuai amanat Sri Sultan Hamengku Buwono ke IX ...' (I will stay here [and] will guard Merapi according to the mandate of Sri Sultan Hamengku Buwono IX ...).
71 Ghaffar, Ibrahim, 'Embah Setia Menunggu Merapi', *Dewan Masyarakat*, July 2006, pp. 54–55.

in abiding by the latter's orders that the *juru kunci* would abandon his post. This of course could only mean that Sultan Hamengkubuwana IX, who passed away in 1988, would have to give his injunction from the grave.

This blind loyalty, not even to a living authority, but to the ghost of a king, may seem far more feudal than one can imagine. And the desire to move steadily towards one's doom, to remain at the place of danger despite all the technology that today makes possible a temporary escape from death, may strike us as a mere case of madness or irrational behaviour. But for Mbah Maridjan and his followers, the life of the villagers is inextricable from the fertile soil. And one can only begin to sense the severity of this bond when villagers refuse to leave their homes, and are more willing to face Merapi's threat to die at the place that has given them life, the source of their clothing and food (sandang-pangan).[72] Their loyalty therefore is wrought not by blindness but gratitude, and it is precisely in acknowledging the mountain's goodwill that Mbah Maridjan urges people not to speak badly of Merapi or resent it for its eruptions. As a friend, Merapi is good (apik), and does not destroy but seeks to build (Merapi kuwi mbangun).[73]

As I see Semar dancing happily on stage, I realize that the philosopher, on this rare occasion, ceases to be the loud and profuse proclamation of ideas and wise adages. Instead, he speaks to me with the silence of an image, a gentle reminder, through the evocations of hot air in the form of 'pohs' and farts and of the mountain that hides from sight and sleeps inside his belly. Semar, as the shadow of the image, is what passes across and beyond the wayang *screen between performance and life and the image of passing, the flickering shadow that commemorates the fire.*

Listening to the phrase manunggaling kawula gusti *being uttered for the umptieth time, I begin to hear, arising from the tiresome repetition of the mantra, the shadow of sound: what resounds is not a new revelation but the echo that rehearses what the Javanese have always known all along: to remain the same and at the same place, and in exchange for the truth of the blinding sun, they seek the fire that consumes and consummates, that brings all of life to conclusion.*

---

72 Ibid.
73 'Duka Bencana Merapi'.

The Animal That Laughs at Itself
False False Alarms about the End of 'Man'
JAMES BURTON

INTRODUCTION

The first two sections of this paper consider a series of Western theories of laughter, identifying and exploring a nexus of themes that resurfaces across different approaches, in particular those that have been referred to as superiority theory, incongruity theory, relief theory, as well as Henri Bergson's philosophical investigation of laughter and the more recent false alarm theory. The recurring trio of themes I identify comprises violence, the human/nonhuman, and error: together, I argue, they can be read as reflecting a certain, partially submerged concern with the instability and demise of the human. However, my aim is not to point to a unifying or universal set of concerns underpinning what, from within a Western academic and historical context might seem a diverse range of approaches; nor to synthesize these approaches with a view to arriving at a unifying or universal theory of laughter. On the contrary, I want to suggest that the transversal recurrence of this set of themes is actually a reflection of how much these different theorizations of laughter share — of the ways they are circumscribed by a common set of cultural and epistemological factors. Notably, these factors converge in the treatment of a culturally specific (if historically and globally far-reaching) notion, image, understanding of selfhood as the universal model of the human.

This particular version of the human derives its key features from a set of bodily, intellectual, and moral ideals that are primarily white, Western, masculine, valuing particular forms of cultural education and social behaviour, and defining itself in part through its self-declared superiority to certain nonhuman others, such as animals, machines, and inanimate objects. The self-identification of this culturally-circumscribed version of the human with the category of humanity per se, its self-universalization, is reflected in its historical tendency to refer to its culturally specific values, regarding morality, education, aesthetics, politics, and so on, using terms such as *humanitas*, *Humanität*, and eventually, 'humanism'. Its masculine idealization in particular is also reflected in the traditional use of 'Man' to refer to humans regardless of gender — and indeed, now that the politics of this terminology have entered the cultural consciousness, leading to its abandonment in public cultural and academic discourse, we may employ the capitalized 'Man' as a shorthand for the culturally specific version of the human to which it has actually historically tended to correspond.

It is this figure of the human — built on an equation of a culturally specific form with a universal category — that, I will suggest, can be said to be implicitly treated as under threat in the prominent Western theories of laughter I will discuss. That is, the recurrence of the above-mentioned trio of themes (violent struggle, the human/nonhuman, and error) can be seen as an index of an implicit shared sense that laughter threatens the self-certainty of this culturally specific (Western, masculinized, civilized, non-animal) version of the human — which is to say, exposes the illusory nature of its self-identification with the human per se, destabilizing its attempt to universalize itself. However, whether this gives laughter, even within the cultural context dominated by this falsely universalized figure of the human, a subversive, critical potential, or affords it a particular capacity for managing and suppressing this threat, is a question, I will suggest, that is ultimately undecidable, yet nevertheless is deserving of attention.

In the third section of the paper I gesture towards the ongoing cultural prominence, as well as the discursive mobility of such approaches to laughter (a quality already highlighted in the second section through references to the slippage between the practical and theoretical functioning of laughter), through the frame of a well-known scene of collective laughter from the film *Goodfellas* (1990). In this scene, in which the thematics of violence, the human/nonhuman, and error converge in formally equivalent ways to their manifestation in Western philosophy and theory, the self-certainty of the Western, masculine, 'civilized' version of the human appears to be under threat — yet is ultimately reasserted through laughter. Thus we may (and I think should) pose, but cannot decisively answer, the question of whether treatments of laughter of the kinds I deal with, whether philosophical, literary, cinematic, or otherwise, reflect a (perhaps growing) sense of the (perhaps increasing) cultural destabilization of 'Man', or simply highlight the ways laughter has figured among the means and techniques by which it has historically managed to reassert itself in the face of the fundamental falsity — and thus the immanent potential cognizability — of its self-equation with 'humanity'.

THE LAUGHING ANIMAL

Contemporary accounts of the treatment of laughter in the history of Western philosophy often start with its categorization into three 'theories': superiority, relief, and incongruity theory.[1] In fact, these are not so much theories as loose ways of categorizing different approaches in order to contrast, oppose, and identify currents between them. Each category has a few particular thinkers who tend to be taken as its primary advocates, regardless of whether their 'theory' of laughter is developed through a sustained treatment of the topic or inferred from a few remarks made in another context. Thus, Thomas Hobbes is frequently cited as a proponent of the so-called superiority theory, '[t]he oldest, and probably still the most widespread theory of laughter', according to which laughter is seen as 'an expression of a person's

---

1   See, for example, John Morreall, 'A New Theory of Laughter', *Philosophical Studies*, 42.2 (September 1982), pp. 243–54; John Morreall, *Comic Relief: A Comprehensive Philosophy of Humor* (Chichester: Wiley-Blackwell, 2009), pp. 1–23; Simon Critchley, *On Humour* (London: Routledge, 2002), pp. 2–3; Mordechai Gordon, *Humor, Laughter, and Human Flourishing: A Philosophical Exploration of the Laughing Animal* (Cham: Springer, 2014), p. 2.

feeling of superiority over others'[2] — despite the fact that he discusses laughter only very briefly. In Chapter 6 of *Leviathan*, Hobbes writes that laughter 'is incident most to them, that are conscious of the fewest abilities in themselves; who are forced to keep themselves in their own favour by observing the imperfections of other men. And therefore much Laughter at the defects of others, is a signe of Pusillanimity.'[3] Such an approach associates laughter primarily with something like the feeling of *Schadenfreude*, or what Aristotle termed *epikhairekakia*.[4] Around the same time as Hobbes, René Descartes made a similar association in suggesting that the observation of evil befalling those who we deem to deserve it arouses a kind of joy 'accompanied by laughter and mockery'.[5]

Given that most statements taken as indicative of a superiority theory approach, despite their dispersal or recurrence over a long historical period, seem to be made more or less in passing, it might be argued that it is only with attempts to 'theorize' laughter in more sustained ways that the superiority approach begins to be characterized *as* a theory, as something for new (counter-)theories to oppose. This begins

---

2   Morreall, 'A New Theory of Laughter', p. 243.

3   Thomas Hobbes, *Leviathan*, ed. by Noel Malcolm, 3 vols (Oxford: Clarendon, 2012), II, p. 88 (Chapter 6). Hobbes also discusses laughter in chapter 9 of *Human Nature*. See Hobbes, *The Elements of Law, Natural and Politic*, ed. by Ferdinand Tönnies (Cambridge: Cambridge University Press, 1928), pp. 28–37 (pp. 31–32).

4   Aristotle, *Nicomachean Ethics*, trans. by W. D. Ross, revised by J. O. Umson, in *The Complete Works of Aristotle*, ed. by Jonathan Barnes, 2 vols (Princeton, NJ: Princeton University Press, 1984), II, pp. 1729–1867 (p. 1748 [1107a]). Here W. D. Ross translates ἐπιχαιρεκακία as 'spite'. In another edition, Rackham uses the term 'malice': Aristotle, *Nicomachean Ethics*, trans. by H. Rackham, Loeb Classical Library, 73 (Cambridge, MA: Harvard University Press, 1926), 73. Contrary to the *Schadenfreude* with which English writers and speakers sometimes like to declare that, since the Germans have a specific word for it, *Schadenfreude* is a particularly German emotion, the English language offers various near-equivalents. For example, the verb 'to gloat' can be used to approximate the German word; Aristotle's term is occasionally rendered in English as 'epicaricacy'; and one might consider the seventeenth-century theological term 'morose delectation' (from the Latin *delectio morosa*) — 'the habit of dwelling with enjoyment upon evil thoughts' ('morose, adj. 2', in *OED Online* (Oxford: Oxford University Press, 2020) <http://www.oed.com/view/Entry/122319> [accessed 1 October 2019]), or more modern terms like 'sadism', as doing similar work in the right contexts.

5   René Descartes, *Les Passions de l'âme*, in Descartes, *Œuvres philosophiques*, ed. by Ferdinand Alquié, 3 vols (Paris: Garnier, 1963–73), III (1973): *1643–1650*, pp. 941–1103 (p. 1003 [II, art. 62]). Descartes suggests that undeserved evil, in contrast, arouses sadness, and seeing deserved or undeserved good in others' lives results in serious joy or envy respectively.

with elaborations of a broad approach that has come to be termed 'incongruity theory', with proponents including James Beattie, Immanuel Kant, and Arthur Schopenhauer, and developed in different ways by a number of recent thinkers. Incongruity-based approaches share the view or assertion that we laugh when faced with something that does not 'fit' with the 'patterns among things, properties, events, etc.' that we have come to expect (provided the incongruity does not have any particular negative significance to us).[6] Alongside incongruity-based approaches, what has been called 'relief theory', associated in particular with writers such as Herbert Spencer and Sigmund Freud, but with elements identifiable at least as far back as the early eighteenth century in Lord Shaftesbury's essay-letter on laughter, suggests that build-ups of 'nervous energy' or 'psychic energy' must find outlets for release, and in certain circumstances do so through humour and laughter.[7]

I would like to draw attention to three features shared by these different types of approach to laughter and humour — features whose transversal recurrence may be less apparent when such approaches are treated as separate 'theories'. John Morreall has argued that salient aspects of the superiority-, incongruity-, and relief-based approaches point towards the possibility of a general theory of laughter, which he summarizes with the formula: 'Laughter results from a pleasant psychological shift.'[8] Like Morreall, I want to draw out features from these different approaches to laughter which seem to point in a certain direction: however, rather than generalizing or universalizing on this basis, I want to tease out the particularity of these different approaches, pointing through this recurring trio of themes to a shared set of underlying concerns that are, in fact, quite culturally specific (even if the culture to which they are specific has had a historically and globally extensive reach).

---

6   Morreall, 'A New Theory', p. 245.
7   Herbert Spencer, 'On the Physiology of Laughter' [1860], in Spencer, *Essays on Education and Kindred Subjects* (London: Dent, 1911), pp. 298–309; Sigmund Freud, *The Pelican Freud Library*, trans. by James Strachey, rev. and ed. by Angela Richards, 15 vols (Harmondsworth: Penguin, 1973–86), III (1976): *Jokes and their Relation to the Unconscious*; Anthony Ashley Cooper, 'An Essay on the Freedom of Wit and Humour — A Letter to a Friend' [1709] <http://www.earlymoderntexts.com/assets/pdfs/shaftesbury1709a_1.pdf> [accessed 1 October 2019].
8   Morreall, 'A New Theory', p. 249. For Morreall's subsequent elaboration and exploration of this general theory, see, among other publications, Morreall, *Comic Relief*, especially pp. 49–68.

The first of these themes is an association of laughter with violence and competition — with a struggle between opposing forces. In superiority approaches, this struggle is primarily social: laughter is construed as a means by which one attempts to establish one's superiority over others, possibly, as in Hobbes's formulation, in compensation for one's underlying sense of inferiority or weakness. In the *Republic*, while discussing the qualities that should be possessed by the guardians of the ideal state, before he gets round to suggesting that drunkenness, softness and sloth are 'most unbefitting', Socrates links laughter directly to violence: the guardians should not be 'prone to laughter. For ordinarily when one abandons himself to violent laughter his condition provokes a violent reaction.'[9] This dimension of social violence remains closely associated with — indeed is in some senses treated as contiguous with — the emphasis on the interplay or opposition between energetic forces in relief-based approaches. In *Jokes and their Relation to the Unconscious*, Freud suggests that, where wit or joking (*der Witz*) is not intended purely to induce pleasure, it is used either to show hostility or produce obscenity. Obscene or smutty jokes, he suggests, arise from a desire to seduce — but one which manifests in an aggressive attempt: 'Through the utterance of obscene words, the person *attacked* is *forced* to picture the parts of the body in question in the sexual act, and is shown that the *aggressor* himself pictures the same thing.'[10] When wit is used in the service of a hostile tendency, it substitutes for the actual violence which social morals prohibit: 'By belittling and humbling our enemy, by scorning and ridiculing him, we indirectly obtain the pleasure of his defeat by the laughter of the third person, the inactive spectator.'[11] And when this kind of wit is used 'as a weapon of attack or criticism of superiors who claim to be an authority', wit can also be employed in response 'as a resistance against

---

9   Plato, *The Republic*, trans. by G. M. A. Grube, rev. by C. D. C. Grube, in Plato, *Complete Works*, ed. by John M. Cooper (Indianapolis, IN: Hackett, 1997), pp. 971–1223 (p. 1036 and p. 1026 [III, 398e and 388e]). Aristotle reaffirms the association of humour with competitiveness in repeating the opinion of Gorgias, that 'jests [...] are supposed to be of some service in controversy. [...] you should kill your opponents' earnestness with jesting and their jesting with earnestness'. Aristotle, *Rhetoric*, trans. by W. Rhys Roberts, in *The Complete Works of Aristotle*, II, pp. 2152–2269 (p. 2268 [1419b]).
10 Freud, *Jokes*, pp. 140–41 (emphasis added, J. B.).
11 Ibid., p. 150.

such authority and as an escape from its pressure.'[12] This emphasis on the relation of laughter, or at least humour, to social constraint and its resistance, had already been emphasized by Shaftesbury, writing in 1709, with the suggestion that restrictions on free expression lead to the use of wit and humour or 'raillery' as a kind of disguise:

> If men are forbidden to speak their minds seriously on certain subjects, they'll do it ironically. If they are forbidden to speak at all on such subjects, or if they think it really dangerous to do so, they will then redouble their disguise [...] Thus raillery comes more into fashion, and goes to extremes. The persecuting spirit has aroused the bantering one.[13]

While relief theories focus more directly on psychic and bodily energy, the struggle between opposing energetic forces remains primary. In Herbert Spencer's physiologically oriented account of the causes of laughter, he focuses on situations in which 'a large mass of emotion had been produced, or [...] a large portion of the nervous system was in a state of tension' — for example, when watching a moving scene in a play. Such tension entails a 'large amount of nervous energy' corresponding to a 'quantity of vague, nascent thought and emotion' which seems destined to be expended in the 'body of new feelings and ideas' that the viewer expects to arise from the next part of the scene.[14] However, if something interrupts the dramatic flow — Spencer imagines a kid goat wandering on to the stage and sniffing the actors at a climactic moment — then 'the channels along which the discharge was about to take place are closed.' (As a contemporary equivalent example, we might think of the supposedly comic 'outtakes' or 'blooper reels' sometimes released after or alongside a film or television production, which so often show an actor forgetting their lines at a tense moment in the drama — usually leading to the interruption of the flow

---

12   Ibid., p. 153.
13   Shaftesbury, 'An Essay on the Freedom of Wit and Humour'. Such examples already point to the relative arbitrariness of the categorization of approaches to laughter into separate categories: Shaftesbury's essay clearly already bears elements of both superiority and relief approaches, which are likewise co-present in Freud's account. At the same time, incongruity — first between social expectations and desires, but also as integral to the psychological experience by which we find something humorous or are given to laughter — play a key role in Freudian and Spencerian relief theories.
14   Spencer, 'The Physiology of Laughter', p. 305.

and sudden outbursts of laughter among cast and crew). The actions of the goat open a new channel for direction of this nervous energy, but one based on ideas and feelings that are 'too small' to absorb all of it: 'The excess must therefore discharge itself in some other direction; [...] there results an efflux through the motor nerves to various classes of the muscles, producing the half-convulsive actions we term laughter.'[15] Freud draws on and develops Spencer's approach in arguing that the joke, in dealing with topics or ideas usually repressed, yet allowing them not to be, results in a discharge of 'static energy' (*Besetzungsenergie*) which would, in other circumstances, have been used in the 'inhibition' of those ideas, but now finds itself 'superfluous and neutralized'.[16]

Approaches that tend to be classed as incongruity theories, meanwhile, can be said to associate laughter with violence in the form of a violation of expectations. Even if this can be construed as a more metaphorical or abstract notion of violence than those central to superiority- and relief-based approaches, proponents of incongruity-based approaches tend to presume that it would be more natural to experience displeasure, discomfort, when suddenly faced with incongruities among things, circumstances, phenomena, or ideas: the ability to find pleasure in such incongruities is seen as a kind of displacement of this more fundamental or natural reaction, and thus a redirection or diversion of a potentially violent experience. (The capacity to enjoy or celebrate ambiguity and incongruity is effectively treated as secondary to the rationalist philosophical tendency to seek to explain or clarify, and thus resolve apparent contradictions, and/or to traditional aesthetic-religious valuations of symmetry, harmony, balance, etc.)[17] The anticipated or implicit violence or discomfort in this reaction to incongruity is displaced into the physiological and psychological form of laughter. Thus, just as Spencer will emphasize the discharge (relief) of 'excess' energy through 'half-convulsive actions', in Kant's version of the incongruity approach, he talks of mental and physical 'agitation': he suggests that a joke works by deceiving us for a moment, so that

---

15 Ibid., p. 305.
16 Freud, *Jokes*, p. 229.
17 Cf. Gordon, *Humor, Laughter, and Human Flourishing*, pp. 19–22.

when the illusion vanishes, 'the mind looks at the illusion once more in order to give it another try, and so by a rapid succession of tension and relaxation the mind is bounced back and forth and made to sway'; the sudden 'snapping' of the metaphorical string causing this swaying 'must cause a mental agitation and an inner bodily agitation in harmony with it, which continues involuntarily, and which gives rise to fatigue while yet also cheering us up.'[18]

The second feature I would like to highlight as being transversal to historically dominant Western theories of laughter is the foregrounding of the boundary — or perhaps it is more apt to say the relationship — between the human and the nonhuman. Historically, this figures as a concern with the relationship between human and animal, emblematized by Aristotle's oft-cited declaration that the human is 'the only animal that laughs'.[19] The logic compressed in this formula situates the human within the category or sphere of the animal, yet only by assigning it its own special sub-category, as isolated from all other animals. Philosophical discussions of laughter in Western thought are, as with many other topics, embedded to a significant extent within the long-running preoccupation with explicating this duality of the human/nonhuman, with distinguishing between human and nonhuman aspects of the human animal (or, increasingly, from the Renaissance on, the human machine). Epitomizing this tendency, Laurent Joubert, in his 1579 *Treatise on Laughter*, distinguishes 'bastard laughter' and 'dog laughter' as false or 'untrue' forms of laughter from the 'true' form which is only available to the human. According to Erica Fudge, this 'true laughter', which 'calls on the workings of the rational soul', but still depends, like bastard and dog laughter, on physiognomy, becomes 'an important aspect of being human' — even 'a microcosmic exhibition of human-ness' — precisely because it is part voluntary and part involuntary — partly subject to the exercise of will and reason, and partly beyond their control.[20]

---

18 Immanuel Kant, *Critique of Judgment*, trans. and introduction by Werner S. Pluhar (Indianapolis, IN: Hackett, 1987), p. 204 [AA 333].

19 Aristotle, *Parts of Animals*, trans. by W. Ogle, in *The Complete Works of Aristotle*, I, pp. 994–1086 (p. 1049 [673a]).

20 Erica Fudge, *Brutal Reasoning: Animals, Rationality, and Humanity in Early Modern England* (Ithaca, NY: Cornell University Press, 2006), pp. 17–18. As she puts it a

This conception of nonhuman entities or agents as characterized by involuntary or deterministic behaviour, in contrast to the rational, wilful, soul-possessing human, was a major factor in attempts from the sixteenth century onwards to draw an equivalence between the animal and the machine. Descartes' thesis of animal automatism, controversial in its time, is one of the best known and most influential — as expressed, for example, in his statement that 'if there were such machines, which had the organs and the appearance of a monkey or any other irrational animal, we would have no means of knowing that they were in any way of a different nature from these animals'; whereas a machine made in the image of a human, able to mimic its actions accurately, would still be absolutely distinguishable from a 'real' human.[21] Contrary to Descartes's apparent intentions, his arguments would eventually become part of the basis for *eradicating* distinctions between humans and machines — culminating in Julien Offray de La Mettrie's 1748 *L'Homme-Machine*[22] — and, indeed, anticipating and establishing some of the conceptual grounding for later posthumanist thought.[23] Thus when Spencer, three centuries after Joubert, likewise

---

little further on (pp. 19–20), for Joubert, 'in laughter, mind and body are brought into potential conflict, but in true laughter the mind takes control of something that is possibly and powerfully out of its control. [...] The laugh may be of the passionate animal body, but the true laugh is certainly of the reasonable human mind'. See also Laurent Joubert, *Treatise on Laughter*, trans. and annotated by Gregory David de Rocher (Tuscaloosa: University of Alabama Press, 1980).

21   René Descartes, *Discours de la méthode*, in *Œuvres philosophiques*, I (1963): 1618–1637, pp. 567–650 (p. 628 [v]).

22   Julien Offray de La Mettrie, *Machine Man and Other Writings*, ed. and trans. by Ann Thomson (Cambridge: Cambridge University Press, 1996).

23   In effect, these two lines of thought amount to mirrored expansions of Descartes's position, leading on the one hand to the (mechanist) notion that the human is simply a highly sophisticated machine, and on the other to the (posthumanist) notion that it is possible to make a machine so sophisticated that it would be indistinguishable from the human (the latter seemingly implying the former). For an historical account of Descartes's animal automatism and the trajectory connecting it to the human mechanism of the eighteenth century as epitomized by La Mettrie, see Leonora Rosenfield, *From Beast-Machine to Man-Machine* (New York: Octagon Books, 1968). Rosenfield notes that Fromondus's critique of Descartes on theological grounds (made just three months after the appearance of the *Discourse*) — that atheists would be able to apply his thinking on the animal soul to the rational soul — highlighted precisely the point from which La Mettrie would draw inspiration a century later. (See ibid., pp. 7–8 and pp. 25–26). Neil Badmington has highlighted the way Descartes's argument, intended to mark a radical difference between human and nonhuman, in fact left open the possibility that, with the right technological advancements, it would 'no longer be possible to

attempts to explain laughter on the basis of physiology, the mechanical has replaced the animal as the involuntary, instinctive, or physiological part of the human, that which is not unique to it and which thus binds it to the nonhuman sphere: the question of the human's relation to the (its) non/inhuman dimension remains crucial to the context in which laughter is discussed.

Whether in the form of the animal or the mechanistic, this non-human — or at least, this (emphasized as) not-uniquely-human — aspect of laughter, based in physiology, can be said to mirror the way in which laughter, in a more symbolic manner but at a no less real, experiential level, *reduces* its human targets, in certain relatively common circumstances, to the status of the subhuman. This parallel recurs throughout the history of theoretical discussions of the nature, function, and cause of laughter, yet is seldom remarked explicitly. How is it — or what is the significance of the fact — that a kind of behaviour viewed as somehow less than human, or minimally human, in both a moral and a biological sense (with neither the moral being exclusive to superiority-based approaches, nor the biological exclusive to relief-based approaches) — serves to enact this dehumanizing effect on the laughter's target? A kind of behaviour, rooted in the human's least human dimension, seems to go through the very human circuit of socio-cultural interaction, and produce, when it emerges at the other end, a symbolic reduction of a human who played no active role in this movement. It may even be that this seeming contradiction — or at least, this unusual parallel — is a factor in the tendency to delineate the so-called superiority theory from the so-called relief theory — as though it were harder to countenance the nonhuman as a decisive feature at both ends of the laughing/being-laughed-at relation. This issue is pursued further in the following section, in particular in relation to Bergson's theory of laughter.

The third recurring feature of theoretical explanations of laughter I want to highlight is probably the most obvious (and yet worth re-emphasizing, especially given the context of this volume): the linking of laughter to error. In fact, we require no theories, no philosophical

---

maintain a clear distinction between the human and the inhuman'. Neil Badmington, 'Theorizing Posthumanism', *Cultural Critique*, 53 (Winter 2003), pp. 10–27 (p. 18).

arguments to convince us that laughter and humour are almost always associated with something 'wrong', something out of place — something that is perceived as being 'in error'. Incongruity theory approaches, as we have seen, make this their direct focus — with much of the theoretical work oriented around explaining how, why, and when experiences that ought to be unsettling — misperception, misunderstanding, thwarted expectations, deception, illusion, incongruity, impropriety — can give rise to a response indicating pleasure or delight. Yet in superiority-based approaches, too, a certain notion of error — albeit moral error — is primary. Indeed, as we have just seen, this primacy is simultaneously highlighted from two seemingly opposing perspectives: on the one hand, the laughter itself is supposed to express some form of contempt or derision regarding that which is lacking in another person — their failings, weaknesses, inadequacies, compared to the one who is laughing; on the other hand, those propounding this explanation of laughter usually seem to view the laugher themselves as morally deficient — ignobly taking pleasure in the misfortune of others (*Schadenfreude*), or compensating for their own insecurities and weakness by putting others down (displaying 'pusillanimity', as Hobbes put it), or lacking rational competence and self-control. Finally, in relief-based approaches, error figures in the form of energetic resources that have been prepared, but are no longer needed; that is, the laugher built up a store of nervous or psychic energy for some purpose, which they then no longer needed to fulfil, leaving that stored energy purposeless: this energy, having nowhere to go, yet still needing to be released, became errant, finding its way into physiological and emotional gestures that must be regarded as useless, except to the extent that catering for the suddenly useless is a useful function.

I have been able to provide only a cursory overview here of the recurrence of these different features of Western philosophical approaches to laughter: competition-based violence (whether viewed as actual or symbolic — and we might question whether violence can *ever* be purely symbolic), the relationship between human and nonhuman, and the experience or recognition of error, in a multiplicity of forms. This brief sampling is hopefully enough, however, to allow us to begin to speculate as to why they recur, together, across what have tended to be separated into different, sometimes opposing theories of laughter. I want to do this based on two propositions, which I will state briefly here before elaborating on them in the following section.

First, while conventional histories of ideas might stress the broad cultural and epistemological differences between thinkers in, say, classical Greece, Renaissance France and twentieth-century Vienna, viewed together — as, for example, from a critical-theoretical, feminist, or postcolonial perspective — they can be said to share a great deal. Crucially, they have a common aspiration to universalism: that is, to understanding certain of their own basic assumptions and values, e.g. with regard to truth, rationality, morality, nature, psychology, as universally applicable. Yet these 'universal' values of course derive from a specific (even if apparently broad) set of cultural and material forms, texts, bodies, modes of thought. The figures of the human and *humanitas* that are thus shaped and presented as universal retain key elements of this underlying specificity — and these are most visible where and whenever some individual or group is denied full inclusion within the (supposedly universal, actually particular) category of the human. Thus 'the human' arising from these aspirations remains more male than female, more masculine than feminine, more European/Western than non-Western, more heterosexual (or at least, familial) than not, more likely to derive its morals or ethics from Judaeo-Christian sources, and so on. Following Sylvia Wynter, I will refer to this falsely universalized human below using the term by which it generally used to identify itself — 'Man' — though now, of course, in order to highlight the specificity that is masked by its historical deployment as the universal representative of the human.[24] Second, given that the various Western philosophical approaches to laughter we have touched on can be said to be largely embedded within this falsely universalized — and then strategically restricted — understanding of humanity/the human, it may form the basis for hypothesizing as to the function behind the recurrent trio of themes I have identified across them. The repeated emphasis placed on the distinction between the

---

24   Sylvia Wynter, 'Unsettling the Coloniality of Being/Power/Truth/Freedom: Towards the Human, after Man, its Overrepresentation — An Argument', *CR: The New Centennial Review*, 3.3 (2003), pp. 257–337. Cf. Rosi Braidotti, *The Posthuman* (Cambridge: Polity, 2013), pp. 13–54.

human and the non/human in such discussions — both attributed to laughter as part of its function, and at stake in discussions of laughter as situated within larger attempts to explain the ideal nature of the human (physiologically, e.g., in Joubert, Spencer; socially, e.g., in Plato, Hobbes; metaphysically, e.g., in Descartes etc) — can be seen as directly connected to the violence or competitiveness that is so frequently at play in these discussions. There is a dehumanizing, overtly or covertly violent struggle to assert the universal but exclusive status of Man, to equate it with, or allow it to dominate, the 'human' per se, and thus to enforce the cultural, social dominance of those self-identifying with it over those others it designates as less than human ('not-Man'). What I would like to hypothesize is that the recognition of error that is crucial in many apparently different ways to the conditions that produce laughter may in some sense consist in the recognition and management of the fundamental error involved in this equation of Man with the human. If this hypothesis carries any weight, a further, consequential and necessary — even if undecidable — question arises: if these accounts of laughter do indeed point to the error at the heart of the Western self-conception as human, do accounts and experiences of laughter in which the primary features of Man feature prominently (i.e., those in which displays of masculinity, cultural and intellectual superiority, sexual and physical domination, are particularly pronounced) render laughter the site of Man's potential undoing, where its false universality is revealed and begins to collapse — or does laughter simply form another means by which Man copes with such destablising threats, and ultimately reasserts its dominance?

'FUNNY HOW?' — FALSE FALSE (FALSE?) ALARMS

Bergson begins his 1900 study *Laughter: An Essay on the Meaning of the Comic* with three general postulates about laughter that will guide the rest of his investigation, and which relate directly to the themes elaborated above, starting with the boundaries of the human. First, he suggests that 'the comic does not exist outside the pale of what is strictly *human*.'[25] Thus he suggests that a landscape is never laugh-

---

25 Henri Bergson, *Laughter: An Essay on the Meaning of the Comic*, trans. by Cloudesley Brereton (New York: Macmillan, 1911), p. 3.

able without figures or subjects, that animals are laughable only by virtue of 'some human attitude or expression', and that if you laugh at a hat, you're not laughing at its material existence but the shape or use assigned to it by humans. For this reason, he suggests that whereas philosophers (following Aristotle's famous formulation, as cited above) have often defined the human as 'an animal that laughs' (*un animal qui sait rire*), in fact a better definition might be 'the animal that is laughed at' (*un animal qui fait rire*).[26] Second, he proposes that laughter tends to be accompanied by an 'absence of feeling' (*insensibilité*).[27] This is not to deny that laughter may be pleasurable, but that it is antithetical to 'negative' emotional states — such as anxiety, despair, or fear; and also to feelings of pity or sympathy for whatever/whoever it is that is the object of the laughter (here we seem to have at least an echo of superiority-based approaches). Third, Bergson agrees with many other thinkers in seeing laughter as something fundamentally social: 'Laughter appears to stand in need of an echo.'[28] Thus even when it comes from a solitary individual, laughter is always 'the laughter of a group' — and specifically, that of a 'closed circle', such that it indicates a 'complicity with other individuals, real or imaginary'.[29]

After establishing these framing presumptions, Bergson goes on to develop his central argument, that the comic, and thus laughter, is very widely and fundamentally associated with the central image of 'something mechanical encrusted on the living'.[30] This seemingly unnatural combination of the mechanical and the living manifests, he argues, in a number of ways, linked by the recurrence of unnatural or incongruous relationships between elasticity and rigidity, flexibility

---

26 Ibid., p. 3–4.
27 Ibid., p. 4.
28 Ibid., p. 6.
29 Ibid.
30 Ibid., p. 37. See also p. 29: 'The attitudes, gestures and movement of the human body are laughable in exact proportion as that body reminds us of a mere machine.' Bergson goes on to suggest that many comic figures are funny due to their exhibiting, like Don Quixote, a certain automatism, an ignorance of self — 'the comic person is unconscious' (p. 16) — and that this inelasticity may be manifest in all sorts of ways — in the physical body, a person's mind, character, behaviour, etc. Later in the course of his argument the scope will be expanded, such that he highlights a recurrent slippage from 'an artificial *mechanization* of the human body' to 'any substitution whatsoever of the artificial for the natural'. (p. 48)

and tension. To give just one example, he suggests that if we laugh at someone falling over in the street, it is because we observe 'a certain *mechanical inelasticity*, just where one would expect to find the wide-awake adaptability and pliableness of a human being.'[31] In Bergson's definition and the many examples through which he elaborates and explores it, we repeatedly encounter the three characteristics we have identified as recurring in Western philosophical discussions: laughter results from an unexpected image or event, violating our expectations and often implying actual physical or emotional violence, caused by an unexpected (erroneous, incongruous) combination of mechanical inelasticity with living pliability — in a 'strictly human' context.[32]

There is an apparent tension here, however — one which might be identified in any of the explorations of laughter we have already considered, but which I think Bergson's investigation makes more central than most — between the 'strictly human' and the encrusting of the mechanical, artificial, and rigid upon the living: that is, between an image or instance of the human as it is expected to appear, and a process of its becoming nonhuman. Thus laughter in the Bergsonian account revolves around an experience of the human that doesn't coincide with itself. Something or someone taken at first non-controversially (probably unthinkingly) to be a human acting in a certain, culturally 'normal' human way, or forming a culturally recognizable human expression, suddenly upsets these expectations, these norms, and thus reveals itself as not fitting the preconceived notion of the human (or of a 'normal' human mode of action, expression, etc.) that initially, probably unconsciously, framed it in the perception of the observer. However, given that the rest of the observer's general expectations (epistemol-

---

31 Ibid., p. 10.
32 Freud fully accepts and endorses Bergson's argument in *Jokes and their Relation to the Unconscious*, although it seems he can't help trying to play down the importance of Bergson's work relative to his own even as he draws on it. The ways thinkers relate to one another's work is perhaps one of the most visible and recurrent sites in philosophical and theoretical writing of 'Man's' competitive need to assert his superiority at the expense of others, whether he agrees with them or not. Thus Freud avers that he can 'include his [Bergson's] view under our own [Freud's] formula' (p. 209); and that the relating of comic effects, via automatism and automata, to the child's toy — in what he condescendingly refers to as 'Bergson's charming and lively volume *Le rire*' — has 'surprisingly enough' been an influence on his own attempt to seek for the 'infantile roots' of the comic, its psychogenesis. (pp. 222–23)

ogy, ontology, understanding of cultural norms) are not shaken by this encounter with the unexpected — everything else seems to continue to 'fit' — they will not go so far as to conclude that what they are observing is actually something nonhuman: the man who falls over due to mechanical inelasticity — e.g., by failing to adapt to obstacles or other changes newly introduced to his environment — is only taken to behave 'as if' he were a machine, a nonhuman; if the observer concluded that he were actually, in this action, revealing himself to be a robot — just as if he turned out to be seriously hurt — the laughter would very likely cease; one would be in the realm of other experiences associated with human/nonhuman, living/non-living encounters — the uncanny, mortal fear, social concern, etc. The observer who laughs does not situate what they are laughing *at* outside the realm of the nonhuman or non-living, but recognizes their preconceived notion of what the human entails to be subject to modification: the man behaving as a machine, and falling over, is funny because he must still be considered a man, a human; the category of what is understood as human is widened to include what was intuitively considered just a moment ago as nonhuman; that prior understanding of the limits of the category of the human is thus revealed as having been too small, restrictive, thus flawed.

All of this begs the question, what particular kind of human is it that is thus unsettled — what preconceptions regarding the normal human have been challenged and opened to modification — in this or that particular laughable scenario? A large number of Bergson's examples are taken from relatively canonical (especially French) modern comic writing — from the plays of Molière, Racine, and Labiche, the caricatures of La Bruyère — as well as popular European comic novels such as *Don Quixote* and *Baron Munchhausen*. These examples very often focus on male (and masculine) figures exhibiting self-confidence or self-certainty regarding their particular outlooks, accompanied by some corresponding character trait(s) from which the comic effects are in part derived — pomposity, arrogance, naivety, hypocrisy, etc.: Don Quixote as identifying himself with the noble hero of chivalric romance and living accordingly despite overwhelming evidence to the contrary; the customs house officers who, on rushing to help passengers rescued from a wrecked steamer ship, adhere rigidly to the rules of their profession by first asking the survivors if they 'have anything to declare';[33] the philosopher who asserts, when faced with people attesting experiences that contradict his arguments, that '[e]xperience is in the wrong',[34] or another who criticizes displays of anger before flying into a rage;[35] the policeman marionette who repeatedly springs to his feet to assert his authority no matter how many times he is felled by Punch's cudgel;[36] Molière's doctors, who would rather hold fast to the authority of Hippocratic medicine than save a patient.[37] In discussing all these examples, Bergson stresses that it is the rigidity of the characters or their behaviour that is found humorous, identifying this with a certain automatism, life or the human behaving mechanically rather than adapting fluidly ('being alive') to changing circumstances. Yet even as he generalizes this notion of rigidity or inflexibility, inserting it within the abstract formula of 'something mechanical encrusted on the living', his examples continue to inscribe it within certain cultural ideals of moral propriety and 'respectability'[38] that tend to be circumscribed in Western, masculinized terms (e.g., those which fetishize heroism, scientific rationality, professionalism, bureaucracy, social order, etc.).

In other words, it is more Man than 'the human' which is having its claim to fully human status challenged here — yet at the same time, this is treated as the basis for the undermining of *any* image of the human. On the one hand, Bergson is probably quite aware that he is dealing with laughter within a culturally specific context, and that there are recurrent tropes in his examples, many of which involve some aspect of European, civilized masculinity being lampooned or 'taken down a peg': he is explicit that the 'natural environment' of laughter is society, and that the premise of its fundamentally social function will be 'the leading idea of all our investigations'.[39] Yet on the other hand, his desire to extrapolate from this a general or universal theory of laughter risks

---

33 Bergson, *Laughter*, p. 46.
34 Ibid., p. 48.
35 Ibid., p. 147.
36 Ibid., p. 71.
37 Ibid., p. 54.
38 Cf. ibid., pp. 125–26: 'To express in reputable language some disreputable idea, to take some scandalous situation, some low-class calling or disgraceful behaviour, and describe them in terms of the utmost "*respectability*," is generally comic.'
39 Ibid., pp. 7–8.

undermining this very specificity — and indeed, risks allowing Man to recover a little of the façade of universality that these comic scenarios are supposed to take away from him.

It is worth emphasizing how the place of superiority (effectively always a prelude to, if not form of, violence) seems to shift constantly through these discourses on laughter. Whereas for those citing Aristotle and Hobbes in support of a superiority approach, laughter is the mark of the coward or weakling attempting to assert his superiority over (an)other(s), in comedies of social manners, the laughter has a 'corrective' role, in that it identifies, exposes — and thus encourages the avoidance of — traits taken as socially or morally undesirable.[40] In other words, the moralizing function implicit in one purportedly *theoretical* way of accounting for laughter passes over to comedic *practices*, which seek to evoke laughter; and, indeed, this moralizing effort is itself a counter to and undermining of the implicit moralizing of the civilized, self-assured figures exposed to ridicule. There is an ongoing, shifting struggle of moral forces that seems to surround laughter in Western culture — especially the literate/literary culture, which, from the classical era through the Renaissance until relatively recently, was both the main prescriptor of *humanitas*, Man, the ideal human, and the means by which one attained to this ideal (through education, reading, cultivation).

This fluidity may mean that we can never take a Western critique of Man at face value, whether conducted through philosophy, theatre, critical theory, or telling a joke: it seems likely that challenges to particular aspects of this multi-faceted figure can always be re-inscribed within a larger scheme of corrective cultivation; one laughs at a flaw in one of Molière's comic figures in order to correct the tendency towards this trait in oneself and one's peers — seeing the illusory equation of 'Man' with the 'human', but only in the end to attain a 'better' ideal version of humanity that is ultimately likely to retain some of the salient traits of Man. Perhaps for the same reasons, it seems that such critiques, in exposing the false universalization of a particular figure of

---

40 Cf. ibid., pp. 87–88: The apparent automatism characterizing the comic 'calls for an immediate corrective. This corrective is laughter, a social gesture that singles out and represses a special kind of absent-mindedness in men and events.'

the human, find it hard to avoid translating this very self-universalizing tendency back into a fundamentally human trait.

Indeed, it is precisely for this reason that attending to the question of what particular version of the human is being universalized (and thus used to particularize the category of 'humanity') is of such importance. This is one of the issues, for example, underpinning Eduardo Viveiros de Castro and Tânia Stolze Lima's critical deployment of 'Amerindian perspectivism' towards a 'requalification of anthropology' (that modern field in which the relation between particular and universal forms of the human has been so consistently a site of struggle and concern).[41] Viveiros de Castro refers to Lévi-Strauss's fascination with the parallel 'anthropological' investigations of the Spanish and the Americans at the historical moment of their first encounter — with the Americans drowning Spanish prisoners to test their material, bodily natures at the same time as the Spanish were sending investigators to determine whether the Americans had souls. For Lévi-Strauss, this scenario made manifest the seemingly paradoxical way in which '[a] kind of congenital avarice preventing the extension of the predicates of humanity to the species as a whole appears to be one of its predicates:'[42] to claim exclusivity for one's version of humanity is a universal human trait; all humans identifying with a cultural group equate it with the human. Whether or not this is so, for de Castro and Lima, there is a critical difference between the Spanish doubt regarding the Americans' possession of souls equivalent to theirs, and the Americans' doubt concerning the Europeans' possession of bodies equivalent to their own. The distinction is something like the equivalent one, in another register, of a Pauline political theology: of determining someone as Jewish or Roman (as counting as human) according to the spirit (*pneuma*) or according to the flesh (*sarx*).[43] One version grants an

---

41   Eduardo Viveiros de Castro, 'Cannibal Metaphysics: Amerindian Perspectivism', *Radical Philosophy*, 182 (November–December 2013), pp. 17–28 (p. 20). Cf. Tânia Stolze Lima, 'O dois e seu múltiplo: reflexões sobre o perspectivismo emu ma cosmologia tupi', *Mana*, 2.2 (1996), pp. 21–47.

42   Viveiros de Castro, 'Cannibal Metaphysics', p. 20.

43   See, for example, Alain Badiou, *Saint Paul: The Foundations of Universalism*, trans. by Ray Brassier (Stanford, CA: Stanford University Press, 2003), pp. 55–64 and *passim*; Giorgio Agamben, *The Time That Remains: A Commentary on the Letter to the Romans*, trans. by Patricia Dailey (Stanford, CA: Stanford University Press, 2005), pp. 44–58

equivalent right to life, affords equality in terms of moral responsibility, the other denies it.

I have been considering Western philosophical and theoretical engagements with laughter that, to lesser and greater extents, when considered together, seem to repeatedly expose, *and extend or repeat*, the violent ways a particular cultural figure of the human — masculine, civilized, Western — uses laughter to assert its superiority over those it considers non- and subhuman (animals, machines, members of other socio-cultural groups). There seems to be something almost innately ambiguous, not so much about laughter (though the non-linguistic, non-propositional form of laughter may be one reason for its aptness in this context) but about such concerns with the particularity/generality of this culturally specific figure of the human. That is, if every exposure of this false, violent imposition of Man on 'the human' simultaneously has the potential to critique *and* reassert it, then it becomes increasingly difficult, if not impossible, to know whether a given instance of this exposure — whether in an experience of humour or a philosophical discussion of laughter — has the function/effect of undermining or reinforcing the violent act of the universalization of Man.

This ambiguity and this difficulty recur with particular force in a more recent theory of laughter. Here again the thematic trio of violence, the human/nonhuman boundary or relation, and an experience of error, converge. The false alarm theory of laughter, which borrows from evolutionary biology, neuroscience, and physiology research, suggests that humans evolved laughter as a means of relieving tension in situations where a perceived danger turns out to be a false alarm.[44] Here is the scenario John Morreall uses to illustrate the false alarm theory in his book *Comic Relief*:

---

and *passim*. Thirty years after his writing on laughter, in a text that nevertheless again centrally treats processes of mechanization as forms of dehumanization, Bergson also makes an equivalent distinction, between closed and open forms of morality — the former extended only to those a cultural group considers to be like them, the latter extended in principle beyond any given material form of the human, extending in the direction of all life, if not further. See Bergson, *The Two Sources of Morality and Religion*, trans. by R. Ashley Audra and Cloudesley Brereton with W. Horsfall Carter (Notre Dame, IN: University of Notre Dame Press, 1977).

44 V. S. Ramachandran, 'The Neurology and Evolution of Humor, Laughter, and Smiling: The False Alarm Theory', *Medical Hypotheses*, 51.4 (October 1998), pp. 351–54.

> A group [of early humans] is sitting around a fire at night, when they see what looks like a horned monster coming through the tall grass. If it really is an invader, then they should be serious and emotionally engaged. Fear or rage would energize them to escape, or to conquer the monster. But what if 'the monster' is actually their chief returning to camp carrying an antelope carcass on his head? Then their fear or rage not only will waste time and energy, but could easily lead to pointless killing. In that case, what they need is a quick way to block or to dispel fight-or-flight emotions. They need to disengage themselves and play with their perceptions and thoughts, rather than act on them.[45]

This 'play' gives rise to laughter, whose value lies not only in relaxing the muscles, releasing the tension, but in communicating to other members of the group that, as V. S. Ramachandran, one of the first proponents of the theory puts it, 'there has been a false alarm; that "the rest of you chaps need not waste your precious energy and resources responding to the spurious anomaly."'[46] This account of laughter actively presents the evolutionary origins of laughter as occurring in a masculinized scene. We need not, of course, presume that those who feel threatened by the perceived invader, becoming 'energized' by it, ready for fight or flight, should be the male members of the group — the 'chaps'. But the prominent features of the scene are identifiable as strongly associated with masculinity in Western culture — the threat of violence, the need to defend the tribe or family, the patriarchal social structure (there seems to be no logical reason, in terms of what the scenario is supposed to say about the origins of laughter, for it to be the chief, as opposed to any other member of the group, who has been mistaken for a monster).

Furthermore, it is precisely the self-certainty of this masculine, assured superiority that has been called into question here — that is, the preparedness and capability of those involved to defend the tribe against a violent invader, which necessarily includes their ability to accurately detect and respond to threats, to distinguish the human from the animal and the monstrous. Laughter arises when members of the group realize that their sense of danger is misplaced and that they

---

45 John Morreall, *Comic Relief*, p. 44.
46 Ramachandran, 'The Neurology and Evolution of Humor', p. 352.

have mistaken something harmless, indeed, something beneficial to the group, for something dangerous. Their own capacity for perceiving, interpreting, understanding their world, has revealed itself as flawed. In this sense, while the laughter seems to be the outcome of a sense of relief — both emotional and physical — it is also an indicator that this flaw remains: had the error not been realized, they might have killed the chief; at any later point, one of them might be wrongly identified as a threat and killed by the others; or, even after the mistake has been recognized and laughed at, were an actual beast to charge the group later that night, they might take it to be the chief or another member of the group replaying the joke, and thus fail to respond in time to defend themselves and their fellows.

Does the laughter in this scenario — and does this account of the origins of laughter — challenge the confidence of a particular type of human, of Man, the alert, discerning defender of his people, ready for action, laughing at the errors of (his own) superstition; or does it reassert it? On the one hand the theory presents a potential arche-scene for the tendency to take the membership criteria of one's own socio-cultural group for the totality of those worthy of life (respect, protection, preservation); and laughter here, again, seems to challenge the effectiveness of this gesture, to expose its illusory, suspect nature, by virtue of the error in the scene whereby a member of the group (indeed, a privileged member, the chief) is misidentified as nonhuman. The ensuing laughter recognizes and communicates this failure of perception and judgment. Yet on the other hand, the laughter also indicates that this human/nonhuman categorization is stable after all: not only has the apparent violent threat disappeared and physical security returned, but Man's security has been restored. There is, in effect, an interminable undecidability as to whether the identification of Man with the human is exposed and threatened, or managed and reinforced by the laughter in this scene, or in the theoretical discussions of laughter that stage it. Thus the apparent false alarm (the perceived threat is not real) can itself be construed as false (the mistaking of the threat for real marks the instability of perceptions regarding the real), and yet this, in turn, may be marked as a 'false falsehood': Man survives the threat to his Manhood, and remains secure in his self-identification with the human in general.

This uncertain, fluctuating, ambiguous relationship between laughter and violence is encapsulated in an infamous scene from the 1990 film *Goodfellas*, itself epitomizing what has become something of a modern cinematic/audiovisual cliché, especially in narratives revolving around violent struggles (which, of course, most often means masculine struggles, and thus, arguably, struggles over masculinity). Tommy DeVito (played by Joe Pesci), a Mafia figure who has recently begun to rise in power, having been 'made' — and who is already known for his volatile capacity for unpredictably becoming extremely violent — is relaxing with his entourage of friends and henchmen in a restaurant. He is in the middle of a long, relatively unfunny anecdote about how he verbally abused a cop. Everyone around him is laughing uproariously, to a degree that the larger narrative, as well as the direction, frames as excessive relative to the comic quality of the account; their laughter is demanded by Tommy's power, status, and personality. After Henry Hill (played by Ray Liotta), the film's protagonist and partial narrator, says, 'You're funny ...', Tommy becomes quiet, and, while at first still smiling, repeatedly asks Henry to explain what he means by this. His tone becomes increasingly aggressive: 'I'm funny how, I mean funny like I'm a clown, I amuse you? I make you laugh, I'm here to fuckin' amuse you? What do you mean funny, funny how? How am I funny?' As Tommy's anger increases, and Henry repeatedly fails to satisfy him, the tension builds to a point where violence seems to be about to break out, before after a final, long pause, Henry declares: 'Get the fuck out of here Tommy!', leading to everyone at the table cracking up with laughter, led by Tommy as he makes out that the whole thing has been a big joke.[47]

On the one hand, this second round of laughter may seem like a perfect illustration of the false alarm theory. It seems to have the direct function of deflating tension, saying — with relief — we are all friends here, the threat has passed; 'the rest of you chaps' can relax. Except that this scene *started* with laughter and camaraderie: indeed, even when the laughter gave way to a sense of menace, this was caused by the

---

47   *Goodfellas*, dir. by Martin Scorsese (Warner Bros. Pictures, 1990). Martin Scorsese and Nicholas Pileggi, *Goodfellas* (London: Faber & Faber, 1990).

basic component of many jokes and puns, the misunderstanding or ambiguity of a word, in this case the word 'funny'. There was no threat approaching from outside the group: it was the alpha figure, the chief himself, who suddenly seemed to sprout horns and become the threat — presumably reminding everyone present that the social hierarchy for which his leadership is the pivot *depends* upon the past acts of violence that got him there — and the future acts that will be needed to maintain his status. In this sense, the laughter that takes place here must *always* be the indicator of a threat that will *always* be internal to and constitutive of the group — at least of a group such as this, built on masculine aggression, violence, and a rigorous adherence to a familial or tribal structure. In laughing, the group is externalizing this threat, somehow simultaneously both raising the alarm and signalling it as false. It is not incidental that the scene eventually ends with Tommy inflicting actual violence upon a waiter of the restaurant who has the impertinence to ask him to settle his tab: just as the laughter may be seen as a release or relief of tension that was built up by the threat of violence, this economy can be turned around, so that the eventual violence against an outsider is a release of the tension that was built up and restricted by the internal moral structure of the group, with the help of the mechanism of laughter.

CONCLUSION

Combining the traditional Aristotelian formula — the human as the only animal that laughs — with the one proposed by Bergson — the human as the animal that is laughed at (*l'animal qui fait rire*) —, we arrive at the following: the human is the animal that laughs at itself. However, in taking this laughter to amount to the human's undermining, in some sense, of its status as human, there is a risk of reinscribing a presumed, universal notion of the human, exactly where its universality is being challenged. That is, if laughter in many circumstances may be said to challenge what a given human or human group takes to be its humanity, we should not take it for granted that there is an implicit, universal understanding of the human that all people share and that is challenged *in general* by laughter. Rather, we should attend to the particularities of the form, image, definition of the human that is opened to challenge, destabilized, in any given instance of laughter, or in any given portrayal or account of laughter and its functioning. In this essay, I have considered a number of philosophical and theoretical approaches to laughter that seek to develop a general or universal theory of laughter — of its function, its role in 'human' society and culture. Viewed together, their shared cultural particularities are clear, though largely unacknowledged by the thinkers and writers themselves. Yet their theories repeatedly point to the notion that laughter is a mechanism directly engaged with these same errors concerning self-understanding and the boundaries of the human. They imply, even argue for, an understanding of laughter as destabilizing the very status of Man that conditions their own implicit and explicit claims to universality.

The question that then seemingly remains is whether this particular form of the human is destabilized by such accounts of laughter and the instances of humorous, laughter-invoking situations they refer to (literary, dramatic, everyday, etc.) — or whether it is reinforced by them. I do not think this is a question that can be settled in general: rather, the potential for both destabilization and reinforcement remains at every stage and in each circumstance; and this, rather than suggesting that we abandon any attempt to account for the functions and effects of laughter, either in general or in this or that context, should encourage us to be attentive to these effects in their local specificity, even and perhaps especially when that locality seems quite broad, i.e., aspiring to generality or universality. The human is the animal that laughs at itself; but 'the human' is seldom, perhaps never a genuinely universal category (even if this very statement implies that it could be). It matters which 'human' is laughing at itself, and whether and to what extent this self-directed laughter undermines its false claim to universality, or, by exposing this claim and making it seem of minor consequence, enables its reassertion.

Not Yet
Duration as Detour in
Emmanuelle Demoris's *Mafrouza* Cycle
ROSA BAROTSI

Mafrouza was a shantytown of around 10,000 inhabitants situated next to the port of Alexandria, Egypt. Built on top of a Greco-roman necropolis that was carved into stone in the fourth century BCE, the neighbourhood also went by the name Gebel — the rock. Mafrouza was one of many shantytowns (or 'Ashwa'iyyat', meaning disordered or haphazard) in Alexandria and one of quite a few 'cities of the dead' in Egypt (most of them in Cairo). The area had electricity but neither running water nor a sewage system. Most of the inhabitants had come from Upper Egypt, from the 1970s onwards, to find work in the city. They would do odd jobs at the port, work at the Misr textile factory, or sort and resell refuse. They were mechanics, carpenters, drivers. Some were better off than others: Abu Hosni was a freelance docker at the port and lived in a perpetually flooded house next to the neighbourhood dumping ground. Mohamed Khattab was more fortunate: a factory worker by day, the owner of Mafrouza's shop in the afternoon, and also the much-loved local imam. In the late 1990s, a French archaeologist discovered a cemetery camouflaging as the foundation of the Mafrouza community of self-produced space. The largest cemetery of its kind in the Mediterranean, it was uncovered during the last stages of the construction of an elevated highway connecting the harbour to the main route to Cairo in 1996. Archaeologists were excitedly working to excavate the site from 1997 until 2000, when the dig was closed down to continue construction work. It was around that time that Emmanuelle Demoris followed an archaeologist to this place where the living were shacking up with the dead. But she soon abandoned the mystique of this cohabitation and spent the next few years filming the people of Mafrouza. In 2003, she had accumulated 150 hours of footage. With the help of her producer, Jean Gruault (famous as the screenwriter of Jacques Rivette's *Paris nous appartient* (1961) and Francois Truffaut's *Jules et Jim* (1962)),[1] she edited and released the first two parts of the five-part, twelve-hour documentary in 2007 around the same time that the neighbourhood of Mafrouza was demolished to expand the port.[2] The inhabitants were relocated to a massive housing project around 20 km from the city centre, which made access to most forms of employment difficult. The heavily criticized project was part of 'Mubarak's promise', a subsidized housing scheme he had announced in the run-up to his election in 2005. Its name, until 2011, was Mubarak City. After the revolution, it was renamed after the old neighbourhood: Mafrouza.

Despite the remarkable cut from 150 hours down to a *mere* twelve hours, one of the first features to stand out is *Mafrouza*'s unusual length. The five-part structure helps make it easier to watch a documentary that is more than six times the length of an average feature film, at a time when streaming services had yet to normalize the consumption of serialised films with feature-length episodes. But within each of the episodes, the distension of time is equally present. Extended temporality is therefore hardly exhausted by the overall duration of the film. An unflinching focus on the temporal pacing of the everyday, as well as an above-average shot length and the single point of view of the DV camera guarantee that time is experienced as unspectacular and loose despite the abundance of people, activities, and micro-stories. Given

---

1 *Paris nous appartient*, dir. by Jacques Rivette (Diaphana, 1961); *Jules et Jim*, dir. by François Truffaut (Cinédis, 1962).
2 *Mafrouza — Oh la nuit!*, dir. by Emmanuelle Demoris (Les Films de la Villa, 2007), *Mafrouza/Coeur*, dir. by Emmanuelle Demoris (Les Films de la Villa, 2010), *Que faire?*, dir. by Emmanuelle Demoris (Les Films de la Villa, 2010), *La main du papillon*, dir. by Emmanuelle Demoris (Les Films de la Villa, 2010), *Paraboles*, dir. by Emmanuelle Demoris (Les Films de la Villa, 2010).

the film's predilection for the quotidian, we could perhaps quite easily imagine a significantly shorter version with tighter editing: skip a *zaffa* (wedding procession) here, one less song by Hassan, no reason to hang out in Mohamed's shop for so long ... But duration is evidently a structural concern for Demoris — although 'to what end' might be a more complex question. Are the twelve hours of the film an attempt to show everything? If so, is the underlying concern to make as transparent as possible the object of observation? Similarly, is the accommodating display of ordinariness an attempt to interfere with the material as little as possible, a form of a quest for authenticity, truth, or empathy? Or, as I will try to demonstrate, does the *Mafrouza* project betray, not so much a longing for realism or 'doing justice', but an anxiety, a hesitation in the face of an effort to establish a different relation to its subject — one that is perhaps (in both senses) positively *in*authentic, because it deviates and defers?

A CERTAIN OPACITY

Demoris, a one-person film crew, used a small DV camera to shoot *Mafrouza*. She talks about the digital camera not in terms we might be more familiar with, such as indexicality, quality of the image, freedom from the predetermined length of the filmstrip, freedom of movement, etc. Instead, she is preoccupied with the modified relationship digital technology forces into motion between gazes, bodies, and machine. She says:

> The camera is too small to rest on one's shoulder. It is therefore the hand and the forearm that carry it. It's tricky to link the eye to the hand. To look is a movement that engages the body towards the exterior but at the same time pulls towards an interior, sometimes down to the neck and shoulders, the gaze pulling its tension out of the chest where it breathes. It's difficult to accommodate this momentum in the hand, which caresses more than it looks.[3]

Along with the displacement of the role of observer to the hand, the small DV camera causes another dislocation, that of the conventional

---

3   Emmanuelle Demoris, *Camera con vista* (Marseille: Shellac Sud, 2012), p. 20.

relationship between documentarist and the filmed subject. She continues:

> No need to bring the face to the eyepiece [...] the screen that folds out on the side of the camera permits to check on the frame without being glued to the camera. [...] Moreover, since it's small, like the camera itself, it doesn't hide you, the person filmed can see you.[4]

A twist on Vertov's 'camera-eye', the cinematic gaze becomes a camera-hand necessitated by technology, which undoes the conflation of camera and gaze. Of course the hand can grasp as much as it can caress. Édouard Glissant is right to point to the manual features of epistemological violence: he speaks of the French *com-prendre* as evoking precisely this violent pursuit of a phantasmatic transparency of relation, which becomes a tool for control.[5] The verb *comprendre*, 'to understand', but also 'to grasp', contains 'the movement of hands that grab their surroundings and bring them back to themselves. A gesture of enclosure if not appropriation.'[6] Nothing seems to guarantee that an empirical, 'fly on the wall' approach to visual representation will lead to social recognition rather than epistemological violence.[7]

Glissant proposes errantry as a way around 'summarizing' the world, a letting-go of the generalizing instinct to sum up or possess the world. Perhaps it is this resistance to summary, with its connotations of cutting down for efficiency's sake, that leads Demoris to the protracted duration of *Mafrouza*. Opacity, Glissant's central term for his poetics of relation, is intimately linked with the erratic, constantly slipping and slithering away from reduction — another term that brings together the meanings of 'bringing back to' and a temporality of economics, of cutting back or trimming down. Demoris similarly talks about the strategy of 'taking one's time' as offering a path for the creation of a

---

4   Ibid., p. 20.
5   Édouard Glissant, *Poetics of Relation*, trans. by Betsy Wing (Ann Arbor: University of Michigan Press, 1997), p. 26.
6   Ibid., pp. 191–92.
7   As Heather Love points out, a similar debate regarding the potential and pitfalls of empirical observation has been ongoing in sexuality and queer studies since the shift to treating homosexuality as a sociological phenomenon rather than a medical one. Heather Love, *Norms, Deviance, and the Queer Ordinary?*, lecture, ICI Berlin, 22 June 2015, video recording, mp4, 47:09 <http://doi.org/10.25620/e150622>.

generous distance from the subject filmed, as opposed to the instant recognition of styles of documentary that, as she says, 'surplombent', overhang or supervise their subject.[8]

Even so, I am aware of the twin danger of appealing to opacity in order to create a framework for some form of 'ethical' representation. On the one hand, this danger has to do with opacity becoming merely another word for othering, especially when the 'right to opacity' does not belong to those represented but is decided and bestowed upon by her who records, the filmmaker. On the other hand (but not unconnected to this), there is a risk of equating opacity with gradations of visibility, a sort of becoming not-quite-invisible. In the Otolith Group's *Nervus Rerum* (2008),[9] for instance, a film essay shot in the Palestinian refugee camp of Jenin, there is a direct appeal to Glissant's concept in order to explain the film's strategy of representation. As a way of turning Glissant's opacity into a visual practice, the filmmakers, Kodwo Eshun and Anjalika Sagar, use a combination of distance (no close-ups, mostly long shots and backs to the camera), lack of diegetic sound combined with an alienating score and a calm velvety voiceover of texts by Fernando Pessoa and Jean Genet, and an eerily gliding Steadicam. They describe this as producing an effect of 'non-empathy. There is a wariness of the idea of the Other speaking for themselves either from a state of victimhood or a state of defiance.'[10] As T. J. Demos points out, there are many risks here:

> Might the embrace of opacity as a strategy of resistance against oppressive identifications [...] end up unintentionally silencing the other, as the unforeseen mimicry of political erasure reenacts the very effect of colonization? And does this invocation of the opaque not also negate positive identifications with Palestinians in the act of collective and transnational solidarity, mitigating or undermining support for their struggle for liberation and self-determination? And if Pallywood cinema [i.e. 'victim reportage'] is deemed ineffective, then what real consequence does the recourse to opacity promise? And

---

8   Demoris, *Camera con vista*, p. 25. She poses this not as an 'axiom' but as 'just another weapon in the resistance'.
9   *Nervus Rerum*, dir. by The Otolith Group (2008).
10 Irmgard Emmelhainz and the Otolith Group (Kodwo Eshun and Anjalika Sagar), 'A Trialogue on Nervus Rerum', *October*, 129 (Summer 2009), pp. 129–32.

where does the evocation of the nondiscursive phenomenological experience of the camp, creating the existential sense of estrangement, leave the viewer, if not in a state of debilitating confusion and alienation?[11]

The gliding camera of *Nervus Rerum*, with which the filmmakers intended to approximate the sense of a 'lost ghost', instead risks placing the spectator in a position of unaffected superiority, of a transcendental point of view compounded by a complete inaccessibility to identification with anything else on screen. The sense of superiority risks being further compounded by the voiceover, which provides abstracted interpretations of 'universal' human suffering in the words of famous European writers.

Nervus Rerum provides an example of the complex effects of a certain iteration of opacity — one that slips too far on the side of obscurity and ends up reproducing the 'impenetrable autarchy' Glissant cautions against. It appears to me that, in order for opacity to have the potential to be operative to some extent (and for the purposes of this essay), we need to posit at the very least that opacity should not be 'conferred upon' and that (to paraphrase Glissant) it should be the by-product of equality and solidarity. In other words, opacity is not about being invisible, just as it is not about being obscure. It is perhaps more accurately, following Ntone Edjade, about a reluctant visibility:[12] reluctant both in the sense of hesitance (which I'll discuss later) and, as per its etymology, resistance.

Demoris is one of a long chain of filmmakers who appeals to some form of 'taking one's time' as an instrument for a — morally, politically, epistemologically — adequate representation. Before I discuss this hesitation I have described as a temporal term operative in *Mafrouza*, I want to give an overview of long duration in western cinema. It will hopefully become clear in the process that the problem of extended temporality in the west has a history of being linked with questions of

---

11   T. J. Demos, *The Migrant Image: The Art and Politics of Documentary during Global Crisis* (Durham, NC: Duke University Press, 2013), pp. 156–57.

12   Moses März, '"Embracing Opacity": Interview with Ntone Edjabe (Chimurenga Magazine)', *AfricAvenir International — African Renaissance, Development, International Collaboration and Peace*, interview conducted on 14 July 2011 <http://www.africavenir.org/nc/news-details/article/embracing-opacity-interview-with-ntone-edjabe-chimurenga-magazine.html> [accessed 5 May 2016].

ethics, both as adequate and (or) realist representation. Inversely, long duration has been intimately connected in western film history with the anxiety of realism, an anxiety which includes the ethical question of 'doing justice'.

THE THREAT OF DEAD TIME[13]

Long duration in Western accounts of cinema has a long and complicated history. Over the course of this overview, I will try to demonstrate that this complication stems partly from the problem of 'dead time' and its double inadequacy: 'dead time', such as when a shot goes on for too long after an action has been completed, is both excessive (that is, redundant, wasteful) and lacking (that is, narratively insufficient). Long duration is most often associated with the technique of the long take. But as ethnographic filmmaker David MacDougall points out, what constitutes a long take is not straightforward and in fact 'is obviously an artificial and somewhat arbitrary concept, formed in relation to an average notion of shot length and affected by content and position as well as by duration.'[14] Even in the strict terms of shot duration one has to allow for historical relativism for example. If we are to trust quantitative studies of average shot lengths, such as those by Barry Salt or James Cutting et al., shot lengths in mainstream US cinema have gotten significantly shorter in the seventy-five years since the Hollywood studio era.[15] One would then assume that our expectations for how long a shot should be in order to be perceived as too long would have also evolved over time. Moreover, the definition of the long take is not exhausted in questions of temporal length, but is largely based on considerations of structure — for example whether or not it is an uninterrupted sequence shot or part of an edited sequence.

---

13 An earlier version of this section appears in Rosa Barotsi, 'Contemporary European Cinema, Time, and the Everyday' (unpublished doctoral thesis, University of Cambridge, 2014).

14 David MacDougall, *Transcultural Cinema* (Princeton, NJ: Princeton University Press, 1998), p. 211.

15 See Barry Salt, *Moving Into Pictures: More on Film History, Style, and Analysis* (London: Starword, 2006); James E. Cutting, Jordan E. DeLong, and Christine E. Nothelfer, 'Attention and the Evolution of Hollywood Film', *Psychological Science*, 21.3 (2010), pp. 432–39.

MacDougall's view therefore is that the long take is 'a method of film construction' rather than a question of shot length.

The filmmaker reminds us that in the very early days of cinema, before editing, the long take was the norm by necessity.[16] Helen Powell traces the advent of 'real time' shots back to those early actualities of the end of the nineteenth century and sees their chronologically 'archaic' positioning as a reason why these shots get perceived as 'regressive' in later production.[17] Mary Ann Doane, on the other hand, sees in the very earliest instances of edited actualities the same use of editing that encapsulates a persistent anxiety in the history of cinema: the exclusion of dead time, 'time which is, by definition, "uneventful."'[18]

Trimming the excess duration around 'meaningful' time was one of the earliest impulses of filmmaking. As Doane rightly points out, however, the existence of uneventful time, that is, time outside the event, implies that the latter is self-evident and clearly definable. Doane suggests, and I agree, that it is more accurate to perceive the singling out of dead time as the condition of possibility for an 'event' to come into being. An event appears therefore to consist of '*eminently meaningful*' material, as opposed to the wastefulness and unproductivity of undramatic time. It seems that this inherent meaningfulness exists *outside* of time, insofar as, despite its actual duration, the event 'is packaged as a moment', or as MacDougall puts it (in terms that remind us of Walter Benjamin), 'a spark or a stab of lightning'.[19]

Like an electric shock, according to this line of thinking, a film shot 'discharges most of its meaning at once'. If the shot continues uninhibited, beyond that 'moment' of recognition, the response of the spectator might range from impatience and annoyance to inattentiveness, boredom, perusal, or distraction. This is, for example, how filmmaker Jackson Mac Low describes his imagined project:

---

16 MacDougall, *Transcultural Cinema*, p. 211.
17 Helen Powell, *Stop the Clocks!: Time and Narrative in Cinema* (London: I. B. Tauris, 2012), p. 22.
18 Mary Ann Doane, *The Emergence of Cinematic Time: Modernity, Contingency, the Archive* (Cambridge, MA: Harvard University Press, 2002), pp. 159–60.
19 MacDougall, *Transcultural Cinema*, pp. 209–10.

> Tree* Movie
> Select a tree*. Set up and focus a movie camera so that the tree* fills most of the picture. Turn on the camera and leave it on without moving it for any number of hours. If the camera is about to run out of film, substitute a camera with fresh film. The two cameras may be alternated in this way any number of times. Sound recording equipment may be turned on simultaneously with movie cameras. Beginning at any point in the film, any length of it may be projected at a showing.
>
> *) For the word 'tree', one may substitute 'mountain', 'sea', 'flower', 'lake', etc.

Most shots are nonetheless not, as MacDougall puts it, 'allowed to' go on for too long.[20] His revealing phrasing reflects a constant anxiety on the part of filmmakers and producers, one that lurks in the most unlikely of places: even schools of filmmaking that championed the ordinary time of everyday life were inherently terrified of the 'dead spot'. He recounts that in *cinéma vérité* and American 'direct cinema' filmmakers 'still contrived to avoid dramaturgical dead spots': they had to defend their 'interest in the ordinary by making sure that the ordinary played well'.[21] In the oft-cited 1960 premiere of Michelangelo Antonioni's *L'Avventura* at Cannes, 'the reiterated shot of a girl running down the corridor brought bellows of "cut"' from the audience, reaffirming that fear of spectatorial response to empty time.[22] By using the long take and undramatic time, Antonioni was of course consciously undercutting spectatorial expectations, by performing a double subversion of cinematic conventions: substituting the temporal ellipses conventionally employed in the name of efficiency and succinctness with ellipses in the narrative. Antonioni was following Roberto Rossellini's interest in distended time and narrative stasis, although the younger director's undercutting of exposition was seen as utilized 'in the best modernist fashion', whereas the Neorealist Rossellini was perceived as reflecting Cesare Zavattini's realist theory of *pedinamento*.[23] Zavattini

---

20 Ibid., p. 209.
21 Ibid., p. 211.
22 Peter Brunette, *The Films of Michelangelo Antonioni* (Cambridge: Cambridge University Press, 1998), p. 29.
23 Ivone Margulies, 'Exemplary Bodies: Reenactment in *Love in the City*, *Sons*, and *Close Up*', in *Rites of Realism: Essays on Corporeal Cinema*, ed. by Ivone Margulies (Durham, NC: Duke University Press, 2003), pp. 217–44 (p. 241).

is frequently quoted as proclaiming that his ideal film would consist of ninety minutes in the life of a man to whom nothing happens. This attitude had moral implications for the Neorealists and Zavattini in particular: his theory indicated a natural link between factual knowledge about fellow humans and a resultant solidarity.

A few years after Antonioni's *L'avventura* was released, Andy Warhol would make a series of real-time structuralist films in which the vacuous time of non-events glimpsed in Antonioni's film would be brought to their radical extreme. A forty-five minute long film portrayed pop artist Robert Indiana consuming a meal in real time; another one showed the poet John Giorno sleeping for five hours and twenty minutes.[24] *Eat* (1963) and *Sleep* (1963)[25] appear to thoroughly enact the principle of non-interference and continuity Zavattini had called for. At the same time, Warhol's structuralist films dramatically undermine the neorealist ethics of observation. The hyperbolizing of duration appears to mock Zavattini's radicalism — after all, as Ivone Margulies points out, the ninety minutes of Zavattini's ideal film merely represent 'the normal length of a commercial feature'.[26] Furthermore, the obstinately fixed camera in Warhol taunts the humanist empathy of Neorealism by transforming it into a politics of passivity, 'the equally ethical, and [...] actively political, stance of indifference'.[27] The Warhol films defy 'transparent representation and the naive concept of realism that has commonly been associated with the long take', by stressing through hyperbole the abstract qualities of real-time representation.[28]

Warhol's use of the long take questions the privileged relationship between cinema and reality expounded by the Neorealists. This *other* legacy of the long take — not as a gateway into reality, but as an enabler of critical distance from that reality — includes European political filmmakers such as Jean-Luc Godard and Jean-Marie Straub and Danièle Huillet. The 'insistence of observation' here, as Brian Henderson

---

24 The film is actually composed of six seamless shots. Malin Wahlberg, *Documentary Time: Film and Phenomenology* (Minneapolis: University of Minnesota Press, 2008), p. 89.
25 *Eat*, dir. by Andy Warhol (1963); *Sleep*, dir. by Andy Warhol (1963).
26 Ivone Margulies, *Nothing Happens: Chantal Akerman's Hyperrealist Everyday* (Durham, NC: Duke University Press, 1996) p. 38.
27 Ibid., p. 37.
28 Wahlberg, *Documentary Time*, p. 90.

has pointed out in relation to Godard's *Week-end* (1967),[29] does not draw the spectator into the image, but keeps them at a distance, from which they can judge it '*as a whole*'[30] and proceed to accept or reject it. In this instance, the spatiotemporal integrity of the long take does not serve to better 'reveal physical reality' in the realist manner,[31] but to present a singular perspective that denies the bourgeois world any depth or complexity.

In the 1970s, Belgian director Chantal Akerman combines Neorealism's equivalence between dramatic and undramatic events with the flat literalness of Warhol and Godard's long takes in order to create films with a feminist micro-politics derived from that oscillation between materiality and presence on the one hand and distance and indifference on the other.[32] As Ivone Margulies argues, through Akerman's obsessive gaze everyday gendered gestures are 'simultaneously recognized and made strange.'[33]

Two issues arise from this overview of long duration in Western accounts of film history. Firstly, the sustained focus on everyday activities through distended temporal structures takes the form of a double frustration. The long take is perceived as both a 'nothing happens' — a lack — and a 'too much' — an excess. We have seen that the question of what to do with 'dead time' has been posed again and again amongst filmmakers. This lack has been nonetheless constantly counterposed with an overabundance seen as inherent to the complexity of the long take: in sustained duration 'one sees more than one needs in order to "read" the image.'[34] The first problem of the long take is therefore that it seems contemporaneously situated at two extremes of redundancy: as overflow and emptiness, 'excess of detail resulting from a fixed stare'[35] versus the deficit of signification resulting from the lack of editing and dramatic events.

29　*Week-end*, dir. by Jean-Luc Godard (Athos Films, 1967)
30　Brian Henderson, 'Toward a Non-Bourgeois Camera Style', *Film Quarterly*, 24.2 (1970), pp. 2–14 (p. 4).
31　Siegfried Kracauer, quoted in Roy Armes, *Patterns of Realism: A Study of Italian Neo-Realist Cinema* (South Brunswick, NJ: A. S. Barnes, 1971), p. 20.
32　Margulies, *Nothing Happens*, p. 23.
33　Ibid., p. 20.
34　Ibid., p. 46.
35　Ibid.

The second issue regarding distended duration is a question of distance and proximity. Different attitudes towards long duration have posited different levels of immersion into some form of the 'real': do distended temporalities act as a probe into reality (Zavattini), a surface literality (Warhol), or an alienating fixity (Godard)?

A FABLE

Hassan and his friend are lounging in the plastic chairs of a café on one of the main streets close to the port, a short walk away from the wall that separates the city from Mafrouza. It's been a long night. After an evening of hanging out, playing games at the theme park situated under the overpass, dancing at a concert, Hassan refuses to put an end to the fun, rejecting his friend's frequent suggestions that some sleep would be in order despite his obvious exhaustion. Not yet. He tells a story:

> The louse and the flea. The louse asks the flea to boil him some water. The flea is taking too long; the louse goes and finds her dead. The louse is sad. A crow asks him why. The louse says, 'I'm sad because the flea is dead.' The crow rips off his feathers and falls into a tree. The tree asks him, 'Why are you sad?' 'I'm sad because the louse is sad because the flea is dead.' The tree snaps in half out of sadness. A donkey comes up to the tree. 'Why are you sad?' 'Because the crow is sad because the louse is sad because the flea is dead.' Desperate, the donkey breaks his leg. He goes to drink some water from the sea. The sea asks, 'Why are you limping?' 'I'm sad because the tree is sad because the crow is sad because the louse is sad because the flea is dead.' The sea dries up out of grief. The fisherman asks, 'What's wrong?' 'I'm sad because the donkey is sad because the tree is sad because the crow is sad because the louse is sad because the flea is dead.' The fisherman hurts his eye, his wife asks him why: 'I'm sad because the sea is sad because the donkey is sad because the tree is sad because the crow is sad because the louse is sad because the flea is dead.' The wife screams, 'My God!' The neighbours come and ask why. 'I'm sad because the man is sad because the sea is sad because the donkey is sad because the tree is sad because the crow is sad because the louse is sad because the flea is dead.'

Hassan's lengthy story traces a series of creatures and elements devastated by the sadness of their interlocutors. When the fisherman, despondent, hears the lament of the sea, I can't stop myself thinking that the story must be coming to an end: the man seems like an convenient last link in this bizarre evolutionary chain of events. But that's not the case. When the man tells his wife, I can't help but imagine this domestic scene will provide the final punchline. But I'm wrong. The wife's misery attracts the neighbours' curiosity. By this point, I have no idea where the fable is heading. I've exhausted my assumptions. It is at this moment that the story comes to an end, just like that. Hassan shrugs his shoulders as if to say 'that's it'.

WHEN IN DOUBT, HESITATE

In *Mafrouza*, the anxiety about the film's relationship to visual justice is performed through duration. This worry is enacted temporally, through what Poor Theory might name a 'working around' intransigent problems, of tinkering with one's subject. Tinkering, such a modest word, evokes a sustained activity of dubious productivity: 'to work as a tinker' means 'to work imperfectly, keep busy in a useless way'. Poor theory is self-effacing and anti-heroic: it pays attention to 'the murky, unsystematic practices and discourses of everyday life', and chooses description over interpretation, in particular 'descriptions [...] that do not leave what is described unchanged'.[36] In *Mafrouza*, the question of the French woman's presence in the shantytown is often evoked, with varying degrees of entertained curiosity and aggressive mistrust. 'The foreigner will make a mockery of us abroad' is a recurring accusation that constantly snaps us out of immersion. Technical errors have a similar effect of distancing and reminding the audience of the presence of the woman behind the camera: we see her fingers slipping over the edge of the lens as she's correcting the light or protecting the camera from the rain, we catch glimpses of the boom, or her silhouette on the wall. More importantly, perhaps, Demoris's limited Arabic meant that a lot of the time she didn't know what people were chatting about. After spending some time in Mafrouza on her own, she recruited a

---

36 Ackbar Abbas and D. Goldberg, 'Poor Theory: An Open-Source Manifesto' (2019), published on the platform 'Foundry', University of California Humanities Research Institute (UCHRI), <https://uchri.org/foundry/poor-theory/> [accessed 16 September 2021].

translator, Rania Berro, who became the routine interlocutor in the film — although she is never shown. Berro would every now and then explain to Demoris what was being talked about, but oftentimes the camera, although often talked at or interpellated, is not fully complicit with what is happening. This fundamental failure is perhaps the most potent performance of the limits of legibility, enacted for instance when Demoris's camera would be slow to follow a developing mise-en-scene by missing out on conversational cues.

Tinkering, this prolonged and constantly imperfect approach that seems to have no end: Demoris had originally thought of calling the film 'Lessa schwaia,' 'not yet,' a ritournelle that people would often use in the neighbourhood. This endless process of ending, to evoke Roland Barthes, can produce as much the paradoxical infinity of weariness that he meant for it to describe,[37] as the pleasure of continuing to tinker pointlessly.

But more than anything, I suggest, *Mafrouza*'s endless ending is 'a way of proceeding', a strategy of deferral when solutions are not discernible.[38] The film hesitates — not yet, not yet — as if weary of the fact that an ending brings pronouncement: By deferring termination, the film continuously postpones the moment when it will become possible to say: 'this film is about ...'. The parallel I am drawing here between end/death and rationalisation/pronouncement, also crops up in Pier Paolo Pasolini's ruminations on the long take. He draws an analogy between montage and death, in which the life of a man remains suspended in ambiguity — the attribute closest to reality, according to him — until the final 'cut' of death. Just as, after their life has ended, it is possible to be conclusive about a person's life, editing in film explains, rationalizes, and undercuts the ambiguity of the uninterrupted long take.[39] The difference of course is that for Pasolini the long duration of the uninterrupted take is (closest to) reality, whereas my assertion is that the extended temporalities of *Mafrouza* — manifesting as total film duration, use of the long take, and a focus on the empty time of the quotidian — showcase not authenticity but reluctance. Joseph

---

37   In Elena Gorfinkel, 'Weariness, Waiting: Endurance and Art Cinema's Tired Bodies', *Discourse*, 34.2–3 (Spring–Fall 2012), pp. 311–47 (p. 315).
38   Abbas and Goldberg, *Poor Theory*.
39   Pier Paolo Pasolini, *Empirismo eretico* (Milan: Garzanti Libri, 2000), p. 241.

Vogl celebrates hesitation as going against a long Western tradition of imperative decision-making that sees it as 'a capricious act that frustrates work.'[40] Vogl hails the 'heroes of reluctance' for standing up for the unproductive and distracted, but I feel that this operation of heroization undermines the premises of the argument: I believe the reluctant and hesitant would find themselves more at home with the likes of the good soldier Švejk and other such petty actors of resistance.[41] The film resists the impossible task it has set for itself — how to 'do justice', what else to do if 'doing justice' does not seem an adequate objective in the first place — by 'using the lag'. Ackbar Abbas suggests this as a strategy for when something threatens to 'outpace our understanding'.[42] But can one also use that lag to suspend understanding?

DIS-ESTABLISHING SHOTS

I think there's something to be said here about this form of durational opacity (opacity created through the accumulation of dead time), which is somehow similar to that accumulation of petty acts that we have been discussing as resisting weakly.

Mafrouza begins with a neighbourhood, a situated locale in Alexandria, Egypt. Yet instead of recounting a community, it gravitates towards a small number of people. Demoris describes the necessity she felt to avoid situating the spectator visually and spatially from the very start. In fact, the first panorama shots of Mafrouza only occur after the first hour. Instead, the film begins by slowly introducing us to some of the people who will reappear throughout the twelve hours. This choice was part of an effort to avoid the pronouncement that

---

40 Maaike Lauwaert, 'Helden van de tegenzin', *Tubelight*, 66 (January 2010) <https://www.tubelight.nl/helden-van-de-tegenzin/> [accessed 16 September 2021], English trans. as 'Heroes of Reluctance: On Hesitation as an Active Act', author's website <http://maaikelauwaert.com/articles/joseph-vogl/> [accessed 16 September 2021]

41 See the discussion of Švejk in Preciosa de Joya, 'The Punakawans Make an Untimely Appearance: In Praise of Caves, Shadows, and Fire (or, A Response to Plato's Doctrine of Truth)', in this volume.

42 Ackbar Abbas, *Poor Theory and New Chinese Cinema: Jia Zhangke's 'Still Life'*, public lecture, Critical Theory Institute, University of California, Irvine, 3 December 2008 <http://www.humanities.uci.edu/critical/pdf/AbbasPoorTheoryStillLife.pdf> [accessed 5 May 2016]

she felt would proceed from opening with establishing shots of the shantytown, which would situate the spectator, unambiguously, in a *bidonville*.

By contrast, the film begins with a misunderstanding. The opening shot finds us walking through a narrow corridor of the neighbourhood. No people are visible yet, but indiscernible voices are heard in both Arabic and French. The first trace of a figure is that of the filmmaker herself. Her voice, unmistakably hers because it is heard from behind the camera, and the unsteady pace of the hand-held camera, are followed by a shot in which the shadow from the boom can be discerned against a sun-lit wall. The rest of the first scene takes place at Ghada and Adel's house. Here, a perplexed Adel is trying to help a French archeaologist figure out the layout of the tomb to which the house is attached. The scene contains a series of entertaining miscommunications. Adel doesn't understand what the archeologist is doing: 'What is he measuring? There's nothing there. He's a professor. What can I say?' The French don't understand what Adel is saying: He asks in Arabic, 'Is this cemetery *important*?' The French debate the meaning of this obscure word. After a while, Adel decides to take matters into his own hands and walks up to the camera, grabs the lens and points it to the area of interest: 'Important, or no interest?' The archeologist replies in his clumsy Arabic: 'I don't understand "important", to the amusement of Adel …

Demoris's use of what we might call 'dis-establishing shots' forces us to confront the ethics of 'making visible'. Making the invisible visible is often cited as one of the underlying objectives of documentary filmmaking that deals with issues, people, or places that are usually disregarded. Yet it goes without saying that this task is not inherently informed by some principle of equality. Who 'makes' visible, for instance? The documentarist, as Trinh T. Minh-ha knows from her own practice, 'in "giving a voice", might forget that she thereby becomes the "giver".'[43] That is one risk. The other risk is that one might take for granted a clear dichotomy between visibility and invisibility. *To whom* does one make visible? How is invisibility constituted? What

---

[43] Trinh T. Minh-ha, *When the Moon Waxes Red: Representation, Gender and Cultural Politics* (London: Routledge, 1991), p. 67.

about visible invisibilities — a recent example being the Lebanese documentary film *Makhdoumin* (2016),[44] where the violently obvious absence of the domestic workers at the centre of the documentary makes a point about their position in Lebanese middle-class society — or invisible visibilities, akin to a Gramscian notion of hegemony as naturalized ideology? Perhaps the challenge would be to break with an easy division between visibility/invisibility or as Trinh suggests,

> not to fall prey to the dominant process of totalization: rather than working at bringing, through gradual acquisition, what has been kept invisible into visibility, one would have to break with such a system of dualities and show, for example, what constitutes invisibility itself as well as what exceeds mere visibility.[45]

As an example, in the first sequence with Om Bassiouni, the woman who bakes bread in an outdoor makeshift oven, the camera introduces us very slowly over the course of around half an hour first to the woman and her daughter, to their struggles with the handmade oven and the persisting rain. Only much later does the scene switch to wider shots of the locale where all this takes place. Since this site is the Mafrouza garbage dump, the film wants us to invest time on Om Bassiouni and her bread-baking before seeing the difficult images of the dumping ground. Demoris insists that if she showed an establishing shot first, we would then only be able to see the garbage dump and nothing else.

And yet, nothing much seems to have changed. At the end of the day, deferring and accumulating is the emphatic perpetuation of a lack and the persistence of a hoarding — too little, too much; diluted, dilated, yet again. But this might just be the point. The durational opacity that results from the accumulation of time and everydayness, twice redundant, places us at the centre of the most fundamental queries regarding cinematic representation. What I appreciate about *Mafrouza* are its impossibilities — in some sense, a film by a Frenchwoman in the bidonville of a country that has been an economic colony of France can never be anything but a failure. In another sense, however, the film

---

44 *Makhdoumin / A Maid for Each*, dir. by Maher Abi Samra (Icarus Films, 2016).
45 Marina Gržinić, 'Shifting The Borders of The Other: An Interview With Trinh T. Minh-ha', *Telepolis*, 12 August 1998 <http://www.heise.de/tp/artikel/3/3265/1.html> [accessed 5 May 2016].

acts as a springboard for a set of important questions. The decision not to begin with an establishing shot of the garbage-filled yard in which Om Bassiouni bakes betrays an assumption that that particular form of visibility would trigger an immediate jump to abstraction: everything else would be blinded by it and subsumed into it. In that sense, abstraction is a form of transparency. Talking about long duration as a strategy of decolonization in the work of Philipino filmmaker Lav Diaz, William Brown notes: 'Applied to films, the process of abstraction can be understood the moment a viewer experiences unhappiness about the length of a film "because they got the film already".'[46] Nevertheless, to claim that there's anything intrinsically ethical about long duration would be naïve, to say the least — the long debates in documentary ethics have done their part in establishing the ingenuity of conflating uninterrupted spatiotemporality with any form of adequate ethical representation. It is my contention that the careful montage work that takes us at a snail's pace from Om Bassioumi to her surroundings has very little to do with preserving any kind of spatiotemporal integrity and is equally irrelevant to any kind of realist impulse that would guarantee access, presence, empathy, or authenticity. Instead, I think its strategy comes closer to an anxious and self-conscious response to the complex issue of the ethics and politics of visibility — and here, the use of long duration and the undramatic temporalities of everyday life become crucial, both as a tool (something with which to) and as a medium (something within which).[47] In other words, accumulation in *Mafrouza* does not operate as the steady acquisition of visibilities — a quasi-Marxian accumulation of understanding as property. Instead, the accumulation of everydayness and dead time pushes the event further and further back as it swells.

I've tried to show that the film attempts to sabotage the landmines it sets for itself at every turn. By using this form of durational opacity, it creates a hesitation that accumulates in order to defer. It doesn't really matter if it fails.

---

46 William Brown, '*Melancholia*: The Long, Slow Cinema of Lav Diaz', in *Slow Cinema*, ed. by Tiago de Luca and Nuno Barradas Jorge (Edinburgh: Edinburgh University Press, 2016), pp. 112–22 (p. 119).

47 Thank you to Claire Nioche-Sibony for this insight.

Incomplete and Self-Dismantling Structures
The Built Space, the Text, the Body
ANTONIO CASTORE

Between 1923 and 1924, a few months before his death, Franz Kafka wrote one of his last short stories, known in English as 'The Burrow'. The English title is justified by the fact that the main character is a strange hybrid creature living underneath the earth,[1] but nonetheless fails to render the rich ambiguity of the original title. In German, 'Der Bau', in fact, has the more general meaning of 'construction', 'building', alongside with that of the English word 'burrow', 'a hole or excavation made in the ground for a dwelling-place by rabbits, foxes and the like'.[2]

---

1   Although we know that Kafka borrowed some features of his main character from the chapters on the 'badger' and the 'mole' of the encyclopaedic work on animal life by Alfred Elmut Brehm (*Brehms Thierleben. Allgemeine Kunde des Thierreichs. Große Ausgabe*, 2nd, rev. and enlarged edn, 10 vols [Leipzig: Bibliographisches Institut, 1876–79] <https://doi.org/10.5962/bhl.title.1067>), he intentionally avoids any precise description of the creature in question, not unlike he had done in the case of the 'vermin' (Ungeziefer) into which Gregor Samsa finds himself transformed at the beginning of 'The Metamorphosis'. The creature of the burrow is not only hybrid because of its unclear belonging to any assignable species; it also shares important, allegedly 'specific', human features, such as rational thought.and technical knowledge, as well as the belief in ancient legends: on this see Hermann J. Weigand, 'Franz Kafka's "The Burrow" ("Der Bau"): An Analytical Essay', *PMLA*, 87.2 (1972), pp. 152–66.
2   'burrow, n.¹', in *OED Online* (Oxford: Oxford University Press, 2020) <http://www.oed.com> [accessed 25 August 2019]

As we will see, this title, defying translation, already contains, in its most contracted form, the essence of the work, which is itself a work on the necessity and the impossibility of the work, a construction that turns itself into its opposite, by undermining its own foundations in the very process of its making.

Like many other tales and novels of Kafka, 'Der Bau' was only published posthumously.[3] It also remained — and this matters even more for the present purpose — very probably unfinished (a point I will come back to later). Its opening words, therefore, carry meaningful overtones: 'I have completed the construction of my burrow [Ich habe den Bau eingerichtet] and it seems to be successful.' With a characteristic move, within the tiny space of one sentence, Kafka lets the first signs of contradiction and doubt emerge, thus warning the reader that the assertive tone of the beginning might be illusory: 'All that can be seen from outside is a big hole; that, however, really leads nowhere.' After these initial remarks, we are introduced by the main character, who is also the narrator, the architect, and the builder, into his dwelling, the burrow: that is, we follow him in all the detours of his thoughts, recollections, fears, plans, actual movements, and building activities as they develop alongside his words during a long present-tense monologue that spans, uninterrupted, many years, from what he calls 'the zenith of my life' at the beginning of the story, to his old age, and his very last hours, in the proximity of death.

It will become clear soon that the burrow is neither complete, nor successful, nor will it ever be. The aim of this paper is to read it precisely as one instance of Kafka's impossible structures, as well as a figure by which the writer (re)thinks his relation to writing and literature; a privileged space that embodies the possibility of an aesthetics of failure; a chapter of an emerging narrative that, in the heart of European modernism, counters the classical ideal of architectural wholeness.

---

[3] First in 1928, in *Witiko. Zeitschrift für Kunst und Dichtung*, 1 (1928), pp. 89–104, then in Kafka, *Beim Bau der Chinesischen Mauer. Ungedruckte Erzählungen und Prosa aus dem Nachlaß*, ed. by Max Brod and Hans-Joachim Schoeps (Berlin: Kiepenheuer, 1931), pp. 77–130. The English edition used here is 'The Burrow', trans. by Willa and Edwin Muir, in Kafka, *The Complete Stories*, ed. by Nahum N. Glatzer (New York: Schocken, 1971), pp. 325–59.

Kafka was not new to the association of writing with architectural elements; textual structures and built spaces mirror each other often in his private writings, in diary entries as well as in letters, in passages often charged with affective investment; on 30 May 1920, for instance, in one of his impassioned letters to Milena, the Czech translator of his story 'The Stoker', he writes:

> Your translation is faithful and I have the feeling that I'm taking you by the hand through the story's subterranean passages, gloomy, low, ugly, almost *endless* (that's why the sentences are almost endless, didn't you realize that?), almost *endless* [...] hopefully in order to have the good sense to disappear into the daylight at the exit.[4]

This passage is noteworthy also because it overturns in an interesting way the conception of maze-like structures characteristic for Kafka's stories, which are usually associated with the idea of a claustrophobic 'closure' of space; in contrast to this, the 'endless' nature of this kind of labyrinthine writing — and reading, consequently — makes us think of a new type of space, created by the very act of being said, which very much resonates with Elizabeth Grosz's elaborations on the concept of space in Bergsonian and Deleuzean thought: 'a conception of space that does not so much underlie or subtend *matter*, functioning as indifferent coordinates of the placement of matter' — rather, a conception of space that functions as an *effect* of matter and *movement*: 'an *unfolding* space defined, as time is, by the arc of movement, and thus a space open to *becoming*'.[5]

Now, I will not argue that Kafka's space should be read as fostering the emergence of liberating energies; still, I see a constant tension at work in most of his texts between a given, even suffocating, closure and the creative and disruptive force of writing, which incessantly strives to open up new paths, embracing the risks as well as the potentialities of becoming.

---

4   Kafka, *Letters to Milena*, trans. and intro. by Philip Boehm (New York: Schocken, 1990), pp. 20–21 (emphasis added, A. C.).

5   Elizabeth Grosz, 'The Future of Space: Toward an Architecture of Invention', in Grosz, *Architecture from the Outside: Essays on Virtual and Real Space*, foreword by Peter Eisenman (Cambridge, MA: MIT Press, 2001), pp. 109–30 (p. 118) (my emphasis, A. C.).

Some years before, in 1917, Kafka had given shape to another incomplete structure in 'The Great Wall of China', a short story that, in my view, belongs to the same genealogy as 'The Burrow'. What these two texts have in common is also, quite meaningfully, the keyword *Bau* ('construction') as a part of their original title, and interestingly enough, a destiny of mistranslation. In the German title 'Beim Bau der Chinesischen Mauer', the emphasis, which gets lost in translation, is precisely on the 'construction' of the wall as a *process* caught up in its becoming. The opening sentence of the story foreshadows that of the later text: 'The Great Wall of China was *finished* off at its northernmost corner.'[6] But as we can by now expect, this first sentence is going to be soon contradicted; and so it is: from the second line onwards, we are told of how the very method employed to carry out the building of the Wall, namely the so-called 'principle of piecemeal construction', or 'building in sections', according to another translation, turns out to be the main cause of the *structural impossibility* for the work to be completed. That is, the wall was not planned to be built continuously from one end to the other; rather, the construction had to proceed independently from the two opposite sides of the Empire, in order to converge and finally meet at a certain point. The work was assigned to small groups of workers; each had to accomplish only small portions of the wall, before being transferred to 'begin building again in quite different neighbourhoods'; but within this general master plan, as if in a sort of infinitely divisible space, between the two extremities, the western and the eastern, the principle of piecemeal construction was replicated, that is, 'applied on a smaller scale', with the result of an inevitably fragmented structure that cannot but fail to achieve its main goal, namely 'to be a protection against the people of the north [...] the nomads'. Unable to provide a distinction between inside and outside, the unfinished/unfinishable wall ends up, very much like a ruin, questioning the very meaning of construction, as well as the metaphysical privilege of presence over absence:

> Naturally in this way many great gaps were left, which were only filled in gradually and bit by bit, some, indeed, not till after the

---

6   Kafka, 'The Great Wall of China', in Kafka, *Complete Stories*, pp. 235–47 (p. 235).

official announcement that the wall was finished. In fact it is said that there are gaps which have never been filled in at all.⁷

I cannot do justice here to the complexity of Kafka's fable, nor can I follow the many subtle hypotheses the narrator formulates and scrutinizes in order to make sense of the 'principle of piecemeal construction'. Indeed, as he remarks, 'the work had not been undertaken without thought'. Yet, there is one point still worth mentioning that helps us relate this story to 'The Burrow'. Although the narrator quickly dismisses it as one of 'the many wild ideas in people's heads at the time', at a certain point he tells us of a 'scholar' who wrote a book drawing a comparison between the construction project of the Wall and that of the Tower of Babel. His main argument was that 'the Tower of Babel failed to reach its goal not because of the reasons universally advanced [...] the tower failed and was bound to fail because of the weakness of the foundations.'⁸ The Great Wall had to be thought, then, as the secure basis on which a new tower of Babel might be erected. The absurdity of conceiving of 'a wall, which did not form even a circle, but only a sort of quarter- or half-circle' as being capable of providing the foundations for a tower is noticed by the reporter himself. Still, this anecdote adds important layers of significance to the whole story and allows us to draw a connection between it and other places of Kafka's oeuvre in which he, more or less explicitly, reflects on — and rewrites — the biblical narrative. Among them are 'The City Coat of Arms' and the sketch, found in a notebook, of a minimal story in form of a dialogue that brings us directly back to 'The Burrow':

> What are you building? — I want to dig a passage [einen Gang]. Some progress must happen [Es muss ein Fortschritt geschehen]. My station up there is much too high.
> We are digging the pit of Babel.⁹

As sketchily outlined as it is, this rudimentary narrative helps us bridge the set of tales revolving around the impossible construction of the

---

7   Ibid.
8   Ibid., p. 238.
9   Franz Kafka, 'Fragments from Notebooks and Loose Pages', in Kafka, *Dearest Father: Stories and Other Writings* (New York: Schocken Books, 1954), § 349 (modified translation, A. C.); a critical edition in German is available as part of the 'Unpublished Works 1922–1924' in *The Kafka Project*, ed. by Mario Nervi (1999–2007) <http://www.kafka.org/index.php?ichentlief> [accessed 5 July 2021].

tower of Babel with the story of the ambivalent, ruinous building of the burrow. Some elements are made explicit here that in *Der Bau* will be veiled by the ambiguity of the word — first of all the equation of the verb 'to build' (*bauen*) with the verb 'to dig' (*graben*). Some others seem to be caught in the middle of a metamorphic process. With regard to the subject(s) involved, as the visibly and distinctly human features gradually recede, all that remains is a voice, answering to an interpellation. No description is provided, no context either: whether it is (still) (a) human being(s) or another kind of creature(s), the subject is only defined by its doing, namely by the activity of building. As well as by its purpose, which is — again — entirely confined within the compass of this activity: to do it further, to do it better, to open a passage, *einen Gang* (to what? to whom? where to?), to progress, make progress, or — more precisely — to 'give' or 'make place' (*donner lieu*, as Derrida puts it)[10] in order for progress to 'happen'. Whoever posits this goal — which is not even a final goal — is a single subject. This is not (yet) the solitary constructor of the burrow though, since at the very end the singular 'I' turns into a first person plural, a 'we' that recalls, even in its most debased and reversed form, the collective undertaking of the construction of the tower of Babel. Yet, in this case, there is no will of elevation or power at stake; on the contrary, one's 'position' has to be *lowered*; if 'some progress must happen', it is in the sense of a *descending* movement, no longer directed upward to the sky but down into the earth.

---

10   This expression, with its emphasis on the act of *giving* (fr. *donner*) as a sort of (impersonal) *gift*, is used by Derrida in his discussion of the concept of *chora* as it is developed in Plato's *Timaeus* (Derrida, 'Khôra', trans. by Ian McLeod, in Derrida, *On the Name*, ed. by Thomas Dutoit [Stanford, CA: Stanford University Press, 1995], pp. 89–127). Meaningfully enough, Derrida proposed to architect Peter Eisenman to read this essay for their collaboration on a garden design as part of Bernard Tschumi's Parc de la Villette project in Paris. Irreducible to the categories of the 'intelligible' and the 'sensible', i.e., to the binary structure of the cosmos as outlined in the *Timaeus*, the *chora* — the Greek for 'space' or 'site' — is nonetheless essential to Plato's theory of creation: it becomes an undefinable and unrepresentable third term, which Plato himself calls a 'receptacle of becoming'. Jacques Derrida and Peter Eisenman, *Chora L Works*, ed. by Jeffrey Kipnis and Thomas Leeser (New York: Monacelli, 1997). For an all-encompassing assessment of Derrida's practical and theoretical interaction with 'architecture', see among others the special issue of *Aut aut*, 368 (2015): *Un matrimonio sfortunato. Derrida e l'architettura*, ed. by Petar Bojanić and Damiano Cantone.

The story of Babel, as told in Genesis 11, in fact narrates in a very condensed form of a collective enterprise, which begins in the name of perfect unity — the unity of people, identity, and place, as it is cemented by the bonds of a common language and a common project — and ends up, after the intervention of God, in the most radical dispersion of humankind and in the emergence of irreducible differences among different peoples.[11] The common project that is bound to fail has to do with the construction of both 'a city and a tower whose top may reach unto heaven', that is, with the foundation of a structured dwelling space (the city) as well as with the edification of an exemplary work (the tower). In order to stop wandering and to keep its unity, the people need to settle down, to occupy and *give form* or 'structure' to a space. The untold violence of this (colonizing) project finds its objective correlate in the erection of the tower, which functions both as a display of power — and a (phallic) symbol of it — and as a means of control over the earth.[12] As is well known, what induces God to intervene is the erection of the tower, or the sheer possibility for the united peoples to achieve that goal. What often remains unnoticed is that the book of Genesis does not report anything about the destiny of the tower, whereas it is said that, after God had 'confounded the language of all the earth', they — the people — 'left off building the city'.

---

11 Genesis 11. 1–9: 'And the whole earth was of one language, and of one speech.[2] And it came to pass, as they journeyed from the east, that they found a plain in the land of Shinar, and they dwelt there.[3] And they said one to another, "Come, let us make bricks and burn them thoroughly." And they had brick for stone, and slime had they for mortar.[4] And they said, "Come, let us build us a city and a tower whose top may reach unto heaven; and let us make us a name, lest we be scattered abroad upon the face of the whole earth."[5] And the Lord came down to see the city and the tower which the children of men built.[6] And the Lord said, "Behold, the people are one and they have all one language, and this they begin to do; and now nothing will be withheld from them which they have imagined to do.[7] Come, let Us go down, and there confound their language, that they may not understand one another's speech."[8] So the Lord scattered them abroad from thence upon the face of all the earth; and they left off building the city.[9] Therefore is the name of it called Babel [that is, Confusion], because the Lord did there confound the language of all the earth; and from thence did the Lord scatter them abroad upon the face of all the earth.'

12 The tower reconfigures the field of visibility: being 'visible' from everywhere, it tautologically restates its sheer presence, hence the monumentality that characterizes it; at the same time, it embodies the (elevated) vantage point from which the whole earth can be viewed, i.e., possessed by the gaze.

This apparent gap of information in the biblical narration has given rise, from early biblical commentaries to the works of writers and philosophers of all times, to a wonderfully varied range of explanations and inventions. Among them, the most common say that, (1) since the tower is not mentioned any longer, it must have been completed, but then, being abandoned, it fell into ruin; (2) it was torn down by God's anger; (3) it was abandoned along with the city and remained unfinished.[13] In any case, at a certain point, the image of the tower seems to be replaced by that of the ruin, another powerful figure of architectural incompletion, which, in the same years of Kafka's writing activity, aroused the speculative interest of authors such as Walter Benjamin and Georg Simmel, who employed it to rethink the mutual relations of aesthetics, history, and modernity.

Just to mention some dates: 1907 Georg Simmel, 'Die Ruine' ('The Ruin', essay); 1917 Kafka, 'Beim Bau der Chinesischen Mauer' ('The Great Wall of China'); 1921 Paul Valéry, *Eupalinos, ou l'architecte*; 1923–1924 Kafka, 'Der Bau'; 1923–1925 Walter Benjamin, *Ursprung des deutschen Trauerspiels* (*Origin of the German* Trauerspiel, published in 1928).[14]

The tower of Babel and the figure of the ruin, which — as I said — seem to converge in the image of the abandoned, unfinished, or demolished work, could also be seen as opposite figurations of architectural failure. The one representing the 'not-yet' of the work, or more precisely, the quintessential impossibility for an ambitious project to be accomplished; the other embodying the idea, to a certain extent opposite to this, of the 'no-longer' complete, of a work as 'fragment', which on the one hand critically and ambiguously points at a former, lost totality, and on the other stands on its own.

---

13   For a detailed discussion on this point in particular, as well as for a historical-political reading of Genesis, 11. 1–9 see the monumental Christoph Uehlinger, *Weltreich und 'eine Rede'. Eine neue Deutung der sogenannten Turmbauerzählung (Gen 11,1–9)* (Göttingen: Vandenhoeck & Ruprecht, 1990).

14   Georg Simmel, 'The Ruin', in *Georg Simmel, 1858–1918: A Collection of Essays, with Translations and a Bibliography*, ed. by Kurt H. Wolff (Cleveland: Ohio State University Press, 1959), pp. 259–66; Kafka, 'The Great Wall of China'; Paul Valéry, *Eupalinos, or The Architect*, in *Collected Works of Paul Valéry*, ed. by Jackson Mathews, 15 vols (Princeton, NJ: Princeton University Press, 1956–75), IV: *Dialogues*, trans. by William McCausland Stewart (1956), pp. 65–150; Kafka, 'The Burrow'; Walter Benjamin, *Origin of the German 'Trauerspiel'*, trans. by Howard Eiland (Cambridge, MA: Harvard University Press, 2019).

'Present form of a past life', according to Simmel's felicitous expression, the ruin is yet no more than a trace, from which neither the past time nor the former structure, towards which the ruin points, can be reconstructed in their wholeness and complete transparency. As the German theorist recognizes, the aesthetic experience of the ruin relies upon an *'antagonism* [between] the disharmony [...] and the formal satisfaction', a *'tension'* between 'purpose and accident, nature and spirit, past and present'. Yet, these contrasts are for him tempered by — and subsumed into — a form of higher justice: the ruin is 'tragic' but 'not sad' because it manifests the 'secret justice of destruction', a return to nature which pays back the violence that was first exerted upon it by the 'will' or the 'spirit' in the very act of construction. In this sense, Simmel seems to resolve the 'ambiguity' that he had originally envisioned — and which instead will become central in the analysis of later theorists. The 'peace, whose mood', according to him, 'surrounds the ruin' is a mood hard to find in Kafka's stories and yet Simmel's remark that its fascination 'goes beyond what is merely negative and degrading' might turn out to be a useful tool for the interpretation of the Czech writer's impossible structures as well. In this perspective, it might be interesting to look at those approaches that tend to keep the tension between opposites unresolved or to problematize it within the frame of a *dynamic* model. Thus, the ruin can be seen as a 'disturbing structure',[15] constitutively 'anachronistic',[16] which not only has the ability of questioning all sorts of *given* 'orders' or (stable) 'structures'; it is also intrinsically ambivalent,[17] being itself a structure and at the same time a moment of an ongoing process — that of 'ruination'. To take into account its double nature of structure/process allows us to see the dyad ruin/ruination as something that 'goes beyond' the absolute annihilation of form and is related to destruction as much as it is

---

15 See Karen Dale and Gibson Burrell, 'Disturbing Structure. Reading the Ruins', in *Culture and Organization*, 2 (2011), pp. 107–21.

16 On anachronism in relation to architecture see Raoul Kirchmayr's elaboration on Derrida's concepts of hauntology and 'visor effect' in Kirchmayr, 'L'arte dell'*espacement*', *Aut aut*, 368 (2015), pp. 62-87 (pp. 82-83).

17 Zygmunt Bauman defines 'ambivalence' as 'the possibility of assigning an object or an event to more than one category', see Baumann, *Modernity and Ambivalence* (Cambridge: Cambridge University Press, 1991), p. 9. For a discussion of the concept in relation to ruins, see Dale and Burrell, 'Disturbing Structure', p. 113.

— in a phantasmatic sense — to both construction (and organization) and *re-ordering*.

The story of Babel was appealing for Kafka, I believe, for its narrative power, rather than for its static figuration. Three elements among others would have caught his attention: (1) the insistence on the activity of building, i.e., on the *process* as well as on the building techniques and materials; (2) the focus on the subjects involved, the builders, the people, and their destiny; (3) the entanglement of the architectural and the linguistic. Kafka's adaptation, translation, recasting of these three motifs in both his private and creative writings contributes to the articulation of a complex imagery that counters the classical ideal of architectural wholeness, even where there is no apparent connection to the story of Babel.

Before descending again into 'The Burrow', I will take a brief detour in order to get a glimpse of the meaning and origin of this ideal. Where does it come from and what does it stand for? What are its implications? And what are the implications of transgressing against it, or denying it, in Kafka's text in particular and his writing in general? And more broadly speaking, what's the cultural and political meaning of such a gesture? This digression should help us at least to bring to the fore the importance of interconnected issues, the web of entanglements that underlies the architectural metaphor: the problem of (1) the text in its material formation and with relation to the quest — and question — of form; (2) reason and thought as the coherent edification of systems; (3) the self in the process of its spiritual *Bildung* and in its bodily relation to life and work.

I want to discuss this nexus of issues in connection — and in contrast with — another complex and fascinating text, namely Paul Valéry's *Eupalinos, or The Architect*, published in 1921. The importance of this comparison for my purpose lies not only in the fact that Valéry was very much concerned with the topic of architecture in itself, to which he would devote more than one work; but also in the fact that in this specific text he addresses many of the questions that are of key concern for Kafka as well, often providing different if not diametrically opposed answers to them. Valéry sees architecture as the most beautiful and *complete* type of activity that a person can imagine. A finished building gives us, at a single glance, the sum of intentions, inventions, insights and forces that imply its existence; it brings to light humanity's combined work of desire, knowledge and ability. Uniquely among the arts, and in an indivisible moment of vision, architecture charges our souls with the sense of human capacity *as a whole*.[18]

The primacy of architecture among the arts seems to depend for Valéry precisely on its inherent capacity to configure wholes — intended both as the material products of its work and as the aesthetic experience it induces; architecture, Eupalinos explains, is, together with music, the only art

which *enclose*[s] man in man; or, rather, which *enclose*[s] the being in its work, and the soul in its acts and in the production of its acts, as our former body was *entirely enclosed* in the creations of its eye, and *surrounded* with sight. With two arts, it *wraps up* itself.[19]

Both Valéry and Kafka are concerned with the problem of 'closure', although their struggle with the form takes different paths and eventually ends up in quite different regions. Valéry's Phaedrus reports Eupalinos's words: 'Destroying and constructing are of equal importance, and we must have souls for the one and the other; but constructing is the dearer to my mind.'[20] By contrast, even if many of Kafka's characters are relentlessly busy with building activities, most of their constructions, as we have seen, reveal themselves to be unrealizable.

Valéry is nonetheless interested in the construction as a process rather than as the end-product of the work. For him, form is formation, *poiesis*. Phaedrus, in reference to Eupalinos's words, says: 'I no longer distinguish the idea of a temple and that of its construction.'[21]

---

18 This passage, quoted in Geert Bekaert, 'Le réel du discours. Eupalinos ou l'architect', trans. by David McKay, *OASE*, 75 (2008), pp. 227–39 (pp. 233–34), is taken from Paul Valéry's introduction to the melodrama *Amphion* (for which Arthur Honegger wrote the music). Written by Valéry in 1929, performed for the first time 1931 in Paris, *Amphion* is, as Bekaert puts it, an 'ode to the *constructive* arts, music and architecture'.
19 Valéry, *Eupalinos*, p. 96.
20 Ibid., p. 70.
21 Ibid.

For Valéry, there's an errancy inherent to language, which the poet must treat as 'irregular blocks' are treated by the architect-builder. There is 'no geometry without words', says Socrates to Phaedrus, but, alongside the 'simple words', which are numbers and allow for the clarity of geometry, there are complex words, their essence being that

> it is impossible to conduct them through sure and far-reaching developments without *getting lost* in their ramifications. [...] So it is necessary to fit these complex words together, speculating on the *chances* and *surprises* that arrangements of this kind hold in store for us, and to give the name of 'poets' to those whom fortune favors in this work.[22]

Although the emphasis is always on the constructive side and on the process by which poetry like architecture gives form and order to matter, Valéry's Socrates does not conceal the violence inherent in such a process: 'The structure of every human creation is disorder', he seems to admit quite surprisingly, as Geert Bekaert observes, because it 'is the result of thought and to think is to disrupt something (*déranger quelque chose*)'. There is, as for Simmel, a necessary violence exerted by thought (Simmel would say: will) upon nature in every (architectonic) creation: 'the artisan cannot do his work without violating or disarranging an order by the forces that he applies to matter to adapt it to the idea he wants to imitate'; yet, since matter holds a complexity that inevitably exceeds thought, and is intrinsically irreducible to the idea, the structure/form of human creations produces 'things which, as a whole, are less complex than their parts'.[23]

Also of great interest for me is Valéry's constant reference, even when it occurs with surprising twists that complicate the scheme, to the powerful ideal of the perfect building,[24] as it has been shaped by

---

22 Ibid., p. 108.
23 Valéry, *Eupalinos*, p. 122 (modified translation).
24 See Valéry, *Eupalinos*, p. 90 for a reference to the body and the 'equilibrium of [its] organs, this true proportions of [its] parts, which make [it] to *be* and to stablish ever anew in the very heart of moving things', but also pp. 128-29 for a reference to the so called vitruvian triad: 'the creations of man are made either with a view to his body, and there is the principle we call *utility*, or with a view to his soul, and that is what we seeks under the name of *beauty*' or with a view to 'the rest of the world' and to 'the movement of nature' and this is when he 'seeks *solidity* or *lastingness*'.

Vitruvius.[25] Here, I just want to sketch out as schematically as possible the main traits of the imagery that from the Roman architect via the humanist rediscovery during the Renaissance has arrived in present times. Above all, it tells of (1) an aesthetics of balance, decorum, and static closure; (2) of a technological dream of complete mastery, (3) of rational control over nature and accidents.

According to Vitruvius's formulation, the characteristics of the well-constructed building — or the 'three conditions' the architect ought to comply with — are: *firmitas*, 'strength', or 'durability'; *utilitas*, 'utility' or 'convenience'; *venustas*, beauty.[26] Such a formulation, which has been for many centuries an unquestioned and powerfully normative formula, is still influential today for our common understanding of the ultimate *telos* of architecture, despite the many attempts of reconceptualizing the field.

The deconstructivist architect Mark Wigley, for instance, in a recent discussion of the language of architecture, has quite surprisingly admitted that

> the very expression 'avantgarde architecture' is probably a contradiction in terms. The word architecture has meaning in our culture only inasmuch as architecture has offered reassurance by resisting time, a dream exemplified by the classical tradition with its supposedly eternal geometries.[27]

If 'solidity' points at the relation of the work to the issue of time and history, by configuring its main goal as an aspiration to 'monumentality', it also addresses the problem of the 'materiality' of the work, that is, in other words, the relation between techniques and matter or materials. Vitruvius, in fact, states: 'Durability will be assured when

---

25   The auratic figure that stands as a putative father to this discourse is the almost legendary Roman architect Marcus Vitruvius Pollio, author of the treatise *De Architectura* (15 BC), which is considered to be the oldest source on classical Western architecture to survive. The peculiar destiny of this treatise as the lone survivor of a long tradition, alongside with its partly normative approach and its capacity of giving concise formulations to some key concerns of the time and their solutions as well, make of it also the starting point of architectural theory and discourse. See Vitruvius, *Ten Books on Architecture*, trans. by Ingrid D. Rowland, commentary by Thomas Noble Howe, Ingrid D. Rowland, and Michael J. Dewar (Cambridge: Cambridge University Press, 1999).

26   Ibid., p. 26 (1, 3, 2)

27   Mark Wigley, 'The Art to Listen to Architecture', in *Eisenman/Krier: Two Ideologies*, ed. by Cynthia C. Davidson (New York: Monacelli, 2004), pp. 119–31 (p. 125).

foundations are carried down to the solid ground and materials wisely and liberally selected'.[28] The same issue, even though rephrased in an idealistic vocabulary, will be central to Georg Simmel's argument in his 1907 essay, where he speaks of 'the great struggle between the *will* of the spirit and the *necessity* of nature [...] between mechanical, inert *matter* which passively resists pressure, and *informing* spirituality which pushes upward'.[29]

For our purposes, the so-called Vitruvian triad is so important precisely because it presents a strong contribution defining a long-lasting model and ideal. Far from remaining confined to its original domain, the model of the ideal building has catalyzed and organized a long chain of concepts from other fields and has become a key figure of Western culture, not devoid of value judgements.

By considering both *utilitas* and *venustas* as conditions for the perfect building, Vitruvius's ideal pursues a balance between 'functionality' and 'aesthetics'. While the recent history of architecture has from time to time stressed the one at the expense of the other, what matters here is the wide range of topics addressed by the classical systematization as well as the constant attempt to 'keep all in balance'. Thus, *utilitas*, usefulness, or 'convenience' is to be intended in relation to both the concrete needs of bodies ('when the arrangement of the apartments [...] presents no hindrance to use'), and a given social and urban order, as well as pre-existing power structures ('when each class of building is assigned to its suitable and appropriate exposure').[30] At the same time, buildings have to comply with a supposedly self-evident concept of beauty, which is ultimately based on the ideal of a harmonious whole: 'when the appearance of the work is *pleasing* and in *good taste*, and when its members are in due proportion according to correct principles of symmetry'.[31] For Vitruvius, the ultimate model of completeness and beauty is the body of the 'well-shaped man':[32]

---

28   Vitruvius, *Ten Books*, p. 26 (I, 3, 2).
29   Georg Simmel, 'The Ruin', p. 259 (emphasis added, A. C.).
30   Vitruvius, *Ten Books*, p. 26 (I, 3, 2).
31   Ibid. (my italics).
32   Ibid., p. 47 (III, 1, 1).

> Symmetry is a proper agreement between the members of
> the work itself, and relation between the different parts and
> the whole general scheme, in accordance with a certain part
> selected as standard. Thus in the human body there is a kind of
> symmetrical harmony between forearm, foot, palm, finger, and
> other small parts; and so it is with perfect buildings.[33]

As Leonardo da Vinci's famous graphic rendering of the descriptions contained in Book III of Vitruvius's treatise emblematically shows, the human (male) body is read, interpreted and re-conceptualized by Vitruvius through the lens of geometry.[34]

It is precisely in this allegiance between the artistic, the technical, and the rational (*ratio* is the Latin term for 'proportion'[35] as well as for 'calculation' and 'reasoning') that nature, represented by its most perfect work, the human body, bridled by the straight line of the square and encompassed by the finite line of the circle, is fixed in a model of wholeness and perfection: static, never-changing, always already made and self-confined, the Vitruvian man expunges error and accident out of his perimeter alone.

The pervasiveness of the ideal of architectural wholeness should not be underestimated. Not only does it stretch out far beyond any strictly historically defined European Humanism. As Kojin Karatani points out, it seems to inform Western thought from its very beginning. By analysing the use of the architectural language in philosophy, mathematics, and economy, in his book *Architecture as Metaphor*, Karatani suggests that throughout the history of Western culture 'architecture' has served less as a name for a peculiar art or practice than as a metaphor, a set of images and figures of speech pointing at the idea of

---

33   Ibid., p. 25 (1, 2, 4).
34   For a revised and critical analysis of the fortune of Leonardo's drawing and for a discussion on the significance of geometry in his thought (as well as in Vitruvius's treatise), see Frank Zöllner, 'L'uomo vitruviano di Leonardo da Vinci, Rudolf Wittkower e l'*Angelus Novus* di Walter Benjamin', *Raccolta viciana*, 26 (1995), pp. 329–58.
35   Admittedly, the etymology of the word *rational* recalled above does not refer strictly to Vitruvius's vocabulary. In particular, Vitruvius does not use the term *ratio* for the concept usually rendered as 'proportion'. Rather, the Roman author opts for *proportio*, which is itself a transposition — and partly a mistranslation, in the wake of Cicero — of the Greek term *analogia*: 'Aedium compositio constat ex symmetria, [...] ea autem *proportione* paritur est, quae graece ἀναλογία dicitur. Proportio est ratae partis membrorum in omni opere tot(o)que commodulatio' (Vitruvius, *Ten Books*, p. 47 (III, 1, 1)).

'formalism' or 'formalization'.[36] In this sense, the secrete force that Karatani sees at work, more or less explicitly, throughout the many domains of Western thought, and that he calls the 'will to architecture',[37] would be basically tantamount to a will to completeness and formalized wholes, 'a way [for philosophers] of grounding and stabilizing their otherwise unstable philosophical systems'.[38]

To 'demolish everything completely and start again right from the foundations', this is Descartes's project.[39] It is the project of the modern, of a thought that conceives of itself as 'critical thinking' and yet cannot endure staring into the abyss (Ab-grund): in order to acquire the dignity of philosophy, thought must be 'grounded', it demands *solidity*; the 'principle of systematic doubt', like any thought aspiring to some form of system — or systematics — first needs to find, or show, that there exists something at the bottom of all critical excavation work, something beyond all doubts, which resists, cannot be shaken by any objection, a 'firm soil',[40] an origin, which might provide the starting point for any further inquiry. It needs to rest at and upon some point, and that point is notoriously for Descartes the assumption that there exists a thinking or doubting substance, the cogito: 'I took this as the bedrock on which I could lay the *foundation* of my philosophy.'[41]

A problem of foundations is also the one raised, no coincidence this, by the 'scholar' in Kafka's 'Great Wall of China', as he claims to know the true reason of the fall of the tower of Babel that was meant to be erected upon the wall. Kafka provides here a radical criticism which points to a double impossibility: by showing the wall as

---

36   Kojin Karatani, *Architecture as Metaphor: Language, Number, Money*, ed. by Michael Speaks, trans. by Sabu Kohso (Cambridge, MA: MIT Press, 1995).
37   Ibid., pp. 5–13.
38   Ibid., p. 5.
39   René Descartes, *Meditations on First Philosophy*, in Descartes, *The Philosophical Writings of Descartes*, trans. by John Cottingham, Robert Stoothoff, Dugald Murdoch, 3 vols (Cambridge: Cambridge University Press, 1984–1991), II (1984), pp. 1–60 (p. 12), cited in Daniel L. Purdy, *On the Ruins of Babel: Architectural Metaphor in German Thought* (Ithaca, NY: Cornell University Press, 2011), p. 87.
40   In one reply to his critics, Descartes explains that when one builds 'where there is a sandy topsoil' he begins 'by digging out a set of trenches from which he removes the sand, and anything resting on or mixed with the sand, so that he can lay his foundations on firm soil'. See Descartes, 'Objections and Replies', in *Philosophical Writings*, II, pp. 63–397 (p. 366) (cited in Purdy, *On the Ruins*, p. 87).
41   Descartes, *Philosophical Writings*, II, p. 366.

structurally interminable, he undermines both the idea of foundation and that of any construction built upon that basis.[42] If seen in this perspective, 'The Burrow' represents an additional step. As is signalled by its untranslatable name meaning both a construction *and* a burrow, this work, which is forged out of a void, built up by digging out, prompts us to recognize as deeply inherent in the (twofold) structure of the *Bau* its being precisely a work *without* foundations.

But further questions are to be answered about the relation of the burrow and its inhabitant and builder to thought. Is this pensive animal a philosopher? Or a parody of it? What kind of reasoning is displayed in the structuring of 'The Burrow'? And what about the very nature of the edifice, the *telos* of the work? What is at stake here, is it the erection of a monument, a fortress, or a dwelling, for thought?

To 'demolish everything completely and start again right from the foundations': Descartes takes the architectural metaphor of destruction-(re)construction seriously. And warns against the risks of a work-in-progress which does not spare any intimate space: 'before starting to rebuild your house, [...] you must also provide yourself with some other place where you can live comfortably while building is in progress.'[43] At stake here is the distance needed for thought to be objective and, more latently, to ward off madness. Kafka's animal will be renovating his burrow without leaving it but for brief periods, during which he will experience the impossibility of looking at his work from the outside. 'At such times it is as if I were not so much looking at my house as at *myself* sleeping.'[44] The initial 'joy of being in a profound slumber and simultaneously of keeping vigilant guard over myself' soon turns into an anguished feeling of dispossession: the 'entrance' of the work, in a way that recalls the doorway in the tale 'Before the Law', 'locks and bars itself against me, the builder and the possessor'.[45] Whatever the burrow *is* and whatever it *means* for its inhabitant and builder, the distance between them tends to decrease

---

42 George Steiner, *After Babel: Aspects of Language and Translation* (Oxford: Oxford University Press, 1975), p. 70.
43 René Descartes, *Discourse on Method*, in *Philosophical Writings*, I (1985), pp. 111–50 (p. 122), cited in Purdy, *On the Ruins*, p. 203.
44 Kafka, 'The Burrow', p. 334.
45 Ibid., p. 340. Kafka, 'Before the Law', in Kafka, *Complete Stories*, pp. 4–5.

over time up to a point of a quasi-identification — 'I and the burrow belong so indissolubly together [...] nothing can part us for long'.[46]

'The double positing of the self as both house and architect', as Daniel Purdy has shown, is a figure of thought that comes from afar, already charged with meaning: its inherently paradoxical structure subtends the major architectural trope of *Bildung* in the eighteenth century. In his *Italian Journey*, Johann Wolfgang von Goethe compares himself to an architect who, in the midst of the construction of a tower, realizes to have laid 'a bad foundation' and needs to amend his mistakes 'before it is too late'; accordingly, he decides to 'tear down all that he has built so far [...], to enlarge and improve his design, to make is foundation more secure'.[47] Even though the metaphor of the house under renovation might allude to Descartes's image, from now on, the self cannot but be entirely dragged into the ongoing process of renovation: the artist can no longer escape his own space, for he is both subject *and* object of the construction work. Goethe overlooks — as the builder of the burrow does — Descartes's warning of finding a comfortable place where to live 'while the building is in progress'. Yet, he does not seem to be caught in the 'paradox of self-indication'[48] in the same tragic way as Kafka's animal. Nor is madness on his horizon. On the contrary, he seems to be confident in the possibility of achieving a complete and successful construction of his work, that is, of the self and the writing of the self in one stroke: he 'looks forward happily to building something that will last'.[49]

'Writing denies itself to me.' The scene of this denial frames the notebook entry of the spring 1922, in which Kafka rephrases the metaphor of the house under renovation and addresses those very issues that Goethe kept out of his sight: the paradoxes of autobiography and

---

46   Ibid.
47   Johann Wolfgang von Goethe, *Italian Journey*, trans. by W. H. Auden and Elisabeth Mayer (New York: Pantheon, 1962), p. 139 (20 December 1786), quoted in Purdy, *On the Ruins*, p. 203.
48   Edgar Landgraf refers to the problem as the 'paradox of self-indication' as the paradox of positing a self that is distinct from the self that posits: 'The self, in order to indicate (think) itself, must make itself different from itself to be able to do so.' Landgraf, 'Self-Forming Selves: Autonomy and Artistic Creativity in Goethe and Moritz', *Goethe Yearbook*, 11 (2002), pp. 159–76.
49   Goethe, *Italian Journey*, p. 139.

the 'self-construction', the need for an experimental form of writing, the risks of a work in progress which engages the whole self, body and mind alike, and which is haunted by the spectres of madness and incompleteness:

> Writing denies itself to me. Hence plan for autobiographical investigations. Not biography but investigation and detection of the smallest possible component parts. Out of these I will then construct myself, as one whose house is unsafe wants to build a safe one next to it, if possible out of the material of the old one. What is bad, admittedly, is if in the midst of building his strength gives out and now, instead of one house, unsafe but yet complete, he has one half-destroyed and one half-finished house, that is to say, nothing. What follows is madness.[50]

Kafka's image of the house under renovation conjures up many relevant features of the burrow. First of all, it displaces the issue of the 'solidity' of foundation, which is essential in both Decartes's and Goethe's enterprises, on to a more general question of the 'safety' of the entire structure. Like in his later text, in Kafka's notebook entry the term 'foundations' is not mentioned at all, whereas the whole house is said to be 'unsafe'. Also, this short narrative privileges the middle phase of the ongoing work over — on the one hand — the initial one of design and methodology (Descartes) and — on the other — the projection onto the final result (Goethe). Yet, the burrow differs from a house under renovation in important ways, mainly because of the sense of undecidability that surrounds the burrow, with regard to both its function and the nature of its inhabitant and creator. While in the sketch of the two houses a purpose for the entire renovation work is clearly stated, to 'construct my self', and this is put in connection to writing, in 'The Burrow' any attempt to pin down the work, to assign to it a unifying meaning is bound to fail.

Neither a house of (pure) thought, nor an image of the Self under construction, even though sharing features of both, the burrow does not coincide with them. It rather escapes classification and eludes metaphorical closure, always showing an excess, or keeping a reserve of meaning which prompts a series of infinite displacements. Instability,

---

50   Franz Kafka, 'Fragments from Notebooks and Loose Pages', p. 350 (Spring 1922).

indeterminacy, hybridity become central to the structur*ing* of the burrow as much as incompleteness turns out to be essential, not merely accidental, to it. Furthermore, conjoining the two figures of the unfinished that we have been dealing with thus far, the 'not-yet' and the 'no-longer' complete, the 'half-destroyed' and the 'half-finished', the burrow instantiates a 'self-dismantling structure' insofar as by revealing the fulfilment of its construction as illusory, it undoes itself in a movement that is both concrete and metaphorical.

The first and more radical ambiguity concerning the burrow concerns its very being and purpose. What the text allows us to say, apart from any interpretation that it invokes and eludes at the same time, is that (1) the burrow is a construction (*Bau*), which in this case means that, being both a process and an object, it is also the exemplary work of its builder's life — and a substitution for it; (2) it is intended to be a dwelling, a home; (3) not only does it provide a shelter; but it (4) is also something of a fortress, if seen through some of his creator's depictions, whereas most of the renovation projects seem to cope with some military arrangements or strategy; (5) it belongs to the order of edification and yet, (6) it is also a dig, a pit, an excavation work; (7) it is shaped as a labyrinth, at least in some of its parts; but (8) it is also a ruin, since it encompasses the remains of 'abortive building attempts'.

There is a final question to be answered: is 'The Burrow' complete or is it a fragment? According to Kafka's friend Max Brod and to Dora Dymant there was to be an encounter that would have ended with the hero's death. As reported by Hermann J. Weigand, Malcolm Pasley asserts that the final page of the manuscript is completely filled without any terminating punctuation mark.[51] This he takes as a proof that there was more to follow. Still, I prefer to see the question as undecidable.

Equally undecidable remains for me the question of the allegedly violent encounter. Is it, as many maintain, the encounter with death? I would prefer to stick to what the text suggests and see it as an encounter with the Unknown, or the Unknowable, the 'event' as the 'Not-yet', towards which Kafka's writing would open the path, give — or make — place for it to be.

---

51 Weigand, 'Franz Kafka's "The Burrow"', p. 164.

Camera Fog; or, The Pendulum of Austerity in Contemporary Portugal
MARIA JOSÉ DE ABREU

One day in early 2012, Portuguese photographer Inês d'Orey was walking in the city of Oporto when she came across a graffiti stenciled on one of the walls of the Carlos Alberto Theatre. It consisted of a map of Portugal overwritten with the ochre-coloured words 'continuamos à espera que o nevoeiro passe' (we keep on waiting for the fog to pass) (Figure 1).

The graffiti inspired d'Orey to make a photography and video series she titled *Limbo*. A statement attached to d'Orey's work expresses it as follows: '*Limbo* contemplates what it is to exist in an indefinite and uncertain state', a reflexive perspective on 'a perplexed and outraged generation'.[1] It refers to what, since the outbreak of the 2007–08 financial crisis and the invigoration of the austerity state, is sometimes referred to as a 'precarious generation', also known in Portugal as *geração à rasca*. Shot in hazy, ethereal light, each photo in the series

---

* Thanks to Iracema Dulley, Patricia Guarda, and my fellow colleagues at the ICI Berlin research project Errans (2014–16). Special thanks to Arnd Wedemeyer for reading and advising, patiently.

1 The statement, along with the photo and video work of the project can be found at Inês d'Orey's artist website <http://www.inesdorey.com/index.php?/projectos/limbo/> [accessed 6 December 2021].

Figure 1. Graffito stenciled on the wall of the Carlos Alberto Theatre in Oporto, Portugal, 2012. Photo credit: Patricia Guarda.

shows a youngster immersed in a canopy of fog, and in an attitude of waiting. (See Figures 2–4.) Generated artificially by a fog-machine mostly within the setting of private homes, fog surrounds the human figure that is located at the centre of each photograph. *Limbo* both draws upon and inverts the classic rules of vignetting in photography, whereby the light marking the image's centre gradually shades off toward the edges. The framing that singularizes each photo is disrupted by the common thread of fog, creating an atmospheric continuum between all of the photographs.[2] Further — and despite its title — d'Orey unsettles more conventional understandings of limbo. To be in limbo often suggests an interruption or break in time, an interval — what classic anthropology termed liminality, as what lies 'between-and-betwixt'. However, d'Orey's alters the concept. As the phrase 'we are still waiting in the fog' evokes, limbo is not what suspends an

---

2   See Maria José de Abreu, 'Still Passing: Crisis, Youth and the Political Economy of Fog in Limbo', *Scapegoat: Landscape, Architecture, Political Economy*, 8 (May 2015), special issue *Weather*, pp. 60–70.

Figure 2. Inês d'Orey, *Limbo*, #05, 2012, 150 × 90 cm, Fine Art Photographic Print. Courtesy of the artist.

order of things but what *extends* a situation in time (a 'still waiting') indefinitely; indeed, because indefinitely, the time of waiting is also a weathered version of time: time rendered as an inscrutable horizon, time as fog.[3]

A sixteenth-century legend known as Sebastianism tells of a sovereign, the awaited messiah, who shall return through the fog in a moment of crisis to restore the country to its glorious destiny. The legend goes back to a foundational moment — or error — in the history of the Portuguese empire: the disappearing of the body of Sebastian, King of Portugal, while fighting the armies of Abd el-Malek in El-ksar-El-Kebir in northern Morocco on 4 August 1578. At just twenty-four years of age, Don Sebastian had been the darling of the Portuguese nobility, but his messianic crusading missions to North Africa would prove disastrous. Despite warnings from his closest allies, the king could not be swayed from invading Moorish territories to the south. The result was an enormous loss of human life, a severe economic crisis, and, as the king left no successor, loss of political autonomy to the rival Spanish court. Never to be found, Sebastian's body grew into a

---

3   As signified by the Portuguese word *tempo* which means both time and weather.

Figure 3. Inês d'Orey, *Limbo*, #08, 2012, 150 × 90 cm, Fine Art Photographic Print. Courtesy of the artist.

site of desire for returns, a messianic-like structure of waiting for what shall reappear through the fog of time; an indeterminate upcoming, paradoxically enclosed in a tomb located in the Mosteiro dos Jerónimos in Lisbon.

Repeatedly promised but always postponed, the attachment to the king's body marks a structure of expectation known throughout the Lusophone world. An epitaph next to Sebastian's tomb written by the Count of Ericeira lionizes the possibility that the tomb might in effect be empty. Written in Latin it augurs, *Conditur hoc tumulo, si vera est fama, sebastus quem tulit in Lybicis mors properata plagis nec dicas falli regem qui vivere credit pro lege extincto mors quasi vita fuit.* (In this tomb lies, if rumour be true, Sebastian, whom premature death took on the Lybian plains. Do not say that those are deceived who believe that the King is alive: for according to law, death is like life for he who has been killed.) Throughout the centuries, impostors would come forth and claim to be the missing one.[4] But just as people went on saluting these

---

4   See Mary Elizabeth Brooks, *A King for Portugal: The Madrigal Conspiracy 1594–95* (Madison: University of Wisconsin Press, 1964).

Figure 4. Inês d'Orey, *Limbo*, #11, 2012, 150 × 90 cm, Fine Art Photographic Print. Courtesy of the artist.

self-styled Sebastians, they would also send them off to the galleys.[5] Its messianic undertones functioned not only as a discourse about an autonomous past but it introduced a foundational narrative where loss, deferral and substitution became relevant notions in providing political and social agendas for the future.[6]

---

5   The legend likewise inspired millenarian revolts, such as the famous example of António Conselheiro who presented himself as Sebastian reincarnated leading up to the massacre of Canudos in the backlands of Sertão perpetrated by Brazil's republican armies of the early twentieth century. On the War of Canudos and the role of Sebastianism, see Robert Levine, *Vale of Tears: Revisiting the Canudos Massacre in Northeastern Brazil, 1893–1897* (Berkeley: University of California Press, 1995). See also Ashley Lebner (2021) 'After the Medium: Rereading Stories on a String and the War of Canudos', *Journal of American Academy of Religion*, 89.4 (December 2021), pp. 1290–1333. Lebner addresses the impact of Sebastianism and cordel poetry. Noteworthy is her critique of the concepts of medium and mediation in light of 'relation', a term she takes from the work of Marilyn Strathern. Lebner writes: 'I am suggesting we take seriously what it means to be unable to know what or whom the medium is' (p. 1296). While fog is not a camera, I am suggesting that we conceive of it as a 'time-weather' medium that confounds content and container, image and photo camera. D'Orey's *Limbo*, for me, renders that confounding precise, thereby framing the non-distinction between medium and message.

6   The legend of Sebastian's return in the future looks forward into the past to find it in the poetry of a sixteenth-century shoemaker and street poet named Gonçalo Anes Bandarra. In his prophetic verses, Bandarra predicted the arrival of a messiah, which although — or perhaps because — forbidden by the inquisition (for the popularity it

In 2006, as signs of the approaching financial crisis began to be felt, a national debate developed concerning the contents of Sebastian's tomb at Mosteiro Jerónimos in Belém-Lisbon. Publishing their findings in a local Portuguese journal, two renowned historians drew public attention to new documents found in the General Archive of Simiancas in Ceuta that attest to the *entrega del cuerpo del rey don Sebastian* (delivery of the body of King Sebastian) to the king of Spain, Felipe II, by Moroccan sheikh Mulei Ahmed on 10 December 1578.[7] In addition to this *acta*, the team also found a manuscript penned by the ambassador of the Spanish monarch confirming the arrival of the body from Morocco to the *Igreja da Trindade* in Ceuta before it was transferred to Lisbon four years later and, finally, a letter of the cardinal-King Dom Henrique addressed to Philip II thanking him for 'all the diligence undertaken by Philip II regarding the recuperation of the body'.[8] The weight of this new evidence — and the ensuing extensive media coverage — opened a public discussion regarding Sebastian and his legend. In line with the popularity of exhumations of historical personalities happening elsewhere at the time, the discussion focused upon how to scientifically verify the contents of the urn.

---

gained among persecuted and converted Jews) were soon incorporated as a political shield against the Spanish rule over Portugal under Philip II. Fast-forward: one of Bandarra's prophetic dates for the return of the 'messiahs' was the year 1888, the year of the birth of Fernando Pessoa, which explains why Pessoa saw in himself the 'Desired' but with a twist! Pessoa's ambition was to build up a 'Fifth Empire' — an empire that is no longer territorial but spiritual, an empire delivered through language and poetic utterance, which, according to Pessoa, 'only a small nation could usefully fulfil' (Pessoa, *Sobre Portugal. Introdução ao problema nacional*, ed. by Maria Isabel Rocheta and Maria Paula Morão (Lisbon: Aticá, 1978), p. 225). And yet, what in Pessoa truly foregrounds any identification between his 'person' (that is, his Pessoa) with the desired messiah (that is, with the myth) is, paradoxically, the possibility to anchor that identification in what Pessoa calls a 'delirious lie', that is, in the false ground of unsedimented heteronomies. What makes Pessoa *a* Sebastian reincarnated is less the aspiration of filling up the vacuum left by the king, than the possibility of staging Sebastianism; less 'the desire to bring forth the figure of originary power' than to show that 'for every tale there is an encounter with the absence of origins'. See Rosalind C. Morris, *In the Place of Origins: Modernity and its Mediums in Thailand* (Durham, NC: Duke University Press, 2000), p. 4.

7   See Emilio Rivas Calvo and Carlos D'Abreu, 'Alacazarquivir. El enigma (o el rescate del cuerpo d'el rey don Sebastian)', *Praça Velha, Revista Cultural da Cidade da Guarda*, 21 (July 2007), pp. 39–59.

8   See Manuel Leria and Ortíz de Saracho, 'El acta de entrega del cuerpo del rey don Sebastián', *Transfretana*, 7 (2001), pp. 135–44.

It was suggested to have a team of forensic anthropologists analyse the body's DNA and 'finish with the myth once and for all'. Progressives called upon the moral responsibility of the state 'to let the truth come out'. Renowned Portuguese historian José Matoso spoke of 'the need to give the myth a face'. But then there were those who repudiated the dissolution of the myth by 'morbid curiosity', advancing reasons of heritage associated with the ethos of a people.

Preparations to open the tomb for a forensic team were going ahead when, as a last moment decision, on 6 June 2006, a phone call from the national branch of the IPAR (Portuguese Institute for Architectonic Patronage) reached the headquarters of the University of Coimbra (where the team of forensic pathologists was based), cancelling the 'exhumation'. The minister of culture had changed his mind.[9] The state's last-minute prohibition fanned the fog of Sebastian all the more, perpetuating yet again what the poet Fernando Pessoa once called a 'postponed corpse that procreates' (cadáver adiado que procria), a death-to-come-but-not-yet.[10] In the following years, as the announcement of austerity packages by the state clashed with the vision of non-state intervention, releasing paradoxical demands of chastisement and extravagant entrepreneurialism, Portuguese society — and the youth in particular — opened the way to a limbo-fog atmospherics characteristic of Sebastinism. And it is that atmospherics that passes through the aperture of d'Orey's camera into the foggy image we see. How do climatic fog, messianic thought, and financial crisis combine in producing a 'precarious generation'? How to comprehend that in the very climax of fierce budgetary calculus under Troika and the austerity state, fog comes to occupy the centre of the picture as the most adequate medium to describe politics and existence?

What follows is an account of how fog connects to the ambivalent semantics of neoliberal austerity in contemporary Portugal. I will argue that fog is the atmospheric counterpart to a rhetorical game paradigmatic for contemporary governance. This game consists in the activation of a form of standstill without dialectics. By this I mean

---

9   Personal communication with Eugénia Cunha, Aeroporto da Portela, 10 October 2010.
10 Fernando Pessoa, *Mensagem*, ed. by Fernando Cabral Martins (Lisbon: Planeta DeAgostini, 2006), p. 33.

a certain logic in governance by which opposites are reaffirmed — not, as dialectic thinking would have it, in order to elevate these to a third, but so as to hollow out the very terms that would secure that opposition. Unlike with modern frames of ideology in which critique involves exiting one's camp into a dialectical tension with an opposing camp, the logic I adumbrate here operates via a kind of torsion where those camps meet at the extremes to form a kind of circular continuum, not unlike the mythical figure of the snake devouring its own tail.

Writing in the context of Italy, Andrea Muehlebach encounters a similar anthropophagic rationale: 'How are we to understand', she asks, 'how leftists relate to the neoliberalism they so vehemently oppose?'[11] Muehlebach shows that this is due to the way in which those political camps meet in the hollowing space of the neoliberal moral state. Opposites entwine like a helix. They are sucked into the large hole that is the neoliberal state. It is the odd political tactic common to neoliberal governance by which opposites fold into the middle and proceed to make of this middle its own extremity. My argument is that this topological operation is compatible with a particular rhetorical figure: the contranym. Contranyms are words with two meanings contradicting each other, homonymous terms that harbour their opposite within themselves.[12] Examples of contranyms are 'swearing' (both an oath and an insult) or 'sanction' (both punishment and validation). Similarly, austerity is a key Janus-faced term in Portugal's governance, an aspect suggested by the definitional camp of the term austerity itself as

---

11   Andrea Muehlebach, '*Complexio Oppositorum*: Notes on the Left in Neoliberal Italy', *Public Culture*, 21.3 (2009), pp. 495–515 (p. 496).

12   See Christoph F. E. Holzhey, 'Weathering Ambivalences: Between Language and Physics', in *Weathering: Ecologies of Exposure*, ed. by Christoph F. E. Holzhey and Arnd Wedemeyer, Cultural Inquiry, 17 (Berlin: ICI Berlin Press, 2020), pp. 3–40, on the political and aesthetic valences of enantiosemic speech, particularly in its ties to weather. As Holzhey puts it: '[T]he OED definitions suggest that the verb "to weather" may be regarded, more radically, as enantiosemic, that is, as having mutually opposite meanings. Such words, which are their own antonyms, are more common than one might expect, and include in English, for instance, "to cleave" (to adhere or separate), "to sanction" (to approve or penalize/boycott), or "to rent" (to purchase use of something or sell it). The verb "to weather" is even more peculiar insofar as it can be said to be doubly enantiosemic and confound oppositions both of activity and quality: Usually signifying a deteriorating change, it can also mean, on the one hand, successfully opposing such a change and, on the other hand, undergoing a beneficial change.' (p. 15)

in the effect of a dryness of the tongue by virtue of it being soaked in wine. Where some might read the 'return of fog' as symptom of crisis, I tend to the performative undecidability internal to the semantics of austerity. I highlight how the term austerity becomes effective because of its capacity to both bring the past back and rehearse the means by which that past was denied.

Austerity was central to Portugal's *Estado Novo* ideology, a key pillar in the perpetuation of what would turn out to be the longest dictatorship in modern Western Europe. For the post-1974 generations, the revolution meant leaving behind the deep-rooted austerity state, its schemes and diplomacies of programmed poverty (through a systematic cultivation of the myth of honourable poverty) and the active embrace of a new era of prosperity. The official independence of Portugal's African colonies in 1975 was politically articulated as a necessary accompaniment to the reintegration of Portugal into a modernized Europe, particularly through the creation of economic pacts with the EEC (European Economic Community). By the late 1970s and 1980s, Portugal was like a parched land craving for its monetary monsoon, effectively enabled by the EU as it became one of its member states in 1986. But how to understand the fact that these liquidities, as deeply associated as they are with the long era of authoritarian rule, end up reappearing at the apex of neoliberalism? In channeling out voices from the field, I follow d'Orey in placing blurriness at the centre of a showing. My argument is that the formal structure of austerity is key to its semantic crossroads. Its efficacy resides not solely in its actual manifestation through policies — e.g., state cuts and shrinking welfare —, as markers of a specific context of crisis *in* time but also in the ambivalences already encoded in austerity, situating individuals in two simultaneous eras at once.

1: HOLLOW

> Sitting at the round table at the kitchen of his family's home in Almada, João Augusto tells me about the oddity of reinhabiting his former bedroom. The bed that belonged to his brother was taken away so that he could have some more space in it for his adult self. He had repainted the walls a light blue, removing the previous light ochre coloration along with the glued rips of

paper and stickers of famous football players he and his brother had had plastered on the walls throughout the years. 'Much to talk about', he says, filling his glass with iced tap water from a jar, 'so you want to know how is it for me to be back with my parents?' João starts by saying that 'it is only a temporary solution' before he will be able to settle again on his own. At least his parents' home is secure, they own the house, an inheritance ... (He drinks water, he offers me some. We both do.) In May 2011, João had to give up the flat in Benfica he had bought in 2004, a third floor in a four-story new building. That year alone, an average of seventeen houses per day were being devolved to banks. Not only did he lose his house, he was not yet out of debt, still owing the debt resulting from the difference between what the bank offered for taking the house back when acquiring the mortgage with Banco Espírito Santo in 2004. 'Lines of credit?', he nodded negatively, (because) 'no-nothing about it is a line but a "ju-mb-le" (um ema-ra-nha-do)', he continued, 'just so you see, the bank takes back houses for a much lower price than the actual cost because banks themselves have run out of money. But because banks ran out of money they have to borrow [ever more expensive cash] from other institutions like the Banco Central Europeu, but [...] in order to do so, banks are using the state as guarantor. Now, [and a pause for water] the reason why the banks ran out of money is not because creditors [like himself] have failed to pay off mortgages and debts, but because "the state that takes the role of guarantor" for the bank loans itself owes millions to those banks, 50 million, which, by the way, is a third of the money that the Bank of Portugal owes to BCE. Do you see how twisted the whole business is, it's like a revolving door ...? So, it is clear that we gentiles (a raia miúda) are the ones paying back, house by house, by house, by house, small business upon small business, et cetera, all in ruin, but behind it all is the state's public debt to the banks. Why do you think the state encouraged *recibos verdes* (green receipts),[13] why do you think the state strangled the local industries? So, when the crisis comes up, we are unable to secure our jobs and our homes, and the cycle of austerity again begins. Job. No job. House. No house. It's like *peixinho-de-rabo-na-boca*. (little fish with tail in mouth) [laughter]. I am a biologist by formation, I have a degree, so

---

13 The official system of freelancing in Portugal created in the 1980s but aggressively implemented in 1992 by the government of the Social Democrat Cavaco Silva, whereby one can formally invoice clients and declare income for tax and social security purposes.

nothing of this world of finance was ever part of my world, you know. My father tried to discourage me from studying biology, saying I should rather be a dentist or a medical doctor if I'm interested in organic stuff or whatever ... Biology seemed like a non-thing to him, neither meat nor fish. Tofu ... [More laughter. Another pause for water]. I persisted and finished my studies with reasonable outcomes but then other opportunities came up and I began working as a computer programmer along with teaching biology to high school students. But with lecturing you never know which part of the country *they* will be sending you and I had bought my house in late 2004 so I started to invest more in web design with the help of one of those EC subsidies and eventually was hired on *recibo verdes* by a company in Vila-Franca-de-Xira. I enjoyed it a lot because it did not feel like my studies in biology had been a total waste but were helping me to think of the organization of the web, ideas of "cellular organization", "growth", "development", "stimuli", "response", you know, there was something really *fixe* (cool) in thinking of computer websites as organic stuff. My labour contract had just been renewed for the third time when my boss told me (he winks meaning matching the rumours) that the company would shut down due to bankruptcy. Then it turned out it didn't, so I guess he just wanted to get rid of me, but then it changed leadership, so it's all very ... unclear. I tried to do some teaching again but was sent to a town outside Lisbon, too far from my residence but also too little [income] for the mortgage. I could do different things professionally ... And then with the austerity cuts in 2011 and after, the situation just went bad to worse. And worse. And worse ... like that feeling that I did the opposite of everything I should have ... So now I am here holding on, each day I go through a myriad of mood swings. My father says "Good morning, biologist ..." but I pay no heed ...'. João brought freshly made coffee to the table and poured some in two cups. He straightened his back in the chair. Then he pointed to the fruit basket lying on top of the fridge as though it were some still life painting. Bananas, mandarins, grapes, kiwis. 'Fruit flies have a peculiar nuptial behaviour', he continued. 'Previously, when a mate wanted to copulate, it would bring a nuptial gift along most likely a prey to seduce the other mate. Then natural selection determined it better to wrap up the gift with some organic stuff so as to potentiate the sexual act, but then, in time, mother nature said that in fact the wrapping is more important than the content. Some fruit flies started to disregard the need for prey altogether, offering only the wrapping. I think there is a parallel to where we stand today.

It is not the content that matters but the wrapping. The inside is hollow.'

2: NEVER WAS

Nuno Assunção is a thirty-five-year-old man with a degree in environmental sciences. In 2004, while still completing his master degree, Nuno started to work on a part-time basis as a conservation biologist for his university department in Algarve. He left his parents' home in Setúbal, a city in the south of Lisbon, and rented out a space in Faro. As an undergraduate student, he went to his parents' home during the weekends, where he also enrolled in a remunerated European Union-funded ICT training course 'in order to cover the basics' for what he saw as the tool for the future. He also took an English language course to improve his curriculum 'since one never knows' (whether one will go abroad or work for a foreign company, he meant). When the financial crisis broke out in 2007–08, he felt secure about becoming part of the permanent staff at his job at the university and so, in spite of the unfolding scenarios of the crisis, he bought a house with the help of a bank loan with a thirty-year mortgage contract. That same year he moved in with his girlfriend who worked for a local bank though she had a degree in psychology. In 2009, however, the scenario drastically changed for him and his partner workwise. While he had been promised he would be made permanent at his job (along with five other interdepartmental colleagues), he was fired from the university. His partner was able to hold on to her job for a while and in fact, began pulling strings to find a vacant place for him at the branch she worked for. She had heard they needed people with ICT knowledge and English would help in a tourist region like the Algarve. They were trying to stay in the city but nothing seemed to work out for Nuno. Eventually his father proposed that Nuno come back to Setúbal for a while. There was a possibility that he take a temporary job at the Lisbon Airport where they were asking for people with language skills such as English and Spanish. Nuno had to ponder things. The good years allowed the young couple to acquire two cars. Nuno could either keep on trying to find work in the south, stay at his parents' home, and drive daily to the airport, then drive down during the weekends to be with his girlfriend or, otherwise, move to Lisbon for the new job and take his girlfriend with him. There was also the possibility of her moving to her parents' home in the Algarve and him moving to his folks', just for the time being, 'until things got more composed [até as coisas se comporem]'. It was unclear what the best solution was in all that. When I met Nuno at Lisbon airport in late 2012, his girlfriend was still living in the Algarve. The situation had been a considerable obstacle for their relationship but now they were bound to each other by a mortgage they had to either pay or rescind. They had to reassess their feelings for one another. In the meantime, before making any radical decision, they rented the house in the Algarve to tourists. He surely missed the future that never was.

3: BACK-AND-FORTH

A. G., forty years old, is the sister of a longtime friend of mine. She studied Social Communication at the University of Beira Interior, a large student town in the hinterland, the central region of Portugal. During her graduate years, she gained a *curso professional* from SENJOR followed by experience as a news reporter for a local radio station. In 2003 she started to work for a small cartoon-colour company as a PR agent in Lisbon, also sometimes drafting copy. Bankruptcy in that year led to the closing down of the company and a proposed exemption of the remaining liabilities.[14] The global ripples of 9/11. By then, she was established in Lisbon and 'to make it through' [para se safar] she found work at ADSE, the state-run health insurance agency. It was supposed to be only temporary until she found something in journalism, which is what she had studied. A little less than a year later, Alexandra and eighty-one other short-term contract employees were fired en masse over the phone ('they did not even bother to write a letter as they used to'). She went on the dole for a while, and soon after, in late 2003, joined her sister who was working as an urban planner for the city of Amsterdam. Once in Holland, she found a job as a childcarer and, parallel to that, decided to pursue a bachelor's degree in fashion design at the Rietveld Art Academy in Amsterdam. She felt pressured to improve her English because 'in Holland everybody speaks English anyways', but things were changing lately with the growing adherence to nationalistic populism there. She reasoned that learning English could be an asset for other places but learning Dutch would help her to put down roots in Holland. She decided for English but

---

14 A system that allows waiving credits on insolvency in order that businesses might start afresh after a five-year hiatus.

soon found a need for Dutch as she was asked to temporarily teach an art class to young kids. She found a home in a squat in the city centre. The rent was low, but having lost her job as a childcarer and unable to find a more permanent job in Holland in either journalism or fashion (and ideally a combination of the two), in early 2012, she went back to Porto. She had high hopes that a degree in fashion design from the prestigious Rietveld Academy would improve her chances in Portugal. Even as the crisis mined the lives of many, there was a peculiar sense that it also called on imaginative opportunities; that rather than limit, the crisis-fog put a challenge to creativity, in harnessing the ability to see through it. And so, she left Holland and went to Oporto with a degree in fashion design. But 2012 was becoming the year of peak unemployment and hopes for a job where she could apply her new degree began to fade away. After a year working for a company dealing primarily with stylized furniture ('but aiming at textiles in the future') the business started to falter. Part-time workers were sent away, clients failed to pay for rendered services, salaries were reduced as subsidies dwindled. Gradually, the company was unable to cover basic expenses like water, internet, and electricity, leading to its closure; having returned from elsewhere, then, she was once again confronted with insolvency. Unable to support herself in Oporto, Alexandra moved into her parents' apartment in the city of Leiria, a town in the centre of the country. She would have to renounce her sense of adulthood and independence, but she would save money on food and shelter. From there she could try to make professional contacts in the business of textiles, to collect local traditional products, which she could remanufacture and relay by reconnecting with distributors and sellers in Holland. But despite initial positive reactions from some of these contacts, things never really took off. Where one business closed, many kept opening up. There was a rhythm: open-close; open-close, open … An opportunity emerged to work in the library of a local penitentiary, but she saw it as potentially even more depressing. The question was: how to 'lateralize' her skills and furthermore what did 'lateralize' mean, in this case? Work on the skills she already had or adapt to whatever might provide better opportunities? Save money by working on a mundane job next door or use her free time to craft things, brand, and sell them, create a name, a style, perhaps back in Holland, where she had made some contacts with textile designers? But the days went by without bringing a sense of restitution, a redemptive outcome that in retrospect could explain decisions taken in the throes of change. She would swing between hope and despair. She decided to get her driver's license, but it literally took her nowhere. Then one day she woke up and concluded that it had been a mistake to leave Holland, where, if nothing else, she could benefit from social security built on her previous work experience there. She moved once again to Amsterdam and enrolled in the system all over again. This time around she is taking a Dutch language course. It gives her a sense that she has come to stay, to lay down roots in one place. There won't be much use for the driver's license in Holland, where 'everybody rides a bicycle anyways'.

4: RE-TORNADO

Joaquim Simão looks like he could be in his early thirties. He has incredibly affable eyes but bats them restlessly. He tells me that he was just back from Angola where he went to work for his father's brother who runs a business in the sector of civil construction. 'I went first to Luanda and then my brother and cousin followed up', he told me, reaching for his Super Bock beer at *Esplanada do Adamastor* in Lisbon. 'We lived in a pre-fabricated modular building in the eastern part of Luanda', he explained, 'where not only Portuguese migrants but also Brazilians and Macauenses lived. We shared the condominium. It was a good deal. We could make [do] because there you just don't have opportunities to spend money, unless you want to mingle with the high society, then you pay up to 200 Euros for an evening meal ... Things were going well, there is a big community of Portuguese in Angola, more than a hundred thousand came there since the crisis, well since 2011 ....' 'When did you move to Angola?' I asked. 'I went there with a contract for five years, just to allow time for the crisis here to pass, but now ... there is crisis there, too. I am now in my second year. 'The supermarkets', he said, 'have been emptied of basic things, from one moment to the other. No oil exported, no food imported. Basic goods are so expensive ... Angola was just a resource. A point of passage.' But now the question for him and his relatives was 'passage to where'? 'Here things go from bad to worse', he frowned, taking a big gulp of his beer. He paused, taking his thoughts someplace else. He asked about me. I said a few things but hurried to steer our conversation back to him. During his stay in Angola, he and his brother were called *retornados* by the locals several times. 'How can I even be a *retornado* if I have never been to Angola before, nor my father or grandfather?

They call me *retornado* simply because I am white and Portuguese. But guess what ... the whites who never left Angola after 1975 call us *retornados*, too. Those are the worst, because they feel that they were courageous enough to stay when the civil war broke out in Angola. The same in Mozambique, Guinea ... They think they are better because they did not return to Portugal. But in fact, they did not suffer the stigma that many who left Africa for Portugal in 1975 did. Anyways, I am not going back ....'. He would live from his savings, from hand to mouth. He had a cousin in Frankfurt who might lead him there. He would wait and see. It feels good to be back home for a while. 'Are you afraid of the future?' I asked him. 'If there is one, yes ...', he replied, awkwardly precise.

5: SHOES

I entered a shoe shop in Aveiro, a coastal city 59 kilometres south of Oporto, to ask about a pair of shoes on display. The shoes look like what during *Salazarismo* would be called *mestre-escola* type. The number on display did not quite fit and the seller, a man in his early thirties, fetched a smaller number from the depot. The shop would soon close for good, its owners were selling. There was an existential melancholy about the place, shoes devalued and unoccupied. The new size fit and we both approached the counter. I have known this shop placed just across Teatro Aveirense since I was a child. 'Why the closing sale?' The seller held the case containing the shoes and began: 'Local artisans are going extinct.' Waiting for a reaction on my part, he continued: 'Shoes have always been a strong article for Portugal's industry but now we are importing shoes and closing down our factories. In 2011 one would open the newspaper or turn on the TV to hear about daily updates of the austerity measures. Now [in 2016] you look around and see the demise of traditional businesses, lots of old homes are empty too. Look at what happened to *AV. Dr. Lourenço Peixinho*, to *Rua Direita*, this street here, it is a different thing today. Funny that people who come here describe our shoes as "austere", because their old-fashioned appearance reminds people of "other times" [he means those of the dictatorship]. A newer version of the "traditional article" is appearing, except that this new "made in Portugal" is no longer for locals but for tourists who come in search of *traditional things*.' As in, 'austerity' itself is now being branded? 'Yes, look at the traditional home-slippers (*chinelo*), which poor people used to make out of rags and that are now being sold in Lisbon and Oporto for tourists as "typically Portuguese". I have them here too on sale but they do not get sold because they are not properly rebranded as "traditional". Well, it is traditional, too traditional ... That's the problem. But I don't blame people because you have to make do with what you can. [...] I know people who studied with me and would not do my job. It is too hard for them to admit that they are jobless. But I have always been a realist about these things ... I am happy to show you the report I am writing for ISCIA.[15] I have a list of austerity cuts with me. [...] In 2012, state workers lost the equivalent of two salaries (Christmas and summer holiday allowances). In the same year pensioners were left without two subsidies ... Shall I go on? Are you not living in Portugal? [...] In 2013, state workers were left without one of the subsidies and increased contributions to the *Caixa Geral de Aposentações* equivalent to a cut of around 14% of gross wages. You know what the minimal wage is *huh*, that it has been frozen because of the *memorando de entendimento* with the Troika? 565,83 Euros. Where did you say you are living ... Berlin ... okay, Berlin, Berlin: the general minimum wage is ... three times more than here, see? ... 2013: private workers' cuts were equivalent to one of the subsidies. In 2013, there were cuts between 3.5% and 10% in state workers' pensions above €1500. Same year, reduction in the number of civil servants by 2% per year. Same year, a total of 168 national public bodies and institutes were either extinct or forced to merge into bigger corporations; cuts in the amount of severance paid; cuts in sickness allowance; cuts in unemployment benefit. Same year, an elimination of four national holidays was decreed ... In 2012, VAT on electricity and gas rose from 6% to 23%. The average value of a family's gas bill (including all taxes and fees) increased by 27% between July 2011 and July 2012. The electricity bill rose 8.8% between 2010 and 2012. Based on the INE survey on household spending, between 2005 and 2011, gas bills rose 76.6% and electricity 25%. With the new rent law coming into being, an increase of 3.36% in rent costs would affect around six hundred thousand families, which will result in hundreds of evictions. Public transport prices rose 20% between 2011 and 2012 ... You get the idea ... I am doing the math. I try to think where the numbers will lead us, to draw a path for me and my girlfriend, for both our families. I haven't taken an academic degree to end up selling shoes but I can

---

15   Instituto Superior Ciencias Informação e Admnistração — Aveiro.

reason why some shoes will sell, others not. Here!' He hands me the shoes.

WHAT REMEDY?!

A well-known dictum inherited from the *Estado Novo* (1932–1974) authoritarian regime extols the ability to 'amend and make do'. A folk lesson in political economy, this disposition to embrace poverty with dignity (*pobres mas honrados*, another proverb goes) is frequently followed up by the phrase 'what remedy?! (que remédio?!)', a way of apostrophizing 'what alternative is there?' Who has spent a year in Portugal without at some point overhearing these expressions in public — on the bus or at the dining table? The verb *remediar* means to heal or plaster with poor means. Its semantic juxtaposing between healing (*remédio*/remedy) and repairing (*remendo*/patchwork), presumes that whatever remedy there may be will not truly cure, but merely 'make up for'. As a solution to the problem, it will never be the best that could come to pass but will always remain provisional, inadequate, derivative. The phrase '*Que remédio?*' is above all apostrophic. It is the lyrical addressing of an absent saviour yet-to-come.

Echoing the times of financial turmoil that brought Salazar to power on 28 May 1926 as Portugal's minister of finance, austerity was officially prescribed as the acrid fix to the financial crisis, the bitter cure to an economy going badly sick. Calls for austerity were so embarrassingly emblematic of other times that the only way to divert away from this fact was by maneuvering directly into it. In October 2011, a few months after winning the national elections that followed the bailout request to the European Troika, Portugal's right-wing prime minister Pedro Passos Coelho stated that the country would only get out of its current predicament 'by becoming poorer'. '[Fortunately] Portuguese people', he proclaimed during another public appearance, 'are immunized against austerity.' It was a peculiar choice of words — 'immunized against austerity' — on the part of the chief-of-state. Everyone knew that at stake was the imputation of sanctions on people's personal economies in the name of saving the public sector — the socialization of costs, as they called it, was but another name for the privatization of costs. But what is involved when the head-of-state rubs salt into the still fresh wound on the body of citizens after nearly a half-century of severe economic contraction under Salazar's authoritarian regime? The logic is comparable to that of a trickster who, having lost all power to seduce his audience, is left with no choice but to reveal his trick in the hope that he will be able to trade off discredit for honesty. In being so patently direct, audiences go on looking elsewhere, perhaps deeper, failing to see that the trick consists in its very disclosure. The use of direct speech has an implosive effect that hollows out what it exposes.

And yet, if the trick works, it is because of historical leverage. The extraordinary longevity of Portugal's dictatorship (nearly half a century) and colonization (nearly five centuries) — indeed, the coordination between both throughout much of the twentieth century — had reached a vexing limit. Portugal's initiation into neoliberalism, in the second half of the 1980s, exploited the sense that its society had reached the extreme of extremes of an era, the utmost stage of a much prolonged situation under fascism a radical separation from which could only happen by an evocation of all the values and principles that were contrary to it: liberty, mobility, autonomy, meritocracy, all of which were premised on a return of republican standards of parliamentary democracy and entrepreneurial economics. Cries for autonomy and emancipation from fascism joined the struggles for independence and autonomy from stalled colonial rule. Freedom from old enduring patriarchal structures, a breaking away from long-term contracts as synonymous with stagnation, provincialism, and nepotism, the dynamization of occupations distributed geographically so as to overcome the notorious separation between littoral and interior, urban and rural, alongside a new emphasis on the circulation of capital, people, and skills: all of these features not only were ripe for being well received in post-1974 Portugal but also, I am arguing, were received in a manner that made explicit the dynamics of extremities as such. What became apparent was not only a society that was ready to flip from one ideology to another — from fascism to neoliberalism — but *how flipping itself could be used as a methodology of governance*, say, as part and parcel of the neoliberal ethos of entrepreneurship. Freedom, mobility, and autonomy were no longer just contents within ideology but principles of administration. Flexibility was not only a horizon to attain but a methodology, not a means toward ends but a means to be ever more efficiently in the middle, or even in the midst; or, better yet, foggy mist.

Such was the logic behind the slippage of precarity as an emerging taxonomy during the financial crisis and afterwards. To live precariously came to mean both emancipation from older patriarchal orders and embracing neoliberal temporalities of work. The normalization of green receipts (*recibos verdes*), a system of short-term contracts partially sponsored by the European Community's special programmes — designed to upgrade less developed southern European countries such as Portugal, Spain, or Greece — stood out as valuable assets when posited against the contractual horizons of the older regime. A record rate of youth unemployment (47%) in 2012 was reached simultaneously with a record of highly qualified young professionals. The categorical distinction between 'job' and 'work' began to widen as young professionals felt reluctant to take up just any menial trade lest it be symptomatic of a personal failure. This is how, in avoiding downgrading their meritocratically acquired status, many decided to embrace voluntary work or philanthropic *assistencialismo* — ironically, as Andrea Muehlebach shows for the Italian case,[16] a much-welcomed initiative by the very austerity state that, in the form of three consecutive austerity packages, had put people in those situations in the first place. In the background appeared the time-worn ethos of charity, as institutions such as *Santa Casa da Misericordia* began to create their own network of benevolences through the coordination of governmental and non-governmental organizations, or the sponsoring of social programmes. Charitable assistance thus was aimed at those austerity hit the hardest, the very highly potentialized generation whose core ideal was to combat the logic that had dominated society under authoritarianism. It is as though the reality of fascism had blown the post-1974 generations with their backs to a future, except that this future, withering from a would-be telos, was now turning into a foggy midst.

Austerity and the restructuring of people's livelihoods to 'pay back' the European Troika was proof that the state had never been absent but (much like Sebastian in his tomb) active in its very absence. In

---

16   Muehlebach, '*Complexio Oppositorum*'.

the new context of economic drainage, calls to 'get the house in order' became imbued with a two-pronged ethical imperative. No longer only 'to amend and make do' as the *Estado Novo* motto had it, but also 'go spend and enjoy'. In the 1990s, citizens were asked to both save and spend, a command that placed individuals at once in the 'society of production' and in the 'society of consumption', both attuned to the father imago of the bygone authoritarian austerity state and repudiating its legacy via the consumption rhetoric. The message was two-fold: refrain from buying *and* watch out for special sales. The crucial thing to understand about the notion of neoliberal austerity is not that it stood — and stands — for a contradiction, but the way in which those seemingly contradictory tendencies entered a torsion dynamic by which the neoliberal *donut* morphed into an austerity *cup*. Like in a topological system, the state's agenda was to apply forms of transformation that would preserve elements in the very act of their deformation. Perhaps this explains why austerity resuscitated the old and already mentioned proverb *peixinho-de-rabo-na-boca* (little fish with tail in mouth) — a hollow system — as much as emblematic cuisine of the poor classes.

The logic here is pendular. In the rhythm of a seesaw, austerity created a confounding scenario. It was not about having a term exit the field through a logic of mutual exclusion, but having one term (authoritarianism) rub against its elected counterpart (neoliberalism) and, thereupon, having the (austerity) haze be released into the atmosphere as if through a fog machine: state *cum* no-state, future *cum* no-future, inside as outside, presence signifying no-presence, crisis also implying opportunity. It is as though the very reasons that ought to distinguish regimes — fascism and neoliberalism — met each other at the extreme limits of that distinction to form a contranym, a coexisting of opposites whose most emblematic sovereign figure could only be rendered through the well familiar undead status of Sebastian: its undecidable, speculative, and limbo-like existence, or else, its atmospheric counterpart, as fog.

Austerity, then, was no longer descriptive but performative. Not mere reaction to bounteous liquidity but an aridity already intrinsic to liquidness itself. Neoliberal flexibility is tricky because it hides itself by drawing attention to its praxis, its own mode of operation: to the production of scenarios, images, dreams, and fantasies, whose edges it then proceeds to blur. Here, then, lies d'Orey's photographic operation. It is this sort of twister apparatus at the core of contemporary political life that makes authoritarianism and neoliberalism not rivals, but bedfellows. Such are the whirling grounds upon which the Portuguese state, in coordination with the market and the media, goes on sustaining the supposition that austerity interrupts neoliberalism, belying what I argue is, in effect, an intensification.[17] Such a topology relates to what Jamie Peck describes as the involvement of the state in its own 'serial underperformance', on the basis of which time and again the rhetoric of austerity — as drought or crisis — persists.[18] The state communicates an image, not of strength, but of vulnerability, turning the latter into its much-cherished apostrophe: 'What remedy?', the lyrical counterpart to the restless Sebastian.

In putting matters in terms of 'immunity to austerity', the state refers to the historical precedent of the dictatorship years. It does so to the extent it wants to recall the salvific role of the family in the old regime, while keeping intact the pressure to spend and enjoy that again leads to austerity. In tacitly suggesting that there is a link between past authoritarianism and present neoliberal governance, the minister implodes the field of signification anew. It is as though at the crest of the comparison between fascism and neoliberalism, he is able to disavow any equivalence between the two. He names the austerity beast, but so as to better ambiguate its contents.

Austerity becomes a borderline notion. In order to make it a borderline notion it is not enough to say that the Portuguese are familiar with austerity. For its ambiguity to be truly effective, austerity must be expressed as 'extremely familiar'. For, only in being 'extremized' can

---

[17] See Luis Mendes, 'Gentrificação túristica em Lisboa: Neoliberalismo, financeirização e urbanismo austeritário em tempos de pós-crise capitalista 2008–2009', *Cadernos Metrópole*, 39 (2017), pp. 479–512; Luis Mendes and André Carmo, 'State-Led Gentrification in an Era of Neoliberal Urbanism: Examining the New Urban Lease Regime in Portugal', paper presented at the conference *Contested Cities: From Contested Cities to Global Urban Justice — Critical Dialogues*, Madrid, 4–7 July 2016, and available at the conference website <http://contested-cities.net/working-papers/2016/state-led-gentrification-in-an-era-of-neoliberal-urbanism-examining-the-new-urban-lease-regime-in-portugal/> [accessed 6 December 2021].

[18] Jamie Peck, 'Austerity Urbanism: American Cities Under Extreme Economy', *City*, 16.6 (2012), pp. 626–56.

austerity flip into its opposite and reveal its contranymic nature. This dynamic allows the neoliberal austerity state to advance the agenda of its own undoing, its hollowing out.

PLANNED BACKWARDNESS

In her second preface to *The Origins of Totalitarianism*, Hannah Arendt refers to the exceptional status 'of Portugal, and her strange ability to continue a fight that other European colonial powers had had to give up'. For Arendt, such persistence 'may be due to her national *backwardness* more than to Salazar's dictatorship'. Arendt's dissociation of the country's 'backwardness' from its dictator serves her theoretical goal. Her thesis is that it was not out of weakness that the British 'liquidated their colonial rule' but by virtue of their sophistication (something Portugal lacked).[19] But Arendt overlooks how forward-looking 'backwardness' was in view of the goals of the *Estado Novo*. Corporatist in nature, the engineering of the regime was entirely construed toward one key objective: longevity. As historian Fernando Rosas puts it, from whatever side one wants to look into the machination of *Salazarismo*, one will come to the same realization about its extraordinary ability to endure.[20] To be able to wake up and say, with each passing day throughout forty-eight years, 'the regime is *still here*' was the regime's true horizon.

Planned backwardness was central to the *Estado Novo* ideology on three fronts: a family ethos of responsibility, its foreign policy, and an investment in colonial rule. Salazar understood that through a tactical articulation of these aspects it would be possible to secure the durability of the regime. The price to be paid was a form of withdrawal on the economic, political, as well as military fronts. First appointed as minister of finance in the coup of 28 May 1926, António de Oliveira Salazar, a professor of economics at the University of Coimbra, went on gaining the trust of several groups, first the rural political elites (especially in southern Portugal), then the small but influential industrial

---

19 Hannah Arendt, *The Origins of Totalitarianism* (New York: Harcourt, Brace & World, 1968), p. xvvii.
20 Fernando Rosas, *Salazar e o poder. A arte de saber durar* (Lisbon: Tinta da China, 2013).

elites. Salazar repeated the core refrain regarding the fragile finances of Portugal, aggravated as they were by sixteen years of anarchy and political turmoil followed by the world financial crash of 1929. Attacking republicanism and monarchism alike, the two main disputed powers, Salazar constructed an authoritarian form of rule according to which he would have the absolute say in the spending of every governmental department. The press and the people called Salazar 'the dictator of finances'.

Unlike other industrialized European nations which understood the role of the welfare state in the lead-up to modernization, the Portuguese Corporatist Social Security held key dimensions like health, education, social and national security to be subordinate to a general policy of austerity. Salazar removed from the previous constitution of the Republic of 1911 (as later from the social insurance model of 1919) the fundamental principle of the 'right to public assistance'. In the new constitution of 1933, Salazar compensated for the privation of public assistance with a proliferation of tightly controlled corporatist bodies with a strong orientation towards charity. Charitable institutions would secure what for the *Estado Novo* was the central unit of society and governance: the family.

Crucial in this arrangement was the actuarial system. Pedro Teotónio Pereira was an expert on actuarial sciences whom Salazar hired to apply his vision of family welfare to the sector of the social security system. Pereira launched 'The Portuguese Corporatist Social Welfare System', a new series of legislations that shaped the relation between economic austerity and family responsibility. Drawing on the terms of the seventeenth-century Elizabethan Old Poor Law system, but with a notorious Catholic twist, Pereira created a model that pivoted around the corporatist integration of the family in pressing its members to survey each other in fighting idleness and to take responsibility for one another in case of misfortune.[21] Pereira stated that 'once the worker no longer had to deal with the state and public money, which could easily allure abuses and bad desires, then he/she would regard the welfare organization of his/her professional household as a work of his/her

---

21   Melinda Cooper, *Family Values: Between Neoliberalism and the New Social Conservativism* (New York: Zone Books, 2017).

own, a result of his/her sacrifices, responsibility and hope'.[22] As for the state, it would monitor the development of new bodies closely, define their technical aspects, helping to form an environment of solidarity, giving them indispensable reputation and solidity.[23] In other words, the role of the state was not to aid families but rather to coerce individuals to extend help to others within the family, their extended relatives, and, even more broadly, within their communities. Appeals to what Melinda Cooper calls 'the ethos of family responsibility' worked in tandem with charities like *Santa Casa da Misericordia*, the *Irmandades, Casas dos Expostos and Mitra* in charge of controlling the spread of 'bad' indigency.[24]

Families were asked to both practice the virtue of poverty and to take on responsibility in assisting their kin. The result was a circular logic of familial dependency that unburdened the state of its responsibility to hamper and socialize risk, which, in turn, reinforced the privatization of care. That is, family responsibility and charity liberated the state from having to pay public welfare assistance. Because the family household was metonymically related to the nation (pátria), efforts from the private realm of families to garnish labour and assistance were posited as public goods. Austerity thus entered a spiraling scheme wherein each level justified the next without ever coming to define the true nature of its centre.

Austerity was not only a feature of the Social Security System but the basis of the larger *Estado Novo* establishment. Salazar renamed charity associations into 'The Portuguese Corporatist Social Welfare System' (PCSWS), institutional organs that drew on nineteenth-century liberal assistance of the Poor Laws in their non-inclusion of social security. Liberal assistance was available only for those who had the economic means and took the initiative to apply to the state. As a

---

22 Pedro Teotónio Pereira, *A Batalha do Futuro* (Lisbon: Livraria Clássica, 1937), pp. 49–50 (my translation, M.J.de A.)

23 António Rafael Amaro, 'The Late Construction of Portugal Welfare State: The Failure of the Social Corporativist State (1933–74)', *Memoria y civilización*, 21 (2018), pp. 437–54.

24 See Marta de Matos, 'Estado-providência em Portugal e as políticas sociais: Avaliação da implementação das cantinas sociais' (unpublished doctoral dissertation, ISCTE — Instituto Universitário de Lisboa, 2014) <http://hdl.handle.net/10071/9008> [accessed 8 December 2021].

liberal minister put it in 1867, the goal of state assistance was 'not to prevent the fall but to provide for "after the fall" and even then, not for all falls'[25] with its skewed patterns of distributive care, well into the late 1970s, thanks to which the ideology of 'remediate and make do' appeared as part of an ethic of care and work.

The cultural significance of austerity was based on the historical relations held between Portugal, other European nations, and the colonies. The refusal of economic dependency vis-à-vis foreign nations translated into heroism on the basis of which the cult of austerity pivoted. One historical episode reappeared with particular vehemence during the 2011 economic bailout request of 78 million euros to the Troika. In 1927, Portugal was on the brink of economic collapse, the result of a combination of the effects of the Great War and the Great Economic Depression. Since the establishment of the First Republic on 5 October 1910 and until the coup of 1926, Portugal had gone through a period of great political turmoil, counting a total of forty-eight prime ministers and eight presidents. This instability, according to Salazar, reflected the evils of liberalism (e.g., individualism, parliamentarianism, capitalism, and socialism), which threatened the natural equilibrium of the traditional oligarchies. But despite economic depression and profound socio-political upheaval, the interim minister of finance at the time, conservative republican military general Artur Ivens Ferraz, personally went to Geneva to decline a large foreign loan negotiated under the auspices of the League of Nations. On his return to Portugal from his role as deputy of finance, General Ferraz was applauded by the crowds at the Rossio Square in Lisbon and congratulated as a true national hero.

In the refusal to obtain external financial help, Portugal delivered on what António Ferro, Salazar's minister of propaganda, called 'the myth of honourable poverty'. In effect, the cult of poverty was used as a screen to maintain the wealthy status of certain traditional families. Salazar engineered an odd form of manufactured backwardness with the aim of dissuading other nations from invading. At the same time,

---

25   Cited in Maria Antónia Lopes, 'Os pobres e a assistencia publica', in *História de Portugal*, ed. by José Mattoso, 8 vols (Lisbon: Circulo de Leitores, 1993-94), v: *O liberalismo* (1993), pp. 500-15 (p. 503) (my translation, M.J.de A.).

Portugal rejected foreign help from the League of Nations so as not to create leverage or indebtedness to other European nations of the League (many of whom viewed aid as a fair trade for meddling with Portuguese colonies in Africa and Asia).

Portugal had a bad reputation as administrator of its empire among other European nations. In Mozambique, for example, Portugal's settlements were largely nominal, with the colonial administration controlling little more than twenty-five percent of the entire territory. The same was true for the hinterland areas. Portugal went on launching expensive military campaigns to contain some of the independence movements then flaring up in the region. But as these counter-independence initiatives ended up consuming most of the available fiscal resources of the state, Portugal resorted to outsourcing schemes in some of its overseas territories, granting the economic exploitation and the direct administration of huge regions to foreign chartered companies.[26] This form of 'corporate feudalism' exposed Portugal's own limitations in dealing with its colonies.

European nations like England, Brussels, or Germany related to Portugal not as a colonial power but as kind of a semi-colony, itself in need of guidance and patronage from other colonial empires. The British Ultimatum of 1890 demanded that the Portuguese give up the inner lands between Angola and Mozambique (what is currently Zambia, Zimbabwe and Malawi), in order to allow the British to build a major north-south railway linking Cairo to Cape Town. The years immediately following this concession to the British saw a massive wave of protests, ultimately leading, as mentioned above, to the conditions that would place Salazar in power. Against the background of Sebastianism, Salazar was idolized as the messiah of finances, a cult that most recently, in 2017, was nostalgically revitalized when Portugal's state television, in collaboration with the BBC, called for a national vote to elect the greatest personality in history: Salazar won an indisputable first place with 41% of the vote.

The *Estado Novo* corporatist system put in place a model beyond liberalism and socialism; it was a third-way tactic, one also

---

26 Malyn Newitt, *Portugal's Third Empire: Portugal in Africa in the Last Hundred Years* (London: C. Hurst, 1981), p. 78.

adopted by ordoliberalism, the German variant of economic liberalism, of the post-war period. Unlike the latter, however, Portugal's *Estado Novo* banned both the welfare state and political democracy. Historian António Amaro is thus right in stating that Portugal would only experience the welfare state by the time neoliberalism was beginning to wither under its own success.[27] The same could be said of its embrace of parliamentary democracy. This trend dovetailed the disposition, after many years under state despotic authoritarianism, to associate progressiveness with decreasing state intervention. Terms such as freedom, private initiative, autonomy, and non-patriarchal meritocracy, which erupted out of the 1974 Carnation Revolution and in the months and years afterwards, jumped onto the neoliberal wagon regardless of the fact that its philosophy was running on tracks laid by countries which had had very different histories than Portugal.

Almost overnight, Portugal went from a long period of fascist rule to aggressive neoliberalism. To prove the temporariness of the austerity crisis, officials set out to calendarize it according to the best predictions of liquidation. It would climb in the course of 2011, reach its peak in 2012, and begin its decline in 2013. Such forecasts allowed the contemporary state to communicate two points: firstly, that it was in full control of things,[28] and secondly, that austerity, like the years of liquidity instigating it, was but a short-term phenomenon. Austerity, too, was an aperture in time, an ephemeral portal in the diaphragm of the machine — certainly in d'Orey's camera-work — through which the messiah might reappear, shrouded in a fog.

---

27 Amaro, 'The Late Construction of Portugal Welfare State'.
28 As Angela Mitroupolous reasons in 'Oikopolitics, and Storms', *The Global South*, 3.1 (2009), pp. 66–82.

Rinko Kawauchi: Imperfect Photographs
CLARA MASNATTA

The oeuvre of contemporary Japanese photographer Rinko Kawauchi is wrought with imperfection. An approach that favours process over product and combines conceptual art with vernacular traditions makes her pictures happily imperfect. Kawauchi's image universe, an aesthetics that has been aptly called a 'poetics of the everyday', is intimate with the world of vernacular, deskilled photography and amateur errors or technical imperfections. Throughout Kawauchi's multifarious experiments in iconicity — encompassing analogue and digital technology, video installation, blogging, slide shows, and, above all, photo books — the notion that a work is an irreversible process ending in a static icon-object fails. Nothing her works offer is perfect, complete, and defined. All is inclusive, expansive, and hypnotically open-ended.

Her oeuvre, in its entirety, is work-in-progress. Kawauchi's latest project, *The River Embraced Me* (2016) materialized her concept of the image in a feat of reverse-engineering that took both the exhibition and book form.[1] Images are transmedial, here spiralling between word and image, but not culminating, for consummation will not describe any work of Kawauchi. Take the title of one of her works from 2013:

---

1   Rinko Kawauchi, *The River Embraced Me* (Tokyo: torch press, 2016). The exhibition was first shown at the Contemporary Art Museum, Kumamoto, from 23 January to 27 March 2016.

4% evokes the theory that only this tiny percentage of the mass of the universe can be perceived; it acknowledges the impossibility of imagining a perfectly complete picture. Infinity for Kawauchi starts with the endlessness of configuration of the elements at hand in the editing of the image. Thanks to the arrangement in sequences of unexpected variation, photography appears as a never-ending process in which the mode of binding is the mode of loosening.

Kawauchi's photographs are radically without frame. Boundary-less images, regularly bound in books, laid out, juxtaposed in a syntax of continuity (itself a form of imperfection), decidedly against linearity, fixed contours, and stable contexts. For Kawauchi, '[p]hotography is a process of continuous choosing', in which 'choosing a photograph from the contact sheet is as important as pressing the shutter release button'.[2] Factor in a grammar just as imperfect as her syntax. These photos speak patois and rhyme without much reason.

Photo books are Kawauchi's cardinal form of producing her emphatically imperfect photographs. Especially in the case of Japan, the dissemination of photographs in book form is more significant and far-reaching than showing photography in galleries. Looking back at the socio-critical history of photography, its beginnings also appear fuelled by photo books.[3] 'Medium' in the modernist, Greenbergian sense fails to provide an adequate description of photography and its variations, in particular, through Kawauchi's photo pages; that is, 'medium' in the sense of a form produced by specific technical means with specific expressive possibilities.

Just as medium-specificity gives way to transmedial photography, photo books instantiate photography's principle capacity to exist in varying copies and with multiple authors, photographer, printer, de-

---

2   Tetsuro Ishida, 'An Interview with Kawauchi Rinko: An Obsession with Time and Memory', in Rinko Kawauchi, *Illuminance, Ametsuchi, Seeing Shadow* (Kyoto: Seigensha, 2012), pp. 125-128 (p. 125).

3   I am of course referring to Walter Benjamin's 'Kleine Geschichte der Photographie' (1931) together with Gisèle Freund's *La Photographie en France au dix-neuvième siècle* (1936). See Walter Benjamin, *Gesammelte Schriften*, ed. by Rolf Tiedemann and Hermann Schweppenhäuser, 7 vols (Frankfurt a.M.: Suhrkamp, 1972-91), II: *Aufsätze, Essays, Vorträge* (1977), pp. 368-85; Gisèle Freund, *La Photographie en France au dix-neuvième siècle. Essai de sociologie et d'esthétique* (Paris: La Maison des Amis des Livres/A. Monnier, 1936).

signer. Books qua photographic dispositif contest an all-too-typical notion of photography and photographs as the single and perfect products of an individual photographer. Recall the signature 'decisive moment' that defined Henri Cartier-Bresson's masterpieces — the formal peak in which all compositional elements in the photographic frame align for the perfect image — it thrives on such a conception of photography.[4]

Kawauchi's photo books come in all shapes and sizes. Some books are hybrid in terms of mixed media, like *The Eyes, the Ears* (2005) coupling word with image; others in larger composition terms. *Gift* (2014) consists of twin volumes. It takes the syntax of facing pages to facing-books-level in order to display Kawauchi's collaboration with Terri Weifenbach. *Approaching Whiteness* (2013) is an exquisite take on the Japanese scroll. It offers a single-themed variation on contact-sheet images very much at odds with *Sheets* (2013).[5] The latter is a book that adds gatefolds to the contact-sheet mimicry, adequately conveyed by black paper and a lower reproduction quality. As the perspective shifts from ultra-distant to a close-up mosaic through layout variation, it invites us to look again, look closer, and further.

Ametsuchi (2012) deserves special mention because it was the first project that Kawauchi originally shot for an exhibition. The work, consisting of seventeen large-scale photographs and a video, is a site-specific project pivoting on the *yakihata* or controlled burning of farming fields that ritually takes place in Aso, Japan. *Ametsuchi* was given new life when Dutch designer Hans Gremmen did the book version.[6] This beautifully manufactured book gave Gremmen princi-

---

4   The English translation of the original French publication — Henri Cartier-Bresson, *Images à la sauvette* (Paris: Verve, 1952) — was chosen by Cartier-Bresson's publisher Simon & Schuster as the title of the 1952 American version, and unintentionally imposed the motto which would define Cartier-Bresson's work. It is present in the epigraph to Henri Cartier-Bresson's introductory text, a quote by Cardinal de Retz: 'There is nothing in this world which does not have its decisive moment'; Cartier-Bresson, *The Decisive Moment: Photographs by Henri Cartier-Bresson* (New York: Simon & Schuster, 1952).

5   Rinko Kawauchi, *The Eyes, the Ears: Photographs and Words* (Tokyo: Foil, 2005); Kawauchi, *Approaching Whiteness* (Tokyo: Goliga, 2013); Kawauchi, *Sheets* (Berlin: Kominek Books, 2013); Rinko Kawauchi and Terri Weifenbach, *Gift* (Tokyo: Amana, 2014).

6   Rinko Kawauchi, *Ametsuchi* (New York: Aperture, 2013).

pality on a par with the artist and the editor, Aperture Foundation's book publisher Lesley A. Martin. For Gremmen, 'The book itself — the way it is printed and bound — asks questions about the medium of the book, and how people tend to use them.'[7] The book is done in a variation of origami or 'Japanese binding'. We slide through it; a feeling of continuity arises through the uncut pages (the sides and bottom part of the page are open, only the top is closed). Moreover, the book has a parallel series of negative images on the inside of the pages. We find images — not all, only the pictures of ritual burning and of starry skies — printed in inverted colours, maroon, blue dashes of purple. The design of the book plays out opposites (rough paper on one side, smooth on the other) that seem to translate the meaning of 'Heaven and Earth' of *Ametsuchi*; it sets a game of repetition and inversion across images and typography alike (the Rinko Kawauchi name and the title of the book appear at both beginning and end, the image on the endpapers repeats, as does the typography, on the hardcover, with Kawauchi's name printed upside down).

Without exception, Kawauchi's books are reshuffle-ready, typically unpaginated, and singularly adept at non-linear narratives. They unfold a certain continuum of time, rather than present individual moments. Isolating a photograph, in fact, is a rather forceful move for the sake of exemplarity. Kawauchi's minimal unit is the tandem, not the single photograph.

In addition to chronological priority (Kawauchi produced handmade photo books before her publishing debut in 2001, with the three volumes *Utanane, Hanabi,* and *Hanako*), the books have epistemic weight.[8] The dominant pairing design has the book layout as matrix, and syncopation for rhyme. While traceable with some insistence, the morphological analogy of pairs is always a bit off, especially compared to the solemn geometry of any New Objectivity series, for example, Renger-Patzsch's *Die Welt is schön*.[9] The effect of her juxtapositions is

---

7   Brian Sholis, 'Interview with Hans Gremmen, Designer of Rinko Kawauchi's *Ametsuchi*', publisher's website <http://www.aperture.org/blog/interview-with-hans-gremmen/> [accessed 10 March 2015].

8   Rinko Kawauchi, *Hanabi* (Tokyo: Ritorumoa, 2001); Kawauchi and Masakazu Takei, *Utatane* (Tokyo: Ritorumoa, 2001); Kawauchi, *Hanako* (Tokyo: Ritoru Moa, 2001).

9   Albert Renger-Patzsch, *Die Welt ist schön* (Munich: Einhorn-Verlag, 1928).

anything but sobering. 'Seeing two images next to each other opens up the imagination and gives birth to something else', declared Kawauchi upon the international release of *Illuminance* in 2011.[10]

The epistemics of colour are key for such dynamics of formation on the fringe of decomposition, pulsing between *Gestaltung* and *Entstaltung*.[11] Colour is unstable — Bauhaus guru Josef Albers warned no normal eye was foolproof against the 'colour deception' of the after-image or 'simultaneous contrast' phenomenon —[12] and colour has the potential to produce multi-sensorial episodes through its vibrating boundaries. Rather than taking colour as deceptive, Kawauchi relishes in the plurality of perspectives: 'I love those ever-changing colours. It can be a metaphor of how the world can transform completely just by looking at it from different angles.'[13]

Consider the vertigo of flowers spiralling in white, mauve, and magenta paired with a seething blue maelstrom, appearing in *Illuminance*. Compare this also to the iconic picture of the man jumping across the puddle where every element in the frame appears perfectly mirrored thanks to his projecting shadow — Cartier-Bresson's 'Behind the Gare St Lazare'. For a description of Kawauchi's vertiginous ensemble, no characterization could be less appropriate than 'the decisive moment' that defines the legendary snapshot, once and for all. Kawauchi offers not marvels of exactness but a galaxy of stills following the fluid nature of colours and producing a *metamorphotography* blurring every fixed contour. The instability of colour harbours the beauty of transfiguration. Perhaps that explains why eggs and hatchlings are a favourite subject of hers, as are butterflies, mutation's winged reminder.

Flipping through the pages of her photo books 'gives birth to something else'; it sets in motion a cinematic, hallucinatory presence.

---

10   Yumi Goto, 'Rinko Kawauchi's Illuminance', *Time.com*, 11 April 2011 <http://time.com/3776240/rinko-kawauchis-illuminance/> [accessed February 20, 2015].

11   For Walter Benjamin, colour was the 'Medium aller Veränderungen'. See Walter Benjamin, 'Die Farbe vom Kinde aus betrachtet', in Benjamin, *Gesammelte Schriften*, VI (1985): *Fragmente vermischten Inhalts. Autobiographische Schriften*, pp. 110–12 (p. 110); and Benjamin, 'Phantasie', ibid., pp. 114–17.

12   Josef Albers, *Interaction of Color* (New Haven, CT: Yale University Press, 2009), chapter 8: 'Why Color Deception? After-Image, Simultaneous Contrast', pp. 22–23 (p. 23). Cf. Ishida, 'Obsession with Time and Memory', p.126.

13   Ishida, 'Obsession with Time and Memory', p. 125.

What Kawauchi's imperfect photographs make visible is as important as what is not manifest, yet can, in principle, be perceived. Her work is an invitation not to look at some stationary object but to 'watch' photographs unfold as we negotiate their signification, even their referent. Her snapshots contain not a slice of time but a thrust of infinity.

The temporality of photo books has been consistently appreciated as closer to cinematic time and motion. The advent of digital technology has smoothed the continuity between photo and film. Filming with a digital camera is now standard practice, and has made quite a few photographers into filmmakers, Kawauchi included. Yet the rapport predates digitalism. Photo books have a particular temporality: Neither the decisive moment of a single photo nor cinema's flow of time. Slide shows are another photographic form that we will find in Kawauchi, similarly imbued with such 'photofilmic' dynamics.[14] Still and still moving, throughout her photo books, materiality marries cinematic illusion.

Photo books are objects thick with materiality that call for manipulation. Unlike an image hung or cast, the book grants us private viewing with plenty of opportunities to linger, to stretch time. Duration fosters the occurrence of metamorphic colour phenomena. On the other hand, the book format is perhaps more prescriptive than that of the exhibition.

If transmediality does not detract from materiality, even less does imperfection. On the contrary, the emphatically imperfect photographs of Kawauchi further advance the materiality of the medium. Ultimately, her imperfect photography amounts to a production of presence, of a presence-effect. But this presence does not refer to the privileged relation of copy and original ('there was referent X') that haunts the discourse of the medium. It is a presence felt, evoked, but not shown. Such evoked presence corrodes the fantasy of an external world independent of the perceiving subject, and undermines the idea of photography as a medium that offers evidence or irrevocable proof of existence by that which appears recorded in the recording device; in

---

14 See *The Photofilmic: Entangled Images in Contemporary Art and Visual Culture*, ed. by Brianne Cohen and Alexander Streitberger, Lieven Gevaert Series, 21 (Leuven: Leuven University Press, 2016).

a word, that eliminates subjectivity. Kawachi's imperfect photography, an image universe tensed between materiality and illusion, is a world not without humans.

Kawauchi's 'poetics of the everyday' has the insignificant as dominant subject matter. With the exception of *Cui-Cui* (2005), her photographs are mostly, uncannily, de-peopled. A bestiary of insects, flowers, children, food, cooked and uncooked, intertwining the urban jungle and the natural world, yield the cosmic in minuscule detail. Her use of a pastel palette and hazy focus blending fore- and background augments the subtlety of the motifs. Delicate fragments form and dissolve into a kaleidoscope of the quotidian. Only in *Ametsuchi* (2012) did Kawauchi drift to an altogether extraordinary planet.

Kawauchi's 'everyday existentialism' has been described as a naïve, amateur, offhand, dilettantish, dream-like, elliptical, fractured, speculative, vernacular, de-aestheticized approach. Her photographs are serene yet disquieting, de-peopled yet full of 'mistakes'. Technical imperfections come forth. Deficient flashlight, a water-splashed lens, magenta-stained images recur — all of them wounds of procedure.

Imperfection must be defined in relation to history — technological and social, that is, cultural — and the set of conventions that shape a repertoire of 'error' in order to advance concrete transformations of error's function and definition. With Kawauchi's, at the same time that the photo book format renders her photos present, her aesthetics conjures presence in the age of digital content. Kawauchi's endeavours have been chiefly analogue as well as contemporary to glitch art, that is, an artistic hacking of sorts that exploits methods to make digital images appear pixelated and thematizes colour blotches or interruptions of figures — a practice for obtaining mutant images. Like many digitally generated works through the manipulation of encoding and compression, Kawauchi's experiments show ways to wake up the latent image, part by chance, part under strict aesthetic control, in her medium of choice.

This roughly sketched present landscape speaks to the post-metaphysical 'material turn' of media theory, which has informed media studies progressively since the 1980s.[15] The material turn (also, 'performance turn' or, alternatively, 'aistheticization') can be justifiably read as a cultural reaction to the promotion of radical absence that an iconophobic tradition has promoted, such as the simulation theory put forth by Jean Baudrillard. Palpable is the love for images in recent *aisthetic* theory, as in the image-making practices including blemishes that reveal material processes while also encouraging viewers to interact with images.

Graphic avatars of imperfection are pregnant with time. They are laden with anteriority and futurity. They evince their own having been made and anticipate their own degradation. When Kawauchi does not get rid of the trace that signals the moment of picture-taking, the temporary status of the image gets uncovered at once. Moreover, imperfections arouse a communion of feelings in the viewer's present. David Freedberg would say that we experience an 'embodied simulation' that kindles empathy, if we can extrapolate the artist's physical gesture in the modulations of paint and sculpt material to photographic images, and spark the feels-*as-if*.[16]

Errors, rather than the infallible photographer, evoke a presence that touches us. We see a round shoulder occupying the right-hand corner of the dysphoric arena as the bullfighting team drags out the bull. 'I don't consider any shot a mistake', Kawauchi tells us[17]. Photography will not, at any given point, be perfect. Perfection promotes distance, reverence, awe. To the extent that we are conscious of the form in a work of art, we become somewhat detached. Aberration, on the contrary, kindles unpostponed emotional involvement. A trembling pulse can move us; an unevenly lit night shot, too. We let down our guard in the face of the magenta-stained image of the waterfalls. Kawauchi's photos embrace the accident, and we embrace them.

Roland Barthes employed similar Brechtian terms to find fault with the 'overconstructedness' of horror presented in 'Shock Photos',

---

15 See Markus Rautzenberg, 'Was ist postmetaphysische Präsenztheorie?', in Rautzenberg, *Die Gegenwendigkeit der Störung. Aspekte einer postmetaphysischen Präsenztheorie* (Zürich: Diaphanes, 2009), pp. 21–45.

16 David Freedberg and Vittorio Gallese, 'Motion, Emotion and Empathy in Esthetic Experience', *Trends in Cognitive Sciences*, 11/5 (May 2007), pp. 197–203.

17 Ishida, 'Obsession with Time and Memory', p. 126.

an essay collected in his 1957 *Mythologies*. The gruesome pictures of political realities on display at Orsay Gallery earned Barthes' distancing disapproval because, 'the photographer has left us nothing' but 'synthetic nourishment' thanks to 'the perfect legibility of the scene':

> Now, none of these photographs, all too skillful, touches us. This is because, as we look at them, we are in each case dispossessed of our judgment; someone has shuddered for us, reflected for us, judged for us; the photographer has left us nothing — except a simple right of intellectual acquiescence: we are linked to these images only by a technical interest; overindicated by the artist himself, for us they have no history, we can no longer *invent* our own reception of this synthetic nourishment, already perfectly assimilated by its creator.[18]

Very much in contrast to these fraudulent 'shock photos', Kawauchi will leave us plenty to invent upon reception. Her photographs, far from 'overindicated', engage with an elliptical visibility that calls for participant viewing. Less sensory detail requires more perceptive completion. Contemplate, for instance, the shattered glass from the *AILA* (2004) series turn magically back into the coffeemaker as our mind's eye intervenes in the reconstruction.[19] The object is evoked, not shown. Non-linearity takes the form of an indirectly constituted object, at once given and withheld.

With such an indirect object, the intensity is cognitive rather than perceptual. Kawauchi lulls us with the art of searching. The instance of reception is decisive for her photography, as if the viewer added the finishing touches to the picture. The viewer must, however, not conceive such finishing as final. Each context grants renewal. The insignificant

---

18   Roland Barthes, 'Shock Photos', in Barthes, *The Eiffel Tower and Other Mythologies*, trans. Richard Howard (Berkeley: University of California Press, 1997), pp. 71–73 (p. 71). Cf. Barthes, 'Photos-chocs', in Barthes, *Mythologies* (Paris: Seuil, 2005), pp. 98–100 (p. 98): 'Or, aucune de ces photographies, trop habiles, ne nous atteint. C'est qu'en face d'elles, nous sommes chaque fois dépossédés de notre jugement: on a frémi pour nous, on a réfléchi pour nous, on a jugé pour nous; le photographe ne nous a rien laissé — qu'un simple droit d'acquiescement intellectuel: nous ne sommes liés à ces images que par un intérêt technique; chargées de surindication par l'artiste lui-même, elles n'ont pour nous aucune histoire, nous ne pouvons plus inventer notre propre accueil à cette nourriture synthétique, déjà parfaitement assimilé par son créateur.'

19   Rinko Kawauchi, *AILA* (Tokyo: Little More, 2004). Excerpts from *AILA*, including the image in question, can be found on the artist's website < http://rinkokawauchi.com/en/works/253/> [accessed 20 August 2021].

form returns and recharges in tireless combinations. The elliptical and insignificant quality itself is key for negotiating both signification and referent. Oblique angles, flattened perspective, overflows of striated morphology, and curious little bits magnify with their imprecision the fact that no de-finition, a specific image even less, could determine Kawauchi's work. Her unsutured images precede and follow as seamlessly as the myriad colours that diamonds cast also in her book's pages. Its title, *Illuminance* (a term referring to the amount of luminous flux per unit area), is perhaps more scientific but less fitting than the 'rainbow-like play of lustrous colours'[20] of *iridescence* when it comes to Kawauchi's work.

Kawauchi's images are gently disorienting. They are at the same time transparent and opaque. Just as syntax is montage in lingo, 'appresentation' is the phenomenological equivalent of connotation.[21] The phenomenon of grasping something over and above what is perceived is defined with the name of 'appresentation' in Edmund Husserl's *Logical Investigations* as the co-presenting not actually given yet produced in perception. As appresentation presupposes a core of presentation, it is a co-presence that is in the spatial field, which Markus Rautzenberg cleverly analogized to connotation. Denotation is the first meaning of a thing, what jumps to one's face, and connotation its inseparable decanting, the meaning at the corner of the eye. Just as connotation and denotation are indivisible aspects of a thing's meaning, every perception simultaneously presents and appresents.

Kawauchi is the doyenne of appresentation. Her artfulness is the antipode of overconstructedness; it is charged by the laconic, implicit semantics of connotation. Kawauchi's strategy exploits and strips bare the mechanics of signification or, which is the same, perception. A

---

20 Ishida, 'Obsession with Time and Memory', p. 125.
21 I am indebted to Markus Rautzenberg for his insights in many writings and his input on an early version of this paper presented at 'Visual Noise: Wandering Artefacts and Aberrant Images', conference at the ICI Berlin, 17 June 2016, organized by Clara Masnatta, in collaboration with Banu Karaca and James Burton <https://doi.org/10.25620/e160617>. The analogy and reference to appresentation is from Edmund Husserl, *Logische Untersuchungen* as quoted by Markus Rautzenberg in 'Die Empfindung eines Objekts als Beobachtung ausgeben. Das Haiku als "Sprachfotografie" bei Roland Barthes und Andrej Tarkowskij', *Kodikas/Code. Ars Semeiotica*, 37.3–4 (2014), pp. 349–60 (p. 351).

figure needs a ground, that is, the immediately surrounding space that frames it and enables the very act of perception. Contexts help decode and co-produce meaning. This is the minimalist approach that flourishes along Kawauchi's parallel reframing. For shades of meaning, Kawauchi is an entire sentimental education.

Over and over, Kawauchi calls forth the hidden sides of a thing that we may not sensuously perceive, but of which we are aware. Her photos pulse between the unseen and the visible, with a non-linear beat. They teach us at once: The stuff that images are made of is not visual. It is temporality that enables the non-manifestation of the image (soon-to-be-unfolded) and the tacit presence insisting throughout Kawauchi's work.

Selections from Kawauchi's portfolio get mixed and remixed in a number of projects. While imperfection spins in the shape of impermanence and recurrence, an image's return seems always fresh and the image renewed thanks to the elliptical visibility at play in the photographic sequences of her books. On the whole, it feels that it is through the choreography of many iterations and associations that we get to uncover things, as we see the varying images dancing on the page. One particular example is the variation on the pincushion full of colourful pins that links *Cui Cui* (2005), Kawauchi's take on the family album, with *Semear* (2007).[22] Originally commissioned by the Museum of Modern Art of São Paulo, *Semear* was to portray the local community of Nikkei immigrants. The pincushion, spotted with hindsight, makes us feel that we are looking at extended family in this later project. Subliminal patterns of such kind (or kin) abound.

In Kawauchi's ceaseless work-in-progress, we never know where the images are going. More often than not, her images do not show where they are coming from. 'Every time I make a book, I leave out many elements that indicate a certain location', she clarifies.[23] A camera can be a geodesic instrument, a compass of sorts; Kawauchi's camera is a magnetic machine at times at the threshold of discernibility. Against all photogrammetry, it produces topographies of sensibility by

---

22 Rinko Kawauchi, *Cui Cui* (Tokyo: Foil; Arles; Actes Sud; Paris: Fondation Cartier pour l'art contemporain, 2005); Kawauchi, *Semear* (Tokyo: FOIL, 2007).

23 Ishida, 'Obsession with Time and Memory', p. 125.

downplaying the charting impulse in the oscillation of the two poles of the medium, *semioisis* and *aisthesis*.

In his book on 'Japan', *L'empire des signes* (The Empire of Signs), Roland Barthes showed that the opacity of signifiers of the system he called 'Japan', in other words, a loss in mediatic transparency entailed a gain in *aisthetic* significance. Kawauchi's body of photography with wounds of procedure gives way to materiality with an emphasis on *aisthesis* that is, too, in detriment of the documentary: not 'This was X' but rather 'Look at this!' Yet the pointing-at is done not with the index but with the little finger. She usually employs a 6x6 medium-format Rolleiflex that gives the child-like perspective: one can typically see the floor in the lower part of the frame. From the perspective of the adult eye, from higher up, this generates a sense of incompleteness, and the mind's eye steps into the breech.

While not really documentary, Kawauchi's style is perhaps in fact diaristic, all snap annotations. If narration is time in textual dress, her work is indeed lyrical, but not elegiac, and never epic. What best describes Kawauchi's art is the interplay of polarities: Unhackneyed clichés, all given at once withheld, serene yet disquieting, prosaic poetics, intimate and domestic but also worldly and universal. As her work oscillates between poles (including, but not limited to *aisthesis* and *semiosis*), we are unable to pin it down. But we come to be certain about the given fragility of a state. Nowhere are these dynamics and the surge of materiality more visible than in her engagement with colour.

The rainbow-likeness describing the shape-shifting iridescence of her work can be misleading. On the one hand, Kawauchi's photography is properly atmospheric. We are at times genuinely immersed in her luminous chromatic expanse. An environmental concept as *Stimmung* — 'the relationship we entertain with our environment' for Hans Ulrich Gumbrecht —[24] chimes with this photography of enveloping feelings. A subtle presence is imparted in the multi-sensorial chromatics of this damp photography full of dense, evaporating light. Images conjure an estrangement comparable to observing life through the glass of an aquarium. It puts us in a mood, like 'the lightest touch that occurs when

---

24   Hans Ulrich Gumbrecht, *Our Broad Present: Time and Contemporary Culture*, trans. by Henry Erik Butler (New York: Columbia University Press, 2014), p. xi.

the material world surrounding us affects the surface of our bodies' that Gumbrecht specified for *Stimmung*.[25]

On the other hand, Kawauchi's palette is restricted to aquamarine greens, blues, maroons, and thoroughly white-splashed. The waxy pastel quality of her pictures produces a coated proximity that allows us to penetrate things with our gaze but also keeps us a coat away from them. Her palette, for Kawauchi, is a way of seeing the world as 'half awake and half asleep'.[26] But is the world that we see opaque or semi-transparent?

Kawauchi's pictures are bright with opacity. A reference to Goethe's theory of colours is in order. Not only because Goethe's *Farbenlehre*, his colour study, is based on perception and engages wholeheartedly with questions of psychology and sensitivity. (To him we owe the confirmation that there is no *Bild* without *Gestaltung*, no picture without consciousness.) Above all, we must refer to Goethe because his notion of white is not the absence of colour, but a pure drop of opaque transparency. To wit, 'Die vollendete Trübe ist das Weiße, die gleichgültigste, hellste, erste, undurchsichtige Raumerfüllung.' ('The highest turbidity is white, the simplest, brightest, first, opaque occupation of space.')[27]

A certain thickness is congenital in whiteness. Thickness slows down the reading of the image; it is troubling. Sometimes shades of white can take over, like the picture of the little albino spider against the corrugated plaster. Other times, white hues can bring dulcification to the riot of colour of a carnival scene. Very often, Kawauchi achieves the pastel quality of her pictures by aiming the lens directly at light sources. But there is more to her white expanses than overexposure. Floods of light bring to her images an 'occupation of space' in particular through the recurring reflections. Reflections are the contagion of two bodies; they give us a being-in-space. The immediate inscription in space that these reflections offer is purposely turned away from the recognizable. White, again, is for *aisthesis*.

---

25   Ibid., p. x.
26   Ishida, 'Obsession with Time and Memory', p. 127.
27   Johann Wolfgang von Goethe, *Entwurf einer Farbenlehre*, in Goethe, *Sämtliche Werke nach Epochen seines Schaffens. Münchner Ausgabe*, ed. by Karl Richter and others (Munich: Hanser, 1986–99), x: *Die Farbenlehre*, ed. by Peter Schmidt (1989), pp. 17–273 (p. 67), my translation.

More often than glass, water appears as Kawauchi's chosen reflective medium. Perhaps because, as everyone knows, meditation and water are wedded forever, the aquatic medium percolates effortlessly into Kawauchi's 'everyday existentialism'. The *Search for the Sun* (2015) series brings aquatic and photographic media nicely together.[28] In this series, shot in Austria, Kawauchi's cerulean palette goes glacier; her aquamarine turns to ice. The crystal blue of this most controlled palette gives the impression of containing natural history, something to be treasured like the moth fossilized in amber.

Reflections emphasize the fact that the image is an illusion that is embedded in a physical object. This also brings us to the realization that photographing involves physical presences in the world. Incidentally, Kawauchi has expressed her preference for arranging her exhibitions as collaborating with space, for the 'wall to look like a large reflection of light'.[29] Augmenting, in this way, the illusion integral to images suggests that the physicality of images is perhaps not best deployed in art shows. It is for sure tangible in the vernacular understanding of photography.

No other work of Kawauchi's is closer to the vernacular tradition than *Cui Cui* (2015), which represents 13 years of day-to-day living picture-taking. *Cui Cui* is a variation on the family album narrative, produced as a slide show and in book form. Because the former is between the banal familial and avant-garde mode of presentation, the projected images combine the vernacular with the conceptual more poignantly. As the slides follow one another against electro-acoustic accompaniment intermixed with chirping (*cui-cui* is an onomatopoeitic French word for the sound of birds), flashing first white and leaving a *turbidus* after-image in our retina, we slowly come to realize that the image carrousel focuses on Kawauchi's own family.

The grandparents are protagonists in this project. The family gets together for dinner, the grandmother cooks in the kitchen, harvests vegetables in the garden, a pregnant woman's belly, scenes of a marriage, the funeral procession, the grandfather reappears, breastfeeding

---

28   The *Search for the Sun* series was shot for the exhibition 'Rinko Kawauchi Illuminance' (20 March to 15 July 2015 at Kunst Haus Wien, Austria). Cf. the artist's website <http://rinkokawauchi.com/en/works/126/> [accessed 20 August 2021].

29   Ishida, 'Obsession with Time and Memory', p. 127.

close-up, and so on. Not only do we get here the vernacular photo par excellence — the wedding picture — together with the impression that culinary shots (behold every kidney bean shining back at us like flash-lit eyes) have been part of photodemotics in Japan long before Instagram made food a universal genre. We also come to appreciate photography as vital part of the domestic architecture; a picture we flipped by can casually appear framed in a room. A photograph is a physical presence in the world. As image-object, it invites physical as well as visual engagement.

Kawauchi's variation on the family album articulates an ecology of images that is in open conversation with how we experience photography as a social and cultural phenomenon. Or, which is the same, photography as snapshots. The simplicity of the composition of snapshots encodes their highly conventional character and reveals that they are artefacts for memory and affect. Snapshots, according to Catherine Zuromskis, are defined by aesthetic simplicity and a certain rhetoric of authenticity; the snapshot's truth is the truth of feelings.[30] A snapshot image is typically drained of its meaning the minute it is contemplated outside its personal frame of reference, Zuromskis remarked, for this move neutralizes the affective charge that defines it next to the simplicity of composition. The snapshot truth-content gets expanded to all images in Kawauchi's serial framework. The genre's constitutive affective charge is rooted in the physicality of the photograph, itself a memory device.

Perhaps the greatest insight into these vernacular workings is the framed photograph of Kawauchi's grandfather carried high by the mourning procession. We are seeing but the ancient talisman of sacred presence as fetishized gadget, the life-like effigy of a dead man in the age of technical reproducibility. This photo will equally grace his tomb, or hold a place of honour in an homage dinner; it is a portable monument.

Snapshots and *Cui Cui* alike feed on authenticity and affect, yet the latter engages in such rhetoric with a distance. Empathy is mediated through the constructed presentation of a cyclical narrative far

---

30   See Catherine Zuromskis, *Snapshot Photography: The Lives of Images* (Cambridge, MA: MIT Press, 2013).

removed from linear temporality. The challenge of continuing after we see the grandfather's corpse and funeral is well sustained through the remaining one-third of the photo-narrative. As the old man reappears, we realize these are rebirths, not resuscitations. *Cui Cui* is really a book on the season-like cycle of birth, growth, death, and the rituals that make up life. The naive immediacy with the personal of the amateur dissolves with the universal.

It is true that documenting and constructing go hand in hand in the snapshooting tradition. Yet Kawauchi's emphasis is on the constructing by way of documenting. Amateur photography and Kawauchi's snaps' paths part as they pave their ways. While Kawauchi's *aisthethic* errors were in detriment of the documentary, the frequent technical imperfections in snapshots testify to their documentary concerns irrespective of (in the modernist sense) the aesthetic, against which amateur aberrations stand. Kawauchi's imagination stands in a third place that is neither the deskilled vernacular nor the aesthetics of high modernism. Her work is at odds with the art paradigm that Barthes upheld before the shock photos, in spite of the opportune comparison. As Ariella Azoulay pointed out, behind Barthes's critique stood an idea of art coterminous with the new.[31] Barthes was unable to shudder before the shock photos because the artist (really any other one) had done this before him. Barthes' cool leaked over aesthetics in the wider sense, that is, perception, sensation, (not) feeling again a feeling that is not new. Against resolution and for reiteration, Kawauchi's work is, in this respect, as well, a sentimental education.

If snapshots are fundamentally true, their truth got reverse-engineered with Kawauchi's most recent project. Commissioned by the Museum of Contemporary Art of Kumamoto, *The River Embraced Me* (2016) introduced engineering between word and image to re-turn to the community present in vernacular photography. Yet the return was not so manifest. *The River Embraced Me* is an uncannily de-peopled representation of community. Their exposure is done in written words, not fixed in images. Words and the logic of performance compounded the programme of this tellingly conceptual work giving precedence to process over product.

---

31   Ariella Azoulay, *The Civil Contract of Photography* (New York: Zone Books, 2008), pp. 163–64.

For the project, the community of Kumamoto was called upon to submit their stories and memories of a place in the region, indicating the corresponding location. Thirty-one memory stories were selected, that is, the best-written ones were chosen, and Kawauchi set off to the places indicated in these stories to make photographs in a shooting 'comparable to a pilgrimage', as curator Haruko Tomisawa put it.[32] She pressed the shutter release when something, anything really, from a story resonated in her in the place. (Reportedly, references to weather, the seasons, and time abounded.) Kawauchi was a distant medium. In addition, Kawauchi produced a poem, an *exquisite corps* of sorts, by extracting lines from each story. One became the title of the project, 'the river embraced me'. At the exhibition, Kawauchi's photographs and the extracted texts were shown side by side, under strict aesthetic control. Also on display were the six sample stories that the Museum made as model for the participation call.

Now, nothing of the process that I am describing is visible in the photographs. To grasp that *The River Embraced Me* is a work of process over product one must read the explanatory text that comes as booklet insert or *separata* with the photo book. Distance gets physically inscribed in the book with this caesura. In fact, words and images here appeared coupled and divorced to a varying extent. While the book kept the site-specific character, the exhibition did not, and included a selection of Kawauchi's previous, more scattered projects (*Utatane, Illuminance,* and *Ametsuchi*). The exhibited images were likewise sequenced in an order different than in the book variant.

Just as the images in *Cui Cui* were far from being snapshots on their own vernacular terms, the photographs of *The River Embraced Me* were, too. The pictures encompass interpersonal intimacies and communities in an unconventional way; they are 'someone's memory place'. The stress falls not on the proximal, but the distant. At the centre lies an absence that is at odds with the sacred presence that came to appear in her earlier project. Still, these images are pregnant with emotions, memories, and the words that conveyed them before mutating like butterflies at the photographer's hands. *The River Embraced Me*

---

32   Kawauchi, *The River Embraced Me*.

cultivates the intensity of the indirect object — in the shape of an ekphrasis in reverse.

But the reversal was not straightforward, or, rather, the substance was not stable and then merely evaporated and condensed. The solicited memory text was a script that eventually was performed in 'visiting someone's place'. The artist retraced movements, thoughts. Her steps' echo in the landscape's architecture of remembrance unleashed the emotions that the memories had recorded. Mimicry and re-enactment mechanics came in play together with involuntary memory in a distorted 'madeleine effect'. Reverberation triggered Kawauchi's own memories; these partially overlapped the recalled fragments, and so — reportedly, at least in the photographer's inner chamber— appeared the images doubly exposed.

This ambitious search was not for a definite kind of temporality, but for time itself: 'Rivers can be a metaphor for time itself, and I want the exhibition to be a place to feel the flow of time', said Kawauchi.[33] The convertibility of past memories into the present of re-enactment, and the certain future drift of these photographs in works to come anchored *The River Embraced Me* far away from the documentary and its preterite.

All along the transmutation *The River Embraced Me* capitalizes on the in-between. It is between one's memory and someone else's capturing, between text and image, that is, between media, and between the lines of the text, in the interlinear and the interstitial. The call for room to recall and air to imagine is not new to this project. Now we breathed the air in between the lines of the multivocal poem; we saw the image and the space between the image and its text on the wall. The potency of Kawauchi's photo books lies in the flipping, between the pages, and in the fringes of images. *The River Embraced Me* thrives in this gap and makes, once again, imperfection photography's finest fire.

---

33 Kawauchi, *The River Embraced Me*.

Inbuilt Errans
What Is and Is Not 'Radical Indifference'
ZAIRONG XIANG

This 'inbuilt errans' points to the two entangled semantic levels, that is, errantry and error.[1] Errans as the erroneous wandering or the drifting error complicates the celebration of movement, fluidity, or 'queering' (at least, queer in its impoverished sense of the flexible gender/sexuality, flirting dangerously with neoliberalism). The rigid or stubborn aspect of *errans*, its erroneousness not only accompanies but also enables its errancy. This 'rigidity' requires scare quotes in order to mark the ways in which these qualities might collapse when a question of 'to whom?' is posed. Similarly, if indifference suggests a strong intention, *radical* indifference points to something else, something unplanned, ambiguous, and weak while at the same time strategic, rigid, and powerful.

SNAPSHOTS

¿Tienes Pluma?

One insignificant moment in those early days of discovering the mesmerizing world of online dating when I was pursuing a master's degree

---

[1] Errans: Latin gerund that assembles two interrelated notions: errantry and error.

in Granada, Spain: a Granada local started chatting with me in a popular gay dating website *Bakala*. My interlocutor was quite amazed to find himself talking with someone from China. His knowledge of China was as sparse as my knowledge of Spain/Spanish even though I had been living there for some months. Now the conversation started, we asked each other our preferences, sexual fantasies and fetishisms. One message from him arrived abruptly and really confused me: '¿tienes pluma?'

With my very limited knowledge of the Spanish language back then, I did not understand immediately what he meant because I didn't (even) know the word 'pluma'. I looked it up in the dictionary. One of the many meanings of 'pluma' is feather or fountain pen. Feather? Pen? It is very unlikely that he was making a mad-woman-in-the-attic pun on pen and penis, nor was I aware of the 'sounding' practice, namely inserting something into the urethra, be it a fountain pen or a feather. My ignorance of the Spanish expression combined with a misconception that a definition standing alone in the dictionary could provide access to the real meaning of any language, made me courageously opt for a quick interpretation: 'tienes pluma?' could mean, 'do you have feather?'. But what would 'do you have feather?' mean? He wants to be tickled?

Why would he want to know if I have a feather or a fountain-pen? None of the direct translations made much sense. I therefore rushed to interpret the phrase 'tienes pluma' — do you have feather — as 'are you hairy?'. Without much hesitation, I answered somewhat proudly, 'cómo voy a tener pluma, soy Chino!' thinking that it meant: 'how could I be hairy? I am Chinese!'. Now, much better versed in Spanish, I can imagine the confused face of my interlocutor: why does being ethnically Chinese guarantee that he does not *tiene pluma*? 'Cómo voy a tener pluma' was articulated with pride and to the ears/eyes of my interlocutor, it must have sounded particularly strange, as strange as the question 'tienes pluma' had sounded to me two minutes earlier.

'Sadako of the People!'

A meme video went viral among Chinese Internet users.[2] The ghost or 'vengeful spirit' (怨靈) named Sadako of the famous Japanese horror film *Ring* is sent by the Japanese army to a Chinese village as a 'secret weapon' to kill members of the Chinese anti-Japanese resistance front.[3] Upon her iconic arrival, that is, crawling outside of the film screen into 'reality', the communist leader welcomes her as the 'comrade'. Dressed in a long white gown with her face hidden under long dark hair, her signature appearance provokes zero fear but full compassion from the other villagers. An elderly woman laments, 'what a good girl and look how terribly the Japanese have humiliated her!' The party leader shakes her hands that were reached out to strangle him (like most vengeful ghosts would do) and promises her 'comrade, trust us! We will definitely avenge the wrong done to you [by the Japanese]!' A male villager-soldier notices her bare feet and shouts, 'look, she doesn't even have shoes! So awful those Japanese! Take, comrade, wear mine!'

Titled '讓貞子生活在我們抗日的這片沃土上，她的心再冰冷也會融化' [Let Sadako live on our fertile land of anti-Japanese struggle and even her frozen heart can be melted], this meme video combines styles of well-known anti-Japanese and anti-Kuomintang films as well as communist revolutionary songs, such as 'Sing a Mountain Song to the [Communist] Party' and 'The Red Detachment of Women'. Wholeheartedly welcomed by the humble villagers who urge her 'don't live in the well, come live with us', Sadako experiences a successful integration and becomes a communist fighter. After witnessing the Japanese bombing of the Chinese village that kills almost everyone, Sadako reappears (again out of the film screen) in the Japanese military headquarter and is hailed as 'the great secret weapon' by the Japanese invaders and their Chinese collaborator. To everyone's surprise, Sadako tears off her white gown and appears in the Chinese

---

2   '讓貞子生活在我們抗日的這片沃土上，她的心再冰冷也會融化' (Let Sadako live on our fertile land of anti-Japanese struggle and even her frozen heart can be melted), online meme video, YouTube, n.d., <https://youtu.be/2gxptjIYRjE> [accessed 29 March 2022].

3   *Ring*, dir. by Hideo Nakata (Ringu/Rasen Production Committee, 1998).

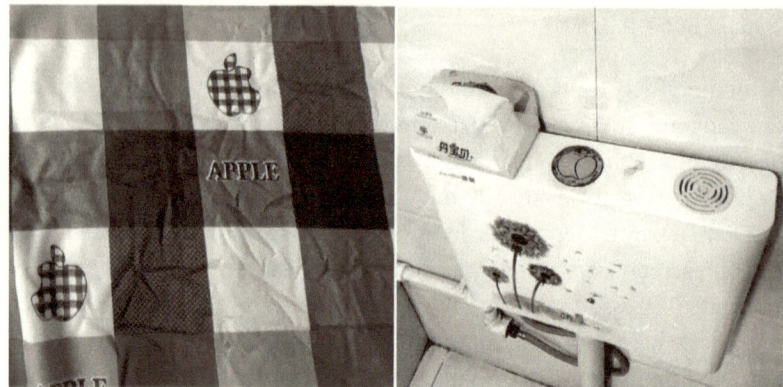

Figure 1. Bedspread in Guiyang, China, and restaurant toilet in South-Eastern region of China, both photographed by the author.

liberation army outfit, opens fire and kills the enemies. The video ends with Sadako posing in typical revolutionary posture with a passionate voice-over hailing: 'Roar, bullets of justice! Revenge, Sadako of the people!'

iFlush, iSheet

The two photos in Figure 1 were taken by me during a trip back to China. The first one was found on an old bed in my hometown Guiyang. The second one was found in the toilet of a restaurant in the South-Eastern region populated mainly by Miao (Hmog) and Dong people. Both feature the famous logo of the US American electronic company Apple: an apple with a bite taken out of it. While in the first one, the iconic logo is filled with cross-patterns and used as a decorative motif for the striped bed sheet, in the second photo, the apple is divided in two and serves as the flush buttons of the toilet. These iSheets and iFlushes belong to a big family of the so called 'Shanzhai' (山寨), together with 'NOKLA' and 'HiPhone' mobile phones or 'Harry Potter and the Chinese Overseas Students at Hogwarts' novel.

THEORIZATIONS

These story could stop here, sufficiently open for interpretation. What happens from now on might indeed be quite irrelevant to the misunderstanding in Granada, misidentification during the anti-Japanese war, and the misplacement in the Chinese factories that produce both iPhones and HiPhones.

The theorization would largely betray these instances in which something that I would call 'radical indifference' occurs. Yet 'betray' is a strong word that betrays the reason behind the textual procession from 'snapshots' to 'theorization'. In the particular case of 'radical indifference' (and other similar instances that are elusive and fleeting), theorization spoils something that, once it's theorized, is lost. As Lady Bracknell, the aunt who certainly is an aunt-in-drag, of Oscar Wilde's *The Importance of Being Earnest*, succinctly points out: 'Ignorance is like a delicate exotic fruit; touch it and the bloom is gone.' Since Lady Bracknell sounds very much in drag, her statement needs to be heard in multiple quotation marks. *The Importance of Being Earnest* brings out, through a dazzling pun inside and outside the play, a constant displacement between name and 'thing', that is to say, empties out any certainty of 'identity', let alone an 'earnest' one. The emptiness that is nevertheless not a *nothing* might resonate with 'the queer' in Lee Edelman's sense. What I want to contemplate here, however, is a more literal hole, which will cause things to crumble and lose their presumed certainty.

~

窾 /Qiao: pronounced as 'ciao';
penetrable cave; bodily orifice.

Qiao 1

窾/Qiao is the word I choose to connote the 'hole' that troubles. Etymologically a cave that is penetrable in Chinese, it is the technical word for 'bodily orifice', one in which sexual differences collapse

Figure 2. Hexagram Tai.

in a superposing hole. In Traditional Chinese Medicine (TCM), the human body in its healthy state is often compared to the hexagram Tai (泰卦) of 易經, *I-Ching* or the *Classic of Changes*.[4] If we let the old English rendering of 'Yi' (易), 'I' of *I-Ching* fall on the ground, we get the basic component of the hexagrams: a stroke: —, which is also the Chinese word for 'one': 一. Lao Tzu, the quasi-mythological founding father of Daoist philosophy, states in *Daodejing*: 'Dao gives birth to one, one to two, two to three, three to one-thousand things' [道生一，一生二，二生三，三生萬物].

One therefore becomes two: there are two kinds of strokes that respectively represent yin and yang, the fundamental propensities of the universe according to Chinese philosophy. Yin is represented by an open line: – – and yang by a full one: —. Yin and yang are in fact the same thing seen from different perspectives. Lao Tzu continues, 'The ten-thousand things carry yin and embrace yang' [万萬物負陰而抱陽]. While yin suggests the propensity to solidify and concretize (which I call identity-formation), the yang propensity is about the tendency to liquefy and vaporize (which, for lack of better words in English, I would call 'queering'). Yin is the tendency in which H_2O as water is turning into ice while Yang is water turning into steam and vaporizing. Each hexagram of the *I-Ching* is made of a free combination

---

4   In 1924, German sinologist Richard Wilhelm published a highly acclaimed translation of the book of changes: *I Ging. Das Buch der Wandlungen*, trans. by Richard Wilhelm, 2 vols (Jena: Eugen Diederichs, 1924). Produced with the help of his Chinese colleague Lao Naixuan, Wilhelm's translation was in turn translated into English in 1950 by Cary F. Baynes and accompanied by an equally influential foreword by Carl Gustav Jung: *The I Ching; or, Book of Changes*, trans. by Cary F. Baynes, foreword by C. G. Jung, Bollingen Series, 19 (New York: Pantheon Books, 1950).

of two trigrams, which in turn are formed by a free combination of the two basic yinyang strokes. In the case of the Hexagram Tai, we find an all-yin trigram composed entirely of yin strokes on the upper level and the all-yang trigram below on the lower level.

The human body in TCM is known through its nine orifices, which are believed to connect with its five inner organs. In one of the classic texts of TCM, *The Yellow Emperor's Inner Canon: Simple Questions* [黃帝內經 - 素聞], Chapter 4, *Jinkui zhenyan* 金匱真言 (the true words from the golden closet), records Qibo the erudite doctor's answer to the yellow emperor Huandi's question: 'The five depots correspond to the four seasons. Do all of them have [something specific] that they collect and receive?' [五臟應四時，各有收益乎？].[5] Qibo's explanation revolves around a seasonal correspondences between five inner organs that explains the connectivity and correspondence between the inner organs (五臟) and the nine bodily orifices (竅), which can be summarized in the following schema[6]:

East — Green-Blue — Liver — Eyes
South — Red — Heart — Ears
Centre — Yellow — Spleen — Mouth
West — White — Lung — Noses
North — Black — Kidney — Two Yin Orifices

The last correspondence in the cardinal point North in particular states:

北方黑色，入通於腎，開竅於二陰，藏精於腎，故病在谿。

The North; black color. Having entered it communicates with the kidneys. It opens an orifice in the two yin [sites]. (Note 49: i.e., the outlets for urine and stool)
It stores essence in the kidneys.
Hence the disease [it brings forth] is in the ravines.[7]

---

5   *Huang Di Nei Jing Su Wen: An Annotated Translation of Huang Di's Inner Classic — Basic Questions*, ed. by Paul U. Unschuld, 2 vols (Berkeley: University of California Press, 2011), I, Chapter 4: 'Discourse on the True Words in the Golden Chest', pp. 83–94 (p. 91).
6   See *Huang Di Nei Jing Su Wen*, pp. 91–93.
7   *Huang Di Nei Jing Su Wen*, p. 93. The editors, Paul U. Unschuld and others, add in note 50, affixed to this passage: '*Su wen* 58 has "The large meeting points of flesh are the

This inner-outer connectivity is illustrated using the hexagram Tai of the *I-Ching*. We observe that the upper trigram made of three open and thus yin lines, representing six orifices, that is, three pairs of orifices of the body: namely the eyes, the ears, and the nostrils; whereas the lower trigram consisting of three yang whole lines represents three single orifices of the body: the mouth, the genitalia, and the anus. The philtrum between these two cosmic realms of yin yang is called 人中, the middle point of the human (body). Yang Yu in *Shanju Xinyu* (山居新語) states succinctly '人中者，以自此而上，眼、耳、鼻皆雙竅，自此而下，口暨二便皆單竅，成一《泰》卦也' (quoted in Qian p.25). That is to say, the human body is made sense of through its nine *qiao*-orifices. Penis is considered to be one of them, undifferentiated from vagina. Anatomically speaking, the penis does contain a hollow space. Considering the urethra, the penis *is* an orifice.

Charlotte Furth calls it the 'generative body' based on her reading of *Huangdi Neijing* or *Yellow Emperor's Inner Classics*.[8] What allows for this in-differentiation or under-differentiation is the bodily orifices (in Chinese, the *qiao*/竅) in which the well-known sexual differences between man and woman are collapsed into a hole. Different from the one-sex model detected by Thomas Laqueur in his history of the Western body, the body-of-orifices is not one based on the model of the male sex.[9]

By representing the human body through its nine orifices, the ancient model announces a radical account of the body that understands that, to quote Paul Beatriz Preciado, 'el sistema tradicional de la representación sexo/género *se caga*'.[10] 'Tradicional', of course, points to a specific tradition. Often only the Western tradition does not feel the

---

valleys; the small meeting points of flesh are the ravines. It is in the parting of the flesh where the ravines and valley meeting points are located." 955/35: "谿谷 is the location in the flesh where water flows and stagnates. Hence in case of diseases affecting the spleen, these 'ravines' are influenced and edemas develop. Li Nian'e commented: '谿 is where the water flows and stagnates.'"

8   Charlotte Furth, *A Flourishing Yin: Gender in China's Medical History, 960–1665* (Berkeley: University of California Press, 1999), in particular Chapter 1: 'The Yellow Emperor's Body', pp. 19–58.

9   Thomas Laqueur, *Making Sex: Body and Gender from the Greeks to Freud* (Cambridge, MA: Harvard University Press, 1990).

10 Paul B. Preciado, *Manifiesto contra-sexual. Prácticas subversivas de identidad sexual*, trans. by Julio Díaz and Carolina Meloni (Madrid: Opera Prima, 2002), p. 27.

need to qualify itself as such. And as we can see, one of the most ancient models of the body used in a medicine that also calls itself 'traditional', does not have a 'sex/gender system' that needs to shit on itself. Of course, this is not a celebration of the 'traditional' as stable and unchanging, outside of history in blissful stillness for the Western nostalgia to indulge its orientalism *and* its critique of orientalism.[11] Anyone who is familiar with TCM knows that it has a complex regime of gender regulation including *Fuke*, a department that could be translated as gynecology.

Qiao 2

Qiao is pronounced like the Italian word 'ciao', which is used as both 'hi' and 'bye'. This double meaning of salutation and farewell shares an unexpected affinity with 'qiao', apart from having the same pronunciation.

I want to return to that moment of 'blissful ignorance' and try to understand the resistive power that is granted in the very moment of the *failure* of understanding. This points to a fundamentally anti-fundamentalist feature of language: its inbuilt errans. Its floating re-signifying process and its rigidity in meaning. When I say language, I mean languaging, which also takes the complex process of representation, interpellation, identification, and dis-identification into consideration.

Only after spending some more time in Spain and with a better command of Spanish, I understood that 'tener pluma' is a slang among gays in peninsular Spanish. It means: being effeminate, probably closely related to the colorful feathers that drag queens, the 'professional homosexuals' use. 'Tener pluma' refers to a kind of embodiment of faggotry (mariconada).

My answer to the Granadino's question now sounds completely absurd. 'Como voy a tener pluma, soy Chino!' If being Chinese and not being hairy might have some logic and empirical ground, although

---

[11] See Zairong Xiang, 'Oracle from 2018: Transdualism, or the A/History of Yin-Yang', *Heichi Magazine*, 23 December 2021 <http://www.heichimagazine.org/en/articles/1067/oracle-from-2018-zairong-xiang-transdualism-or-the-a-history-of-yin-yang> [accessed 29 March 2022].

even that can be contested, being Chinese and being effeminate (or for that matter, being hairy and being effeminate) do not have much of a connection. After spending some considerable time in the gay world of the West however, I have been routinely discriminated against, for the sheer ethnic identification as the 'Asian' (although 'Chinese' often stands as a separate racial category and 'Asian' is a very loose category). I have learnt that the Chinese man or, for that matter, the conveniently generalized ethnic 'Asian' man, for the racist gay mainstream in the Western world, is the quintessential embodiment of 'tener pluma', being effeminate. 'Tener pluma', Asian or otherwise, gets on the nerves of the 'straight-acting' gay mainstream.

The Granada moment of misunderstanding strikes me as miraculously innocent, on both side of the absurd conversation. At that particular space and time, there was little knowledge from either side about the other: my anonymous interlocutor in Granada did not immediately assume that since I am Chinese, *tengo pluma*. He checked it first as he would do with any other person. I didn't shun from outing myself as the hair-less Chinese (*tener pluma* or not) without knowing that this could have gotten me nowhere. This trivial instance later struck me as a form of, albeit precarious, resistance: an unplanned and involuntary resistance to racial stereotyping.

Apart from an interest in critical observation of the ethnographical event, the main purpose of online dating for me was to get some good sex. The promise of promiscuity in online dating and casual sexual encounters in general through cruising and other means, however, has grown gradually bitter, and the sole purpose of getting a good fuck has left behind more frustration than satisfaction. The critico-ethnographical wish to observe has gained more power over the years than the wish for sexual satisfaction. The initiation into the racist discourse of the gay mainstream in Western Europe, where I have lived for seven years, has been overall a humiliating experience. Instances of 'No Asians', explicitly stated or not, emerge as not incidental or singular but widely enacted. The representation of the (desirable) gay male in popular media has almost unanimously agreed to exclude any Asian subjects. And for this statement, I refuse to give concrete examples to allow critical nuances. It is neither nuance nor soothing, even if it is the good-intended 'Really? I think you are exaggerating!' — uttered sometimes with an example of an exception: 'but my friend Joe is really into Asian', or 'well, many Asians are not into Asians themselves', which could suggest that the fact that some of the Asianphobes are Asian themselves (which is empirically grounded) makes the critique of racism invalid or unnecessary.

After these years being interpellated into the racial apartheid in the gay world of the West, I could no longer reply to the gay world with the same degree of innocence and conviction: 'como voy a tener pluma, soy Chino!' No matter how much I try these days, *tener pluma* in that sentence can no longer be unlearnt as 'having feather — being hairy'. The 'effeminate gayasian' was stabilized as a stubborn marker in my self-identification and disidentification once I became part of the game, as I participate in it or as I resist it, by for example, proving that Asians are not effeminate, or by appropriating effeminacy as empowering 'turning the master's tool around to dismantle the master's house'.

The Granada story is one of ignorance and lack of information. It was not intentional and was entirely unplanned. I couldn't help but miss the point. 'Sadako of the People', however, is a different case, that of a misrecognition. What lets Sadako down in her attempt to scare and strangle the Chinese villagers is, paradoxically, her 'monstrosity'. The villagers clearly see her as one of them, the disfranchised ones who are suffering under the imperialist atrocities committed by the Japanese. Their misrecognition of her monstrosity is based on solidarity, that is to say, on identification, which in turn serves the purpose of community building towards the common struggle if not that of forming a kind of class consciousness to be mobilized against Japanese imperialism, which, as the video later shows, has sent Sadako back as a secret weapon to scare/strangle the Japanese. The first example shows that there is no conscious resistent subjectivity prior to or later than the resistent moment of 'radical indifference'. Ignorance in the first instance, however, cannot be transplanted to the second instance. There is nothing ignorant about the villagers' identification with the ghost, the repressed. 'Radical indifference' is not always based on a model of ignorance.

What links the floating signifier to the fixed error, the infinite potential of misunderstanding to the rigid 'degree zero' of the hole? The rigid or stubborn aspect of *errans* — its erroneousness — not only accompanies but also enables its errancy. If 'wrong' is to stray off course, the straying itself is made possible by a reference point to that which is 'wrong'. This 'rigidity' requires scare quotes in order to mark the ways in which these qualities might collapse when a question of 'wrong/off course to whom?' is posed. Similarly, if indifference suggests a strong intention, *radical* indifference points to something else, something unplanned, ambiguous, and weak — while at the same time strategic, rigid, and powerful.

This 'inbuilt errans' points to its two entangled semantic levels, that is, errantry and error. Errans as the erroneous wandering or the drifting error complicates any celebration of movement, fluidity, or 'queering' (at least, queer in its impoverished sense of the flexible gender/sexuality, flirting dangerously with the demands of neoliberalism).

What makes the incident with the *pluma* in Granada particularly unforgettable is perhaps the unintended subversiveness my misunderstanding and mistranslation of the question 'tienes pluma?' entails. Likewise, in the Chinese video meme, the villagers of anti-Japanese struggle completely misrecognize the point of Sadako's 'scary' looks. She is seen as one of them, *disfranchised* and having the same enemy. Misunderstanding in the first instance and misrecognition in the second all depend on a version of what is correct in terms of linguistic signification or visual representation. Yet the dialectics of the mutual dependency between correct and erroneous, rigidity and fluidity is not what interests me here.

ON RADICAL INDIFFERENCE

The particular form of misunderstanding or mishearing I want to analyse here can be rephrased as a kind of indifference, a 'radical indifference'. However, it cannot be paraphrased as 'I don't care'. Resistance is at best its implication and consequence, but not its intention. Radical indifference as resistance is not really a strategy in the sense that it does not follow a conscious and voluntary plan. 'Resistance' or even 'weak resistance' are almost too heavy in this regard. Radical indifference comes from an error that cannot be corrected: a stubborn taint that cannot be cleaned and/or an elusive possibility of sullying that can never been ruled out.

It is worth noting here that 'radical indifference' does not heroically resist interpellation. We shall have a quick look at the concept of 'interpellation'. Rey Chow develops Louis Althusser's classical notion of interpellation to bear an understanding of the process of racialization. She argues, 'an ethnic person's practice of internalizing a cultural stereotype of herself may conveniently be explained by way of [...] interpellation'.[12] Yet, distancing herself with Slavoj Žižek from 'the usual critical move premised on a resistive subject or individualistic agency', Chow contends, 'what the subject always resists is this *terror of complete freedom* rather than the ideological, institutional process of being interpellated'.[13] Despite the rather unexamined privilege of being afraid of the so-called 'complete freedom', what is convincing in Chow as in Žižek's argument is their critique of the assumption of a subject prior to the resistance against interpellation. What is not convincing and politically dangerous is to assume, reiterate, and therefore reify interpellation's omnipotence and its intelligibility.

Instead of asking Chow's set of questions: 'Does the ethnic have a choice of not responding? What happens when she responds? [...] What happens if she does not respond?',[14] I insist that the ethnic might not understand or simply mishear the hailing. 'hey you!' could be heard as 'Hey Jude!'. Or she might not even know that she is an 'ethnic subject'. She might not speak English (well enough) to understand that 'hey you' means 'hey you' or for that matter, that 'hé, vous, là-bas!' means 'hey you'. The hailing might be heard as, say, '嘿呦 (*hei you*)!' — an exclamation commonly used in Chinese to express surprise and/or pain. For example, the 'ethnic' subject might have heard 'hey you' as '*hei you*' and thought that the policeman had broken his throat or leg and that the sudden pain provoked him to groan: '嘿呦 [hei you]!'

If until now it sounds like 'too much freedom', in the sense of being terrifying (as Žižek and Chow suggest), a kind of discursive horror vacui, it must be emphasized that the freedom to be indifferent

---

12   Rey Chow, *The Protestant Ethnic and the Spirit of Capitalism* (New York: Columbia University Press, 2002), p. 108.
13   Ibid., pp. 109–10.
14   Ibid., p. 110.

is grounded in the material conditions of im/possibility. For example, one does not have a good command of a (foreign) language or is ignorant of relevant information and context. That is to say, radical indifference dwells at a space-time (instant or constant) that is radically *different* in relation to a particular ideological and discursive system that interpellates.

Radical indifference as a strategy for resistance cannot be planned or organized and can hardly be appropriated and commodified as portable, as universally applicable. Erik Bordeleau, via Isabelle Stengers and Gilles Deleuze, astutely articulates a similar model of resistance through the figure of the idiot:

> The idiot does not resist for the sake of resisting: as practitioner, she is simply in her element *'à son affaire'*, absorbed by her matter of concern in ways that are never reducible to any common good. The idiot is but another way of affirming the radical locality or mattering of practices.[15]

The 'radical locality' of the 'idiot' leads me to think about radical indifference as a central feature of 'radical elsewheres'. José Rabasa develops this concept through several works in which he engages with Nahua culture, especially the pictorial writing system *tlacuiloliztli* of the pre-Hispanic Mesoamerica. He argues: 'The Mesoamerican key [...] remains inaccessible to modern scholars even in their hermeneutic willingness to understand the world of the *tlacuilo* [the native painter/writer, Z. X.] in and on her terms.'[16] Rabasa uses '*elsewheres*' to theorize 'a spatio-temporal difference that cannot be conflated with the knowledge we Western-trained academics construe about objects and subjects [...] that remain — in fact, must remain — outside the languages and methods we privilege in our positive knowledge, hermeneutics, or ontological definition of the world'.[17]

What I am trying to do in thinking about 'radical indifference', is to push Rabasa's *elsewheres* further (or in fact, *closer*) and envisage a

---

15   Erik Bordeleau, 'Soulful Sedentarity: Tsai Ming-Liang at Home at the Museum', *Studies in European Cinema*, 10.2–3 (2013), pp. 179–94 (p. 186).
16   José Rabasa, *Tell Me the Story of How I Conquered You: Elsewheres and Ethnosuicide in the Colonial Mesoamerican World* (Austin: University of Texas Press, 2011), p. 204.
17   Ibid., p. 1.

spatio-temporal *elsewhere within*, an irreducible, unconquerable space-time of radical in/difference, of an uncorrectable error within. In this sense, radical in/difference brings about not only the figure of the 'idiot' but also the feminine, the pagan, the queer, the animal, the monstrous, and the Mr. Hyde. Here is where a radical elsewhere resides not radically *elsewhere* but rather *inside*, in-built, *hydden*.

Like *plumas*, words float and wander. An instant of acoustic vibration, the word is (mis)heard, but is already gone. Once the written word is seen as a scribble, as itself, it escapes meaning. 'Radical' misheard or misread as *radicalis*, a root and an origin, secretly resides in the closet of linguistic mastery, threatening to come out and stain its nationalistic, racist, and queer-phobic hygiene. Inside the here and now, the metaphysics of presence, the logos, the phallus, the law, whatever you want to call it, there is always a stubborn and rigid space of indifference to the process of interpellation and signification. 'We are here; we are queer.'

Radical indifference is a decolonial response to the 'there is nothing outside of modernity'. 'Como voy a tener pluma, soy Chino' did neither participate in nor resist the racial stereotyping of the Asian. The Granada moment exemplifies the 'radical indifference', especially its resistent power that is grounded in the possibility of misunderstanding, by an error that is inherent to language or any other process of socialization.

Radical Indifference as a political strategy: again, aligning with the indeterminacy of the hole (*trou, tour* — towards destruction/construction), is not only a strategy of the 'subaltern' (although the examples I give might suggest so) but can be misused by governments and the powerful as an excuse of, for example, not providing basic needs, being indifferent to refugees, etc. Hence the 'radicality' of radical indifference. It can never become a planned, conscious strategy, which in turn could be co-opted. That is, much like the subaltern for Gayatri Chakravorty Spivak, the elsewhere in Rabasa, 'radical indifference', once co-opted, categorized, and strategized, loses its radicality. This space of inappropriatability, impossible to educate, to colonize, to inscribe a meaning that does not betray the thing described (objectified?) is radically outside, in however fragile a state. This points to the core of language and languaging, the process in which that radically indifference space is both lost (representation-sceptic) and retained (precisely because of being lost). The process of losing it pertains to errantry and the process of rigid fixity pertains to errancy (error), the hole without solution.

WHAT 'RADICAL INDIFFERENCE' IS AND IS NOT:

> 一颗螺丝掉在地上
> A screw fell to the ground
> 在这个加班的夜晚
> In this dark night of overtime
> 垂直降落，轻轻一响
> Plunging vertically, lightly clinking
> 不会引起任何人的注意
> It won't attract anyone's attention
> 就像在此之前
> Just like last time
> 某个相同的夜晚
> On a similar night
> 有个人掉在地上
> When someone plunged to the ground
>
> 《一颗螺丝掉在地上》
> 'A Screw Fell to the Ground'
> 9 January 2014
> by Xu Lizhi 许立志[18]

The Foxconn Technology Group, the world's largest provider of electronics manufacturing services, made global headlines in 2001 for the collective suicides among its workforce. The Chinese factory manufacturing the iPhone for Apple was known worldwide. In 2010 alone, 18 young assembly workers attempted suicide, with 14 of them succeeding. The deplorable working condition, unfulfilled promises of benefits, and the psychological blackmailing from exacting managers are among the main reasons behind these suicides. Both Foxconn's and Apple's responses to these unfortunate cases have been jaw-droppingly

---

18 Text in original Chinese and English translation (with modifications) are all quoted from 'The Poetry and Brief Life of a Foxconn Worker: Xu Lizhi (1990–2014)', *Nao blog* on *Libcom.org* <http://libcom.org/blog/xulizhi-foxconn-suicide-poetry> [accessed 4 August 2017].

poor and evasive. Since 2010, Foxconn is reported to have built nets around high-rise buildings in its factories to catch the falling bodies. Steve Jobs was asked to comment on the collective suicides, which he found okay since the number of dead seemed to him much lower than the national average.[19]

Xu Lizhi also known as the 'Foxconn poet', who committed suicide in 2014, wrote, not long before his death, the poem 'A Screw Fell to the Ground' quoted above. 'It won't attract anyone's attention', neither the screw that fell from the assembly line to the ground nor the young worker's life that 'plunged to the ground', would attract too much attention from 'anyone'. It was another 'dark night of overtime' with the uneventful falling of the screw that made a light clinking sound. The repetition and its seeming unimportance are reinforced by 'last time/on a night like this'.

If the iSheets, iFlushes and HiPhones could be temporarily theorized as a kind of 'radical indifference' in the practice of counterfeiting/shanzhai, in which the creators freely borrow (a word in Chinese that involves the word for 'fake') signifiers as shared knowledge rather than individual property, the bitter, harsh, and dark surroundings where these almost campy 'radical indifferences' are most common, is not.

---

19   Brian Merchant, who had managed to sneak into the Foxconn Longhua complex, published his findings in *The One Device: The Secret History of the iPhone* (New York: Little, Brown and Company, 2017); the Guardian published an extract from the book: Merchant, 'Life and Death in Apple's Forbidden City', *Guardian*, 18 June 2017 <https://www.theguardian.com/technology/2017/jun/18/foxconn-life-death-forbidden-city-longhua-suicide-apple-iphone-brian-merchant-one-device-extract> [accessed 20 September 2017].

Errant Counterpublics
'Solidarność' and the Politics of the Weak
EWA MAJEWSKA

> The cyborg incarnation is
> outside salvation history.
>
> Donna Haraway, *Cyborg Manifesto*

> It was not long ago that Poland's name echoed throughout the whole civilized world, that its fate stirred every soul and provoked excitement in every heart. Lately one no longer hears very much about Poland – since Poland is a capitalist country. Do we now want to know what became of the old rebel, where historic destiny steered it?
>
> Rosa Luxemburg, *The Industrial Development of Poland* [1898]

> Errant, he challenges and discards the universal.
>
> Édouard Glissant, *Poetics of Relation*

This chapter follows the unfolding of a particular event in recent Polish history — the beginnings of the 'Solidarność' movement (1980–81)

— as a transformation of the public sphere by weak, non-heroic, and errant counterpublics. In the following pages I discuss the early days of 'Solidarność' as non-Western, transversal, and emancipatory counterpublics, thus allowing decolonial and feminist arguments. I address theories of Jürgen Habermas, Alexander Kluge and Oskar Negt, and Nancy Fraser in order to build the notion of counterpublics, and notions of errantry, *mestisaje* and territory, developed by such authors as Édouard Glissant, Gloria Anzaldúa, Gilles Deleuze, and Félix Guattari. The work conducted here can be seen as a search for new, transversal political theoretical tools crossing geopolitical borders, as well as overcoming the limitations caused by gender and class inequalities. Jacques Rancière's theory of disagreement is a vital element of this effort. The concept of 'errant counterpublics' suggested here is a result of analysing these theoretical possibilities in connection to a particular political mobilization.

1. ERRANT AS IN POWERLESS

In the famous essay 'Power of the Powerless' by Václav Havel, the Czech dissident and later also president of his country, a description of the former Eastern Bloc is proposed. It allows a reading of 'Solidarność' as a non-heroic and yet radical event, leading to a concept of 'errant counterpublics'. Havel offers 'an examination of the potential of the "powerless"' and argues that it 'can only begin with an examination of the nature of power in the circumstances in which these powerless people operate'.[1] He depicts the existing communist system around 1978 as so overwhelming that nothing can be done within its norms and structures, and a sense of 'dissent' so strong that it needs to be expressed. In the opening paragraph Havel paraphrases the first lines of the *Communist Manifesto*:

> A spectre is haunting Eastern Europe: the spectre of what in the West is called "dissent." This spectre has not appeared out of thin air. It is a natural and inevitable consequence of the present historical phase of the system it is haunting. It was born at a time when this system, for a thousand reasons, can no longer

---

[1] Václav Havel, 'Power of the Powerless', trans. by Paul Wilson, *International Journal of Politics*, 15.3–4 (Fall/Winter 1985–86), pp. 23–96 (p. 23).

base itself on the unadulterated, brutal, and arbitrary application of power, eliminating all expressions of nonconformity. What is more, the system has become so ossified politically that there is practically no way for such nonconformity to be implemented within its official structures.[2]

Havel depicts the world as governed by two superpowers, possessing claims to historical and ideological legitimacy, which do not need any 'heroic' confirmations. He argues that the Eastern Bloc has a very tacit and indirect way of inducing its main principles on the population: 'if an atmosphere of revolutionary excitement, heroism, dedication, and boisterous violence on all sides characterizes classical dictatorships, then the last traces of such an atmosphere have vanished from the Soviet bloc.'[3] Because of these characteristics of the Soviet Bloc, Havel decides to call it a 'post-totalitarian system'. He suggests a certain automatism whereby both ordinary citizens and state rulers function in a completely mechanical way. The image of a greengrocer suddenly contesting the *status quo* — central for Havel's essay — is not one of heroic bravery. It comes as a refusal to present a political slogan in the window and is depicted as 'a threat to the system not because of any physical or actual power he had, but because his action went beyond itself, because it illuminated its surrounding.'[4] Living in truth becomes Havel's formula for a possible political agency in the deheroicized post-totalitarian system: 'every free expression of life indirectly threatens the post-totalitarian system politically.'[5] Havel argues that the political confrontation does not happen between two superpowers in 1968, nor in the movement around Charta 77. The political power is with the state apparatus, the people do not have it. This causes a paradoxical tendency for a far greater political effectivity on the side of ordinary people, rather than professional politicians.

Such investment of all political power on the side of the sovereign is a very typical element of contemporary radical political theory. In the works of Giorgio Agamben, Slavoj Žižek, and Louis Althusser, the state apparatus is 'fully operational' all the time, while those submitted

---

2   Ibid.
3   Ibid., p. 27.
4   Ibid., p. 40.
5   Ibid., p. 43.

to it are deprived of any power and it is logically impossible to imagine them having any political agency at all. In *Who Sings the Nation-State?*, Judith Butler and Gayatri Chakravorty Spivak challenge this one-sided image of political agency, demonstrating that the oppressed and excluded actually generate potential for resistance.[6] In her discussion of Agamben's political theory, Butler stresses the importance of understanding life as political always, even under the restrictive measures of the sovereign. She argues:

> We can argue that the very problem is that life has become separated from the political (i.e. conditions of citizenship), but that formulation presumes that politics and life join only and always on the question of citizenship and, so, restricts the entire domain of bio-power in which questions of life and death are determined by other means.[7]

I believe that there are two important parts of her argument, one insisting on the inclusion of elements of the embodied social life, such as gender or ethnicity/race, in the realm of the political, and another, not detached from the first one, implying that life cannot be stripped of politics even as a bare life (Butler asks, whether life can be bare at all). Thus the notion of biopolitics seems impossible to combine with the concept of *homo sacer*. And what follows is that the very idea of stripping someone from all political agency is simply unthinkable, although the agency remaining after the sovereign's violent execution of his power might be weak, passive, or minimal.

Similarly, Antonio Negri's and Michael Hardt's theory of empire opens ways for the multitude to act even in the conditions of misery and exploitation.[8] In Jacques Rancière's meticulous depiction of French proletarians in the nineteenth century, we witness the same shift of power.[9] My reading of Havel is directly inspired by these authors and their reading of oppositional political agency as coming

---

6   Judith Butler and Gayatri Chakravorty Spivak, *Who Sings the Nation-State? Language, Politics, Belonging* (Calcutta: Seagull Books, 2007), p. 40.
7   Ibid., pp. 39–40.
8   Michael Hardt and Antonio Negri, *The Commonewalth* (Cambridge, MA: Harvard University Press, 2009).
9   Jacques Rancière, *Disagreement: Politics and Philosophy*, trans. by Julie Rose (Minneapolis: University of Minnesota Press, 2004).

not just from the structures of existing power, but also from the oppressed. Differently from Havel however, I think that these weak acts of resistance can sometimes lead to massive social mobilizations and political changes, and that they should not be seen as detached from one another, but rather as interconnected.

In Havel's words, genuine politics should happen on the level of 'life'. This sounds strikingly similar to the preoccupation of Oskar Negt and Alexander Kluge with the lived experience of proletarians in their theory of proletarian counter public spheres, published in 1972.[10] Havel's essay was written in 1978, it was smuggled to Poland in 1979, and in 1980, it performed the fantastic task of inspiring political opposition. Zbigniew Bujak, one of the key figures of the 'Solidarność' workers' unions, emphasizes the importance of Havel's text for the making of 'Solidarność' in 1980. He remembers it in rather heroic terms:

> Then came the essay by Havel. Reading it gave us the theoretical underpinnings for our activity. It maintained our spirits; we did not give up, and a year later — in August 1980 — it became clear that the party apparatus and the factory management were afraid of us. We mattered. And the rank and file saw us as leaders of the movement. When I look at the victories of Solidarity, and of Charter 77, I see in them an astonishing fulfilment of the prophecies and knowledge contained in Havel's essay.[11]

The management could not possibly be afraid of the workers. It had all the means necessary to stop their fight. Instead, what finally happened is a new constellation, a new assembly allowing more dialogical and experimental forms of agency. The direct cause for the strike on 15 August 1980 at the Shipyard in Gdańsk was the firing of Anna Walentynowicz, a crane operator respected and liked by many other workers, just three months before her retirement. Other factors were the rise of food prices and the workers' general sense of disempowerment on the level of their work conditions and their very limited

---

10 Oskar Negt and Alexander Kluge, *Public Sphere and Experience: Toward an Analysis of the Bourgeois and Proletarian Public Sphere*, trans. by Peter Labanyi, Jamie Owen Daniel, and Assenka Oksiloff (Minneapolis: University of Minnesota Press, 1993).
11 Zbigniew Bujak in Václav Havel, *Open Letters: Selected Writings 1965–1990*, ed. by Paul Wilson (New York: Knopf, 1991), p. 126.

possibilities of expressing dissent. It was a solidarity strike already in the sense of supporting a colleague and speaking up about basic daily matters. It should be remembered that at that time some 30% of the shipyard workers were women. It would be hard to say how many of them actually stayed in the shipyard for the two weeks of the strike that came later, but definitely many did. The workers of other professions, nurses and local transport drivers in particular, decided to back the Shipyard. What happened later was an avalanche of events, which I will discuss as the making of a proletarian, errant counterpublic.

2. ERRANT AS IN DECOLONIAL AND HETEROTOPIC

Connecting the postcolonial (or, more generally, the history of colonization) and the post-socialist or former East still seems extravagant or new. In most writings making such connection, an article from the year 2001 is quoted.[12] However, there are theories and entire paradigms that draw large-scale comparisons between the history of colonization and the development of Eastern Europe and there also exist direct encounters between individual representatives of these otherwise distant locations and contexts.

Several authors from Eastern Europe use postcolonial theories as a comparative context with the Soviet presence in their countries – politically, it leads to particularly strong anti-communist consequences, like in the work of Mykoła Riabczuk concerning Ukraine.[13] For others, the postcolonial references are necessary to depict Central Europe as a space in-between. Maria Janion analyses Polish history as one of a double experience of being colonized and colonizing, in the process of Christianization (around the year 1000, Christianity came to Poland, first as a conquest, then also as a more peaceful process, and it was spread in later centuries to the East) and industrialization.[14] These analyses emphasize the particularly perplexing routes of colonial processes, therefore shifting the usually linear postcolonial critique into a

---

12   David C. Moore, 'Is the Post- in Postcolonial the Post- in Post-Soviet? Toward a Global Postcolonial Critique', *PMLA*, 116.1 (2001), pp. 111–28.
13   Mykoła Riabczuk, *Ukraina. Syndrom postkolonialny* (Warszawa: Kolegium Europy Wschodniej im. Jana Nowaka-Jeziorańskiego, 2014).
14   Maria Janion, *Niesamowita Słowiańszczyzna* (Kraków: Wydawnictwo Literackie, 2006).

more rhizomatic one. And these approaches seem particularly inspiring and similar to the task of my own project.

In his *Poetics of Relation*, Édouard Glissant emphasizes the importance of 'the thinking of errantry and totality (relational, dialectical)'.[15] This way of combining the systemic dialectics and the antisystemic rhizomatic logics builds a particularly inspiring semantics that makes it possible to unpack the political mobilization of 'Solidarność' in Poland in 1980 without assimilating it to the West. It also enables a shift from an assimilative strategy of subsuming this mobilization as monolithic into a genuinely hybrid event with elements not only coming from different origins, but also never blending in an effort to become one.

Nomadism as presented by Glissant does not have happy and innocent roots. In the conquest, even the voyage — as in Homer's epics — there is an oppressive aspect, which errantry can escape. Between the slave ships and the forced stabilization of the Blacks suddenly transformed into mere commodities by the colonizers, we should imagine the brutalized 'arrowlike nomadism'.[16] Postcolonial thought and politics thus appear as a reactive force, directed at some uncertain prospect of reconciliation via the revisiting of the 'roots'. Errantry on the other hand, is neither renunciation nor frustration about the supposedly deterritorialized origins.[17] It is multilingual, as any relation, Glissant argues further.[18] It is discussed in relation to the famous notion of rhizome, which Deleuze and Guattari propose as an alternative to that of the root, one, which 'is not one', which has no centralized structure, and in which all elements matter. In Glissant, errantry is the 'poetics of relation'. What is perhaps most paradoxical, is the relation between the errant and totality: it is a dialectical relationship, in which claims are maintained and at the same time contradicted, in which the universal is at the same time particularized, and the individual shaped in relation. Such relationality, dialectics understood not as imposition of binary, petrified oppositions, but as a (historical and materialized) process of overcoming what at a given moment appears as contradiction, seems

---

15 Édouard Glissant, *Poetics of Relation*, trans. by Betsy Wing (Ann Arbor: University of Michigan Press, 1997), p. 18.
16 Ibid., pp. 11 and 5.
17 Ibid., p. 18.
18 Ibid., p. 19.

to be the essence of errantry. It is not guided by a concept of progress, rather by one of liberation or emancipation.

This kind of dialectics is actually quite typical for any form of decolonial thinking. Unlike postcolonial theory, in which the exposure of exclusion and its possibly never ending repercussions is always undermining any possibility of emancipatory projects, critical discourse, and/or reparative action, decolonial theory aims at legitimizing and projecting ways of building an alternative. The decolonial project is therefore similar to the concept of utopia, but leaning towards heterotopia, an alternative based on the existing norms of the often compliant and deeply non-utopian reality. Foucault depicted heterotopia as follows:

> There are also, and probably in every culture, in every civilization, real places, actual places, places that are designed into the very institution of society, which are sorts of actually realized utopias in which the real emplacements, all the other real emplacements that can be found within the culture are, at the same time, represented, contested, and reversed, sorts of places that are outside of all places, although they are actually localizable. [...]
>
> The heterotopia has the ability to juxtapose in a single real place several emplacements that are incompatible in themselves.[19]

Such a multiplicity of spaces is something that decolonial theorists also emphasize and juxtapose to the linear vision of the 'first, second, and third world' as well as to the supposed clarity of the dialectics. This does not necessarily mean rejecting Hegelianism entirely, however the notions of progress or development, central for the dialectics, are questioned or openly undermined. A great example of the vision of 'decolonial subjectivity' built on contradictions can be found in Gloria Anzaldúa, who often explicitly claimed unity in resistance and integrity in struggle: 'Who, me, confused? Ambivalent? Not so. Only your labels

---

19   Michel Foucault, 'Different Spaces', trans. by Robert Hurley, in *Foucault, Essential Works of Foucault, 1954-1984*, ed. by Paul Rabinow, 3 vols (New York: New Press, 1998–2001), II: *Aesthetics, Method, and Epistemology*, ed. by James D. Faubion (1998), pp. 175–85 (pp. 178 and 181).

split me'.[20] This sentence and Anzaldua's theory of *mestizaje* are a non-linear, unruly form of political agency, overcoming contradictions in a labour of emancipation. This seems to be a legitimate depiction of the lived experience of someone inhabiting a heterotopic space 'laden with qualities, a space that may also be haunted by fantasy'.[21] The intense and mixed spaces combined with the contradictory biographies unable to stretch and form a straight line tend to silence certain subjectivities, as Gayatri Spivak has shown, discussing the Subject of the West.[22]

3. ERRANT AS IN SEMI-PERIPHERAL

The beginnings of 'Solidarność' are in many ways twisted and erratic. They contain some major 'errors', such as an effective political mobilization of workers, women included, counting some ten million participants in a supposedly backwards country in Central Europe – all these are unforeseen elements in classical theories of the public sphere. As an early element of the collapse of the Soviet Bloc, which Claus Offe rightly characterized as a-theoretical, they did not bring much theory and perhaps they could not.[23] They have brought however an exciting plethora of erratic, iconoclastic, and contradictory effects, resulting in building one of the most exciting proletarian counterpublics in history.

In the 1950s and 60s, the Warsaw historical school of Witold Kula and Marian Malowist developed comparative studies of South American and Eastern European development in Early Modern times, highlighting not only dependence on the West but also a system of colonial relations with the East, that preserved some key elements of the feudal system much longer than in the West, blocking the development of industrial capitalism and/or constituting these regions of the world as providing supplementary resources for the West.[24] Their theory of dependency was later continued by Immanuel Wallerstein in his world-

---

20 Gloria Anzaldúa, 'La Prieta', in *The Gloria Anzaldúa Reader*, ed. by AnaLouise Keating (Durham, NC: Duke University Press, 2009), pp. 38–50 (p. 46).
21 Foucault, 'Different Spaces', p. 177.
22 Gayatri Chakravorty Spivak, *A Critique of Postcolonial Reason* (Cambridge, MA: Harvard University Press, 1999).
23 Claus Offe, 'Capitalism by Democratic Design? Democratic Theory Facing the Triple Transition in East Central Europe', *Social Research*, 71.3 (2004), pp. 501–28 (p. 503).
24 Przemysław Wielgosz, 'Od zacofania i spowrotem. Wprowadzenie do ekonomii politycznej peryferyjnego miasta przemysłowego', in *Futuryzm miast przemysłowych*, ed.

system theory, where the concept of semi-periphery appears in 1976.[25] In Wallerstein's view, the semi-periphery's basic characteristics are: trying to become a part of the core, making all efforts not to be seen as periphery, and being kept in an in-between position while being constantly lured with promises of joining the centre soon. Poland is enumerated as one, along Argentine and Brazil.

From its beginnings, the concept of 'semi-periphery' signified a double function — that of being colonized and colonizing; depending and forcing others into dependency. It actually captures the majority of contemporary states struggling between development and/or crisis and marginalization. In world-system theory, the semi-peripheries are situated between the core countries and the peripheries, between the zones of 'concentrated high-profit, high-wage and high technology diversified production' and spaces of 'concentrated low-profit, low-technology, low-wage'.[26] Wallerstein argued that the semi-peripheries act like peripheries to the core countries and like central countries to the peripheral ones; they are also capable of taking more advantage from global economic crisis than the two other kinds of countries. Wallerstein emphasized: 'In moments of world economic downturn, semi-peripheral countries can usually expand control of their home market at the expense of core producers, and expand their access to *neighboring* peripheral markets, again at the expense of core producers.'[27] He also explained how semi-peripheries that are successful in transforming the economic crisis into their gain need to appropriate the gains of other semi-peripheries to their advantage. The closing sentence of the paragraph where these matters are discussed reads as follows: 'This is simply the state-level adaptation of the traditional "dog eat dog" workings of capitalism. This is *not* "development" but successful expropriation of world surplus'.[28]

---

by Martin Kaltwasser, Ewa Majewska, and Kuba Szreder (Kraków: Korporacja ha! Art, 2007), pp. 241–53.

25 Immanuel Wallerstein, 'Semi-Peripheral Countries and the Contemporary World Crisis', *Theory and Society*, 3.4 (Winter 1976), pp. 461–83.
26 Ibid., p. 462.
27 Ibid., p. 464.
28 Ibid., p. 466.

Wallerstein's analysis of the semi-peripheral countries in many ways differs from the famous definition of Central Europe formulated by Milan Kundera in his 1984 essay 'The Tragedy of Central Europe', which is still one of the most popular expressions of Eastern European identity. Kundera's definition is built on a metaphysical distinction between the cultural and the social, where culture is understood as a supposedly immaterial realm: 'The identity of a people and of a civilization is reflected and concentrated in what has been created by the mind — in what is known as "culture"'.[29] Kundera emphasized that unlike Western Europeans, who seem to partly neglect the values of their tradition, Eastern Europeans are ready to 'die for Europe', as it was proven in all the actions of opposition against communism in Poland, Czechoslovakia, or Hungary between 1945 and 1990. It should be stressed that in the Marxist view presented by Wallerstein in *European Universalism* the precious 'universal' values of the West always prove to be particular or limited to the core countries and their inhabitants; they are constitutive of what Spivak aptly called the installation of the subject of the West as Subject.[30] Those who 'die for Europe' are therefore in fact victims of the ideological apparatus always presenting the West as central and Western values as the most compelling. Unfortunately, the majority of political and sociological analyses produced in the semi-peripheral countries seems to comply with what Wallerstein defined as 'European universalism' and the unquestioned beliefs both in the necessity of 'joining the West' and in doing so 'at any price'.[31]

The semi-peripheral is errant in the very general sense, that it is contradictory and incoherent, its development is not linear, there are feudal and neoliberal aspects in contemporary semi-peripheries, which exceed their counterparts in peripheries and central countries. Semi-peripheral histories proceed in jumps, not as regular progress and their allegiances can shift, just as their economies can suddenly fall. Such

---

29 Milan Kundera, 'The Tragedy of Central Europe', *New York Review of Books*, 31.7 (26 April 1984), pp. 33-38.
30 See Gayatri Chakravorty Spivak, 'Can the Subaltern Speak?', in *Marxism and the Interpretation of Culture*, ed. by Cary Nelson and Lawrence Grossberg (Chicago: University of Illinois Press, 1988), pp. 271-313.
31 Immanuel Wallerstein, *European Universalism: The Rhetoric of Power* (New York: New Press, 2006).

errancy also allows sudden appearance of emancipation or utopia – as it did in Haiti (then Saint Domingue) in the early nineteenth century or in 1980 in Poland.

4. ERRANT AS IN ICONOCLASTIC, PLEBEIAN, AND FEMININE

The beginnings of 'Solidarność' and its structure are also somewhat perverse insofar as they offer a complete *détournement* of the traditional structures of power. As a directly democratic entity — produced without preoccupation with gender and class distinctions, private and public divide, hierarchies, etc. — it performed precisely the same function as iconoclasm does in the world of art. It is only logical that in history, which has always been written by the victors, a declaration of the oppressed has some iconoclastic value, as in it they would actually overcome the state of exception to which they are condemned, and they actually would produce a claim.

In his analysis of contemporary and historical forms of iconoclasm, W. J. T. Mitchell speaks about its two basic forms:

> [T]he first is the condemnation of idolatry as error, as stupidity, as false, deluded belief; the second is the darker judgment that the idolater actually *knows* that the idol is a vain, empty thing, but he continues to cynically exploit it for the purposes of power or pleasure. This is the perverse, sinful crime of idolatry. Thus, there are two kinds of idolaters — fools and knaves — and obviously considerable overlap and cooperation between the two kinds.[32]

For Mitchell, iconoclasm constitutes a vital element of contemporary politics, since even the war on terror started with an attack on symbols of the Western power — the Twin Towers in New York in 2001. The beginnings of 'Solidarność' in 1980 were iconoclastic in several ways. They were a scandalous demand to create independent workers' unions in a state that had declared itself communist (with state-run unions, which never questioned the institutional powers); they were a transformation of the public sphere performed predominantly by the

---

32   W. J. T. Mitchell, 'Idolatry: Nietzsche, Blake and Poussin', in *Things: Religion and the Question of Materiality*, ed. by Dick Houtman and Birgit Meyer (New York: Fordham University Press, 2012), pp. 112–26 (p. 114).

proletarians, not by the bourgeoisie or 'intelligentsia'. They constituted a grassroots mobilization in a country governed in a centralized way. They were the first Polish massive political mobilization that started not only because of a woman (Anna Walentynowicz's firing made other workers of the Shipyard of Gdańsk begin the solidarity strike with her), but also because an excessively high quota of women were involved and recognized.

My line of thinking about 'Solidarność' was influenced by the work of Jacques Rancière, whose search for agency and autonomy of the French proletarians is an exceptional effort to localize political dissent outside of the social elites.[33] The workers, who decided to go on strike in 1980 Poland, and then united and engaged in a deliberative process of transforming the political order — not only in their work places, but also on the regional and later also national levels, starting on 15 August in the Shipyard in Gdansk — broke several principles of the public sphere's sanctified ideal, as it was defined by philosophers, from Aristotle until to Habermas and later. Their crucial 'offense' was perhaps that they not only entered the domain reserved for upper classes (or — in the supposedly classless Polish society of the time — social elites), sanctified by power position and privilege — the domain of the 'public' — but also that they actually made this public happen in the workplaces, which are – *par excellence* places of 'private' character in liberal political narrative. The public and private divide obviously was questioned by the state ideology of the People's Republic of Poland, but it was also rather well preserved in the social practice, especially after the hard Stalinist era, which ended around 1956.

Both in Aristotle, but to an important extent also in Habermas, labour is private, because it serves the task of sustaining basic needs. If an individual needs to provide this labour on their own, they do not belong to those, who have, as Aristotle aptly puts it, and as Rancière mercilessly criticized it, the freedom to engage in the public matters, in and the debate of the common good.[34] Such exclusivity of politics, later thematized by Rancière as the 'hatred of democracy', works on several levels:

---

33 Rancière, *Disagreement*.
34 Jacques Rancière, *The Hatred of Democracy*, trans. by Steve Corcoran (London: Verso, 2014), p. 2. (my emphasis, E. M.).

> Indeed it is as old as democracy itself for a simple reason: the word itself is an expression of hatred. It was, in Ancient Greece, originally used as an insult by those who saw in the unnamable government of the multitude the ruin of any legitimate order. [...] And it is *still today* for those who construe revelations of divine law as the sole legitimate foundation on which to organize human communities. The violence of this hatred is certainly on the contemporary agenda.[35]

The disorderly workers refusing to work and demanding the right to practice politics as well, is an image still threatening the order of things today, it is an error possibly leading to a major system collapse. Obviously, such 'disorder' should be seen as a mere reverse of those who occupy a more privileged position, be it in class- or supposedly classless societies.

'Disorderly' is actually a word used by Jean-Jacques Rousseau to depict women, as Carole Pateman reminds us in *The Disorder of Women*, a book that still provides useful knowledge about the highly non-linear routes of fears patriarchal society develops about women.[36]

The making of political claims and democratic procedures in the shipyards, factories, and other striking workplaces in Poland in August 1980 has moved the political agora from its traditional, exclusive, and central locations within institutionalized political order towards the margins, such as factories or — in the case of 'Solidarność' — shipyards and other workplaces. Rancière takes several issues with what he perceives as evasive pseudo-politics — various forms of Platonism, Aristotelism, and Marxism — all of which consist in not analysing the political by means of evading it by focusing on the future ideals, elitist exclusions, or petrified essentializing.[37] As he argues in *The Philosopher and His Poor*, 'The philosopher's city has one real enemy, a character held in low regard: the parvenu.'[38] For the philosopher, aristocrat, and political activist, the plebeian is the raw material to form, the —

---

35   Ibid., p. 2.
36   Carole Pateman, *The Disorder of Women: Feminism and Political Theory* (Cambridge: Polity Press, 1989).
37   See Jacques Rancière, *The Philosopher and his Poor*, ed. and intro. by Andrew Parker, trans. by John Drury, Corinne Oster, and Andrew Parker (Durham, NC: Duke University Press, 2003).
38   Ibid., p. 30.

here I refer to Gregory Scholette's analysis of the contemporary system of artistic production — dark matter, or — to bring in another context — the 'dark continent of femininity', as Irigaray would depict the mysterious world of women, referencing Freud.[39] Rancière raises an important issue, which constituted the core of debates about the concepts of the public sphere: who participates in the public debate? Who is the public?

The iconoclastic practice of proletarians united under the countless banners of 'Solidarność' consisted also in engaging in politics in a grassroots way, deeply unwanted in the former Soviet Bloc. Such reversal of hierarchy first enacted from a position of a minoritarian counterpublic, which later became the most general transformation of the public sphere imaginable, with ten million Poles officially registered as 'Solidarność' members by March 1981, was unprecedented, it was a scandalous moment. The months between August 1980 and 13 December 1981 would later be remembered as the 'Carnival of Solidarność', because the level and amount of political participation was genuinely unforgettable. I should also mention that the Polish Communist Party (PZPR) had approximately three million members at the time. In a country of approximately thirty-six million at the time this meant a general revolution.[40]

Habermas's early work on public sphere is by his own definition an analysis of the 'bourgeois' public, therefore it might be assumed to have less relevance to the struggles I am depicting here than for example the theory of 'proletarian counterpublics' of Negt and Kluge. Yet, several scholars, including Elżbieta Matynia, claim, that 'Solidarność' should be discussed as a transformation of the public sphere.[41] As much as I appreciate this rich and important suggestion, redirecting the majority of previous interpretations of 'Solidarność' towards the analysis of its discursive impact and general reshaping of the political public in Poland and also globally, I also find it somewhat misleading, as Haber-

---

39   See Gregory Scholette, *The Dark Matter: Art and Politics in the Age of Enterprise Culture* (London: Pluto Press, 2013); Luce Irigaray, *Speculum of the Other Woman*, trans. by Gillian C. Gill (Ithaca, NY: Cornell University Press, 1985), p. 19.

40   Elżbieta Matynia, 'The Lost Treasures of Solidarity', *Social Research*, 68. 4 (2001), pp. 917–36; and Matynia, *Performative Democracy*.

41   Ibid.

mas's theory focuses on the bourgeois public sphere and depicts the proletarian publics as 'historically insignificant'.[42] The transformation of the public sphere offered by 'Solidarność' was one of a far greater inclusivity than any former oppositional agency in Poland and the region, it also surpassed the mobilizations initiated by the communist party. Kluge and Negt critically addressed Habermas's public sphere as ideological, and introduced the concept of proletarian counterpublics as a production-based public sphere, oriented at the experience of labour.[43] Fraser emphasizes the problematic oneness of Habermas's public sphere, as well as the exclusions (of women, workers, and other groups), on which it is based.[44] Both critiques of Habermas's public sphere however focus on Western societies, thus demanding another vision of the counterpublics, in which non-Western countries could be discussed.

While the genuine class antagonism is, as Marx observed, one that can only be resolved by an open conflict, the controversy between the Polish Communist Party and ordinary workers or the society in general was one, in which the class difference was dispersed between both sides. The growing alienation of workers was certainly resulting in a paradoxical reconstruction of the clash between the 'working class' as opposed to the 'ruling (party) elites'. Yet paradoxically the very same communist party elites, whose power, economic situation, and entitlement was far greater than that of the ordinary workers, were providing the workers with a narrative of the 'power of the people'. The communist daily press *Trybuna Ludu* (the Tribune of the People) had the subtitle 'Proletarians of all nations, unite!'. Ironically, they did unite, in a general strike against the ruling party, in August 1980.

Much has been said about the exclusion of women from both: traditional theories of the public sphere and 'Solidarność'. Habermas aptly summarizes the conditions of possibility of this kind of marginalization, when he writes in the context of the ancient Greece, that:

---

42 Jürgen Habermas, *The Structural Transformation of the Public Sphere: An Inquiry into a Category of Bourgeois Society* (Cambridge: Massachussetts: MIT Press, 1991), p. xviii.
43 Kluge and Negt, *Public Sphere and Experience*.
44 See Nancy Fraser, 'Rethinking the Public Sphere: A Contribution to the Critique of Actually Existing Democracy', *Social Text*, 25/26 (1990), pp. 56–80.

Status in the *polis* was therefore based upon status as the unlimited master of an *oikos*. The reproduction of life, the labor of the slaves, and the service of the women went on under the aegis of the master's domination; birth and death took place in its shadow; and the realm of necessity and transitoriness remained immersed in the obscurity of the private sphere.[45]

We could object that this is Habermas's depiction of the ancient Greece, not of contemporary society. However, his theory of the public sphere (I focus here on his early work) does not give sufficient proof of any mechanisms revising these sharp distinctions. On the contrary, Habermas's exclusion of what he contemptuously calls 'plebeian public spheres' as historically insignificant, and his argument that only those with bourgeois education and *habitus* can truly engage in the matters of the public, show to what extent his vision of the public sphere was rooted in the exclusivist, aristocratic ideas of such defenders of oligarchy, much as it was for Aristotle.[46]

In the context of such class and gender bias, Habermas's theory of the public sphere does not provide the inclusivity necessary for democracy. This argument, in a slightly different formulation, was developed by Nancy Fraser. For her, however, the central problem of Habermas's theory of the public sphere from the perspective of democracy was his preoccupation with the oneness of the public sphere. Fraser argues, rightly, that the multiplicity of public spheres is crucial for democracy.[47]

'Solidarność' was in many ways a plethora of public spheres — one could argue, that the multiplicity of strikes, conducted in different parts of Poland, by different workers, with a variety of social statuses, professions, etc., was a set of counterpublics and public spheres rather than one public, event though it — at the same time — can be seen as one massive transformation of the public sphere. Jadwiga Staniszkis called the events of 1980–81 in Poland the 'self-limiting revo-

---

45 Jürgen Habermas, *The Structural Transformation*, p. 3.
46 See ibid., p. xviii and Chapter 6. I discuss the class bias of Habermas's theory of the public sphere in more detail in another article: Ewa Majewska, 'The Utopia of "Solidarity" Between Public Sphere and Counterpublics: Institutions of the Common Revisited', *Utopian Studies*, 2.29 (2018), pp. 229–47.
47 See Fraser, 'Rethinking the Public Sphere'.

lution'.[48] This concept captures a difficulty legal theorists have with the classification of these events. Staniszkis's notion allows to see the contradictions inherent in 'Solidarity', which was: one labour union, composed of many smaller unions, often of very different character, a revolution and a reform at the same time; a non-violent revolution; a non-bourgeois institutional politics (!); an egalitarian, worker's mobilization fuelled by religious references; a rupture and continuation of state socialism etc. etc. The social composition of this counterpublic is also interesting — as women were there all the time, sometimes particularly visibly. The majority of 'Solidarność' activists were workers with very low education, thus not fulfilling the bourgeois *habitus* so emphasized by Habermas in *Structural Transformation of the Public Sphere*.

Several feminist attempts have been made to analyse the role and position of women, all of them emphasizing the exclusions and marginalization of women and their role in 'Solidarność'.[49] As much as I appreciate these analyses, I would like to argue for a necessity of contextualizing the situation of women in 'Solidarność', of applying some comparative perspective, and, above all, of distinguishing between the early days of this workers' union (the years 1980–81) and the times after 1981. It is important to know, that 1980 was quite particular for women's political participation also on the institutional level: in the parliamentary elections in March, for the first time in Poland, more than a quarter of the MPs were women; in 1979 Poland signed the UN Convention to Eliminate All Forms of Discrimination Against Women (CEDAW), there was perhaps a general sense of gender equality. The first days of the strikes in 1980 brought to public attention the names of at least three women: Anna Walentynowicz, the crane operator, whose firing became the direct cause of the strike in the Gdansk Shipyard in August 1980; Alina Pieńkowska, a nurse and opposition member; and Henryka Krzywonos, a young tramway driver, who became famous after stopping her tram in the middle of Gdańsk to spread the

---

48 Jadwiga Staniszkis, *Poland's Self-Limiting Revolution*, trans. by Jan Gross (Princeton: Princeton University Press, 1984).
49 See Shana Penn, *Solidarity's Secret: The Women Who Defeated Communism in Poland* (Ann Arbor: University of Michigan Press, 2006); Ewa Kondratowicz, *Szminka na sztandarze. Kobiety Solidarnosci 1980–1989* (Warsaw: Wydawnictwo Sic!, 2001).

news of the strike in the shipyard, when telephone communications were cut by the authorities — her words: 'this tramway ain't going any further' became idiomatic. None of the previous Polish uprising had any women recognized by name, apart from someone who could actually be seen as the first Polish drag king, Emilia Plater, who joined the November Uprising in 1830 dressed as a man, with her female companion (which could lead to wild speculations concerning her sexual orientation, which I cannot pursue here). After 1980, some more women became publicly known as important members of the opposition, including the Warsaw-based editors of the 'Tygodnik Mazowsze' magazine, Helena Luczywo, Anna Dodziuk, Anna Bikont, Ludwika Wujec, Joanna Szczesna, and Elzbieta Regulska; the opposition activists such as Barbara Labuda, Joanna Duda-Gwiazda, Grażyna Staniszewska, Jadwiga Staniszkis, Joanna Wojciechowicz, and many others. After the introduction of martial law in December 1981, the 'Tygodnik Mazowsze' magazine became the main underground press of the delegalized 'Solidarność', its members and sympatizers. Without these women's incessant work, courage, and care the continuation of this movement would have been impossible, yet for many years they were excluded from historical accounts of 'Solidarność'.

Shana Penn and Ewa Kondratowicz rightly emphasized the role and involvement of women in the political work of 'Solidarność', yet it is also correct that they criticize the exclusion of women from historical accounts of 'Solidarność', as well, as from political agency after 1989.[50] They should, however, also mention that 'Solidarność' was the first event in Polish history where women were visible and recognized, at least in the first year of the union's existence. Some women were — in the role of the supporters and affective labourers — providing for their partners and relatives. This care and affective labour had tremendous impact on the survival of the opposition, particularly during the years of martial law.

This intense and multilayered political agency of women actually had an anticipating episode, which is always neglected in accounts of the history of 'Solidarność'. As Małgorzata Fidelis aptly recollected, some 500 000 persons went on strike in Łódź in February 1971, and

---

50 See Shana Penn, *Solidarity's Secret* and Ewa Kondratowicz, *Szminka na sztandarze*.

some 74% of the textile factories workers were women.[51] By forcing the men in the government not only to come to Łódź and discuss their demands, but also exposing them to the unheated factory halls, leaking ceilings, and broken windows on a freezing winter day, they undermined the official propaganda of equality, clearly demonstrating that the poverty of their work conditions is definitely not familiar to those, who were supposed to be their equals, representatives of the people. Here again, the ordinary, everyday, and the common entered the stage of history, as a blasphemy or iconoclasm undermining the unquestioned absolute of patriarchal, elitist political practice of the declaratively communist state.

5. ERRANT AS IN TERRITORIALIZING: THE REFRAIN

Borrowing the crucial strategic elements from the striking female workers of the textile factories in Łódź in 1971, which consisted in passive refusal of to work and demanding negotiations to be held at the workplace, the workers of the Shipyard of Gdansk and other striking workplaces first in Gdansk and then in the entire country performed a general strike with more women involved, than in any former Polish uprising, and genuinely Marxist postulates, combined with several liberal ones, such as demand of freedom of speech and gatherings. In this sense, they were a perfect hybrid, at least politically, combining, but not assimilating, elements of a circuit, not a blend. This sudden unity of all these groups and political currents that would generally not cooperate, could be seen as a deterritorialization, a *ligne de fuite*, a subsumption of newly composed elements into a way out of the oppressively reterritorialized communist idea, for example. I would like to explore the image of territorialization instead.

In *Mille Plateaux* Deleuze and Guattari built their concept of territory in a chapter about the *ritournelle* (refrain) in reference to romanticism, as the new beginning — of music, of politics. The very beginnings of 'Solidarność' could, I think, be very well depicted with a passage from *A Thousand Plateaus*, the opening paragraph of the chapter *On the Refrain*, where Deleuze and Guattari write:

---

51 Małgorzata Fidelis, *Women, Communism, and Industrialization in Postwar Poland* (Cambridge: Cambridge University Press, 2014), p. 248.

> A child in the dark, gripped with fear, comforts himself by singing under his breath. He walks and halts to his song. Lost, he takes shelter, or orients himself with his little song as best he can. The song is like a rough sketch of a calming and stabilizing, calm and stable, center in the heart of chaos. Perhaps the child skips as he sings, hastens or slows his pace. But the song itself is already a skip: it jumps from chaos to the beginnings of order in chaos and is in danger of breaking apart at any moment. There is always sonority in Ariadne's thread. Or the song of Orpheus.[52]

As we might remember, the new beginnings in Deleuze's and Guattari's thinking are not marked by the heroic masculine figures claiming their rights and fighting for them.[53] They actually start in a moment of disappointment and weakness, in confrontation with an overwhelming fear, where the scariest is perhaps the possibility of literally anything happening. The song of the little boy marks a transformation, begins a new constellation, a new assembly. It is not a triumphant anthem of a new nation opposed to a clearly defined enemy. It is a silent tune aimed at survival, not at victory. These are risky practices, of deeply ambivalent character. Deleuze and Guattari comment: 'This synthesis of disparate elements is not without ambiguity. It has the same ambiguity, perhaps, as the modern valorization of children's drawings, texts by the mad, and concerts of noise'.[54] They also suggest a particularly weak character of territorializing practices, arguing, that 'we can never be sure we will be strong enough, for we have no system, only lines and movements'.[55]

In Deleuze and Guattari's description, the territory is a kind of sublation, an overcoming of the ultimate solitude of the terrified child,

---

52 Gilles Deleuze and Félix Guattari, *A Thousand Plateaus: Capitalism and Schizophrenia*, trans. by Brian Massumi (Minneapolis: University of Minneapolis Press, 1987), p. 311.

53 In his lectures about the *ritournelle* from 1977, Deleuze emphasized the role of the non-heroic: 'Wagner, c'est encore d'un bout à l'autre l'éducation sentimentale. Le héros wagnérien dit: "Apprenez-moi la peur." Nietzsche ce n'est pas ça. Il n'y a que des hecceités, c'est-à-dire des combinaisons d'intensités, des composés intensifs. Les hecceités ce ne sont pas des personnes, ce ne sont pas des sujets.' Gilles Deleuze, 'Anti-Œdipe et Mille Plateaux. Cours Vincennes: Sur la musique' (8 March 1977), transcription, *WebDeleuze*, ed. by Richard Pinhas and Benoit Maurer <https://www.webdeleuze.com/textes/183> [accessed 14 September 2019].

54 Deleuze and Guattari, *A Thousand Plateaus*, p. 343.

55 Ibid., p. 350.

an artist, possibly also a population in despair, in the creation of some new quality. A boy sings to himself a song to overcome fear. The chapter begins with an image of a scared child, in a moment of weakness, powerlessness, despair. It references the practice of marking territory, by animals, even plants. It is an image of overcoming fear and deprivation, in many ways oppositional to the one we know far better, at least in Europe — that of the dialectics of slave and master, which in the last 200 years became not only paradigmatic, but also petrified in its heroic version of a 'fight'. The beginnings depicted by Deleuze and Guattari are different, they develop as a creative process, beyond any fight, as an expression of sound, and reaction to fear. It would not be hard to imagine such practice as one marked by heroism or aggression, yet this is not the image offered in *Mille Plateaux* and perhaps this is better – not just for the political analysis, which can profit of such weak image of a beginning, but also for the possible reinterpretation of Hegel, in which the struggle between the slave and the master for recognition would not emphasize bravery and heroism, but rather the mundane, the non-heroic, and the weak?

The rather poetic suggestion of opening the territory to the Cosmos might and perhaps should be read as a suggestion of historical change. Deleuze and Guattari are quite surprised by the somewhat Hegelian sound of the chapter they write, which they explicitly mention.[56] A very important characteristic of territory is that it always produces its deterritorialization, thus it seems strangely dialectic: 'Produce a deterritorialized refrain as the final end of music, release it in the Cosmos — that is more important than building a new system.'[57] Possibly against the intentions of Deleuze and Guattari, who discuss artists and children rather than massive social movements, in the chapter '1837: Of the Refrain' of *A Thousand Plateaus*, I would like to think 'Solidarność' as a making of territory, with all the ambivalences of such a process.

Jacques Rancière explored the comparison between art and social practices in his efforts to build a theory of the partition of the sensible. The way I would like to think is more preoccupied with the erratic

---

56 Ibid., p. 342.
57 Ibid., p. 350.

status of the territory, the lack of power at the core, actually a deep fear, which is not expressed neither in conservative interpretations of 'Solidarność' as a 'self-limiting revolution' nor in the liberal ones, in which the male heroes once again openly oppose authoritarianism. Even the Marxist depictions of 'Solidarność', recently coined by authors such as Janek Sowa or earlier by David Ost, still dwell on the exceptionality and heroism of this event, which — like so many others — supposedly came from a confrontations of two forces.[58] Well, as we saw in the essay of Vàclav Havel on the power of the powerless, and also in other elements of the making of 'Solidarność', there was no such thing, as 'heroism' or even hope to win. Instead, there was fear, solidarity, and many forms of weak resistance, of powerless agency, which nevertheless allowed a great transformation of the public sphere by means of errant counterpublics. It was therefore from weakness and a sense of failure that this movement emerged.

While deciding to begin the strike, the shipyard workers of Gdansk were not thinking of fighting the Soviet Empire, and they certainly did not hope to win such a fight. On the contrary, their state was one of unheroic mobilization, one that comes from what Jacques Rancièere perceives as the core of the political, namely disagreement, and they began a new territory, singing songs of solidarity and persistence in struggle rather than fight. Their strategy was definitely one of resistance, but also of creating a completely new formula for political agency, of protest, and of political organization. In doing so, they crossed the ultimately critical competences of the public sphere, and produced an alternative, a series of errant counterpublics, which was too diverse and hybridic to only be named after just one group or aspect that seemed crucial.

---

58 David Ost, *The Defeat of Solidarity: Anger and Politics in Postcommunist Europe* (Ithaca, NY: Cornell University Press, 2005).

'The Exile from the Law'
Keeping and Transgressing the Limits in Jewish Law
FEDERICO DAL BO

In the present essay, I will try to answer the question whether an understanding of Jewish Law as exilic, as freed from the Land of Israel, is possible without any — projected or supposedly realizable — return from exile. This endeavour requires a review of many aspects of Jewish tradition — interpretive principles, hermeneutic provisions, messianic expectations — that are usually characteristic of Orthodox Judaism. By 'Orthodox Judaism', I mean here not simply the nineteenth-century opposition to secularizing Judaism but also the self-representation of observant Jews since the beginning of Rabbinic Judaism and especially since the dissemination of the Talmud as the most authoritative Jewish handbook of law.

The Talmud is central to Orthodox Judaism. Every elementary handbook of Orthodox Judaism emphasizes the pious commandment — traditionally addressed exclusively to male Jewish individuals — to read, study, and comment on the Talmud.[1] Studying was regarded to

---

[1] Much depends on this discriminatory assumption. The most congruent response to Orthodox Judaism with respect to Talmudic literature can be found in the ongoing project 'A Feminist Commentary on the Babylonian Talmud' (FCBT), established by Tal Ilan (Freie Universität Berlin). I contributed to the project: Federico Dal Bo, *Massekhet Keritot: Text, Translation, and Commentary*, A Feminist Commentary on the Babylonian Talmud, v.7 (Tübingen: Mohr Siebeck, 2013).

be as important as praying and in many respects represented a variance of the Biblical model of priesthood that obviously required the existence of the Temple of Jerusalem. After the destruction of the Second Temple, of course, the priesthood as permanent service in the Temple was terminated and its social importance diminished. It survived transfigured into the pages of the Talmud that typically discuss questions of purity that the Pharisees extended *a fortiori* beyond the perimeter of the Temple to ordinary, everyday life. Albeit in ruins, the Temple did survive as the ideological centre of Rabbinic Judaism together with its rules, norms, and prescriptions.

Yet the historical and textual origins of the Talmud seem to contradict these ideological assumptions but nonetheless allow for an understanding of Jewish Law as an exilic product, as well, freed from the Land of Israel. Indeed, many pages from the Talmud exalt the cultural superiority of Babylon with respect of the Land of Israel up to the point that Talmudic Judaism progressively emerges as a diasporic product. These pages constitute a first effort to understand the Talmud according to its 'eccentric' nature, despite the centripetal force of attraction of the Land of Israel.

1. A THEOLOGICAL PARADOX: THE CENTRALITY OF (AN) EXILIC LAW

At the beginning there is paradox. The paradox of Jewish Law consists in the fact that it was redacted in exile — in Babylon — but it mostly pertains to ritual and legal issues related to the Land of Israel. True, the Pharisees allowed to extend the notion of purity beyond the boundaries of the Temple of Jerusalem since the beginning of the common era. And yet the primitive idea was to extend the rules of purity outside the Temple, but not beyond the perimeter of the city of Jerusalem or, by extension, beyond the Land of Israel. At the time, the Pharisees could hardly assume that the Temple would be destroyed and purity rules would be followed outside the Land of Israel — 'in exile'.

The question was not philological: there was obviously no difficulty in the fact that Babylonian Rabbis could redact Jewish Law 'in exile' and maybe manifest a nostalgia — a desire to return to the Land of Israel. Indeed, whoever opens one of the dense volumes from the Babylonian Talmud cannot help but be impressed by the number of references to the Land of Israel — its institutions, its society, its customs, and, why not, its political utopia. And yet the question was rather more subtle. The Jewish Law redacted in the Land of Israel — the so-called Talmud of the Land of Israel — was monumental, yet still only a minor product of the rabbis from the first centuries of the common era. The Talmud of the Land of Israel will never enjoy the unparalleled prestige of the Jewish Law redacted in Babylon — the famous Babylonian Talmud — that would be written 'in exile', centuries after the destruction of the Temple of Jerusalem, when it had become quite clear that it would never be rebuilt, at least not before messianic times. And yet none of the Jewish sages ever considered the Babylonian Talmud as an 'exilic code': the Babylonian Talmud could emerge from the diaspora but was still an illustration of 'Jewishness' with respect to the (destroyed) Temple of Jerusalem. The *centre* of Jewish life was marked by a centenarian absence, on the ruins of the Temple. In a stark contrast, Orthodox Judaism has generally cautioned against the assumption that Jewish Law could be outdated, inasmuch as it contained rules pertaining to a destroyed Temple. Therefore, they often suppress — if not explicitly correct — the latent suggestion that Jewish Law could be seen as a product of 'exile'. On the one hand, the complex, contradictory nature of the pre-Talmudic Jewish law has generally been 'assimilated', from a textual point of view, by the redaction of the encyclopedic, emphatic, and hypertrophic Babylonian Talmud. Rabbinic literature that escapes the omnivorous Babylonian Talmud was not simply 'removed' from the intellectual history of Judaism. Rather, it is bound to a more subtle destiny — 'put to the margin' of Jewish Law and treated only as a repository of legal decisions. As a consequence of this, several pre-Talmudic legal handbooks — the *Sifra*, the *Mekhilta*, the *Sifre*, the *Tosefta*, the *midrashey halakhah* — were harmonized within the Babylonian Talmud, which is to say: reduced to a specific ideological monopoly. The costs for this harmonization were significant: all these texts virtually disappeared as autonomous legal productions together with their respective different ideological and exegetical orientations; everything 'eccentric' was tamed to conform to the general frame of the Talmud; centuries of previous exegesis were turned into a repository of legal decisions. On the other hand, the less articulate Palestinian Talmud was undoubtedly put to the margins, if not removed both from Jewish life in favour of the Babylonian Talmud. This re-arrangement of the pre-Talmudic legal material involved Scripture only indirectly, since Talmudic masters used to quote from the Bible in order to justify their legal decisions, but actually competed against it with the intention to pose itself as the supreme canon for Jewish Law.

I would like to emphasize once more that the Talmud was itself located 'in exile' without ever being considered 'exilic': the self-representation of the Talmud is always consistent with the idea that Jewish Law might be redacted in diaspora but is still centred on the Temple of Jerusalem. Therefore, there is no such *legal concept* as 'exilic code'. A tentative translation of this expression into Hebrew could be: *galut ha-halakhah*. Interestingly enough, this Hebrew expression would also resonate with the modern notion of 'Halakha in Exile', a very rare expression, invented in recent times by the neo-Orthodox Romanian-born Rabbi Eliezer Berkovits with the specific purpose of designating the progressive detachment of Jewish law from the needs and necessities of modern Jewish life as well as the defensive and passive condition from which the law suffers while being confronted with a world dominated by non-Jews:

> [F]or the time being, Halakha is in exile in the land of Israel as it was before in the lands of Jewish dispersion. It is still the Halakha of the *Shtetl*, not that of the State. As yet you have not become worthy of *Torat Eretz Yisrael* [Law of the Land of Israel]. The reasons are to be found in what happened to Halakha during its *Galut* [exile].[2]

Therefore what is literally called 'the exile of the law' (galut ha-halakhah) would imply an 'exile *from* the law'. Clearly, Berkovits coined the English expression 'Halakha in Exile' in order to awaken the Rabbinic intellectual elite from its self-indulgent torpidity and to expose it to the necessities of modern life and have it be more congruent with it. In other words, Berkovits militates for a 'return' from an intellectual 'exile' with the hope of confirming both the practical and

---

2   Eliezer Berkovits, *Not in Heaven: The Nature and Function of Halakha* (New York: Ktav Publishing House, 1983), p. 91 [translation of Hebrew terms added, as elsewhere, F.D.B.].

intellectual 'centrality' of Orthodox Jewish Law — born and redacted in Babylonian exile. The Hebrew expression *galut ha-halakhah* was not intended to resonate with the mythical and mystical notion of *galut ha-dibbur* (the exile of the speech), developed in Zoharic literature, which designates the perdurability of God's *word* in exile and implies that God is in exile, too, together with Israel. On the contrary, Berkovits intended only to invoke the need for the Babylonian-born Talmud to finally 'return' to the Land of Israel, as an act of re-harmonizing Jewish Law with contemporaneity.

I have insisted on the notion of *galut ha-halakhah* because it stems from a legal context and does not treat exile in metaphysical terms. An interesting, albeit quite unique treatment of both a legal and mystical notion of 'exile' can be found in a brief passage from the Zohar that describes the structure of *sefirot* during the divine exile — God in exile together with Israel — and after the messianic advent that will reunite the *sefirot*. The passage that I am going to quote formally belongs to the Zohar but, philologically speaking, to a later stratum of Zoharic literature, which was mainly devoted to the description of the 'divine palaces' (heikhalot) and produced two quite similar texts: *Heikhalot Bereshit* and *Heikhalot Pequdey*. Both these texts intended to resume some principles from the pre-Talmudic exoteric descriptions of the 'divine palaces' and harmonize them with the system of *sefirot*, fully developed from the thirteenth century onwards. The question was quite complex: connecting cosmological representation of the divine (the 'divine palaces') with a metaphysical system of emanation (the *sefirot*). Both texts offered a strikingly simple answer: the 'divine palace' would consist in lower 'cosmological' structures that lay beneath the superior, 'metaphysical' structure of the *sefirot*. The believer's soul could progressively enter each single 'palace' and eventually ascend to the superior system of the *sefirot*.[3]

One passage from the second, possibly later text — *Heikhalot Pequdey* — is not content with the mechanical description of ascending from lower to upper structures, that is to say: from the 'divine palaces'

---

3   For a general insight into thirteenth-century Spanish Kabbalah, see: Federico Dal Bo, *Emanation and Philosophy of Language: An Introduction to Joseph ben Abraham Giqatilla* (Los Angeles, CA: Cherub Press, 2019).

to the *sefirot*. At a specific point, the text asks about the localization of Jewish writings within the system of the *sefirot* and ventures into a suggestive and yet problematic description of the future of Jewish Law, after the reunification of the divine:

> [H]ere pertains the sublime mystery of the *baraitot* [external sources] that we have mentioned and when a person reaches the tree [of the bottom of the *sefirot*], he kneels. 'Blessed are You, YHWH, who restores the *Shekhinah* [divine presence] to Zion.' Then, the *baraitot* return to Mishnah, and they are blessed as one (we-ha hakha ahadru brayytey le-matnitin we-itbarkkhan ke-chada).[4]

It is necessary to read this short passage with caution. On the one hand, it is unique in Jewish literature; on the other hand, it makes a formidable assumption: each component of Jewish Law is determined metaphysically, and therefore depends on messianic expectations.

When examined in greater detail, the passage abides by the need to justify every aspect of Jewish culture in association with the superior structure of the *sefirot*. Therefore, it is not surprising that the composite nature of Jewish Law — the Mishnah, its Aramaic commentary by early Talmudic scholars, the use of 'external sources', and so on — is projected unto different portions from the system of the *sefirot*. At first, the passage identified Scripture with the superior *sefirah* 'Tiferet'; then, it couples it with the lower *sefirah* 'Shekhinah', which is associated

---

[4] Zohar 2. 261a–b. For the translation, see: *The Zohar*, trans. and commentary by Daniel C. Matt and others, Prizker Edition, vols. 12 (Stanford, CA: Stanford University Press, 2003–2017), XII (2017): *Zoharic Compositions*, trans. by Nathan Wolski and Joel Hecker, pp. 167–68. This composition on the 'divine palaces' runs from Zohar 2. 245a to Zohar 2. 268b, according to traditional pagination. This composition is traditionally inserted into the commentary on Scripture, specifically on the weekly Biblical portion from *Pequdey* (corresponding to Exodus 38. 21–40. 38), and hence called *Heikhalot Pequdey*. The modern editor and translator of the Zohar, Daniel C. Matt, has decided to remove this composition from the main body of the Zohar and to publish it as an independent 'Zoharic composition'. For a discussion of this decision, see Daniel Abrams, 'The Invention of the Zohar as a Book', in Abrams, *Kabbalistic Manuscripts and Textual Theory: Methodologies of Textual Scholarship and Editorial Practice in the Study of Jewish Mysticism* (Los Angeles, CA: Cherub Press, 2010), pp. 224–428, especially pp. 264–359. For a detailed treatment of this portion from the Zohar, see Federico Dal Bo, 'La mística de los palacios divinos en siglo XIII. Los *heikhalot bereshit y heikhalot pekudei* en el *Zóhar*', in *Kabbala judía y mística Carmelitana. Encuentros en Sefarad*, ed. by Sancho Fermin (Avila: Grupo Editorial Forte & CITeS - Universidad de la Mistica, 2020), pp. 169–93.

with the Mishnah. The exegetical justification is quite simple: there is a *first* Law, the Written Law, that is located almost on the apex of the *sefirot*; then, there is a *second* Law, the Oral Law here epitomized in the Mishnah, that is located on the bottom of the *sefirot*. The unoriginal wordplay between 'second' (sheniah) and *Mishnah* (literally: 'repetition') is instrumental to establish the correlation between them. And yet the crucial point is the identification of the external *sefirot* with two discrete textual and historical realities: the 'external sources' (baraitot) and the Amoraim or the early Talmudic teachers. Both these realities appear to be slightly diverted from the central axis running along the central line and connecting, say, the lower with the superior *sefirah* — in fact joining Oral Law with Written Law. Both the 'external sources' (baraitot) and the early Talmudic masters dwell on the 'margins' of the system of the *sefirot*, and accordingly will be affected by its eventual reunification after the messianic advent. This is clearly stated in this unique sentence that has no parallel in the entire Jewish literature: '[T]hen, the *baraitot* return to Mishnah, and they are blessed as one' (we-ha hakha ahadru brayytey le-matnitin we-itbarkkhan ke-chada).

This is a unique representation of Jewish Law that emerges both as a central legal product and a metaphysically exiled reality. Jewish Law is understood to be central to both Jewish life and the metaphysical system of the *sefirot*, since Oral Law and Written Law run along the same *central* axis. And yet exile is described as an almost 'physical' reaction of the divine against evil, and therefore as a temporary condition that will be emended in messianic times. The consequences of this understanding of Jewish Law are formidable and yet paradoxical. This theological representation suggests that Jewish Law is simultaneously exilic and promises reunification with the Land of Israel. And yet this theological dialectic contrasts with the history of Jewish Law and its structure: 'external sources' and early Talmudic scholars — here located on the external margins of the system of the *sefirot* — are not incidental but rather constitutive of Jewish Law. Therefore, this assumption — they will eventually converge into the main body of the *sefirot*, and therefore disappear or be assimilated for a greater good — is problematic and ultimately incompatible with the notion of Jewish Law itself. Indeed, what would Jewish Law be without its 'external sources'?

A collateral question is whether there is an alternative to the fundamental paradox —whether Jewish Law would be central to Jewish life and yet, at the same time, an 'exilic' product, possibly enriched by a metaphysical undertone. Shall Jewish Law then be accepted in its paradoxical nature at the expense of marginalizing everything that is not, *strictu sensu*, Talmudic — especially Babylonian Talmudic? On the contrary, if there is such an alternative, what are its costs?

The elaboration on a notion of 'exilic' Jewish law is indeed possible. It is possible to assume that Jewish law has not only been born 'in exile' but that it also has an 'exilic' nature. Of course, this would have a severe impact on the traditional assumption that the Talmud has to be the 'central' part of Orthodox Jewish life — in particular as long as the notion of 'exile' remains intrinsically annexed to the political, religious, and theological hope of a return to the 'homeland'. If this 'return' is traditionally described, in Hebrew terms, as a 'conversion' or *teshuvah* — what then would be the ethical impact of an 'exilic notion' of law? Should it perhaps even exclude 'conversion' altogether?

A notion of 'exilic' Jewish Law requires first of all the mobilization of different textual, hermeneutic, and philosophical strategies that deeply revise the Orthodox notion of a 'law' that is based on the criterion for 'drawing a line' between 'right' and 'wrong'. The metaphor of a 'line' drawn between what is legitimate and what is not is particularly powerful in Jewish Law; it usually involves a number of collateral assumptions: that everyone is able to distinguish between 'right' and 'wrong', that this ability is both ethical and intellectual, that Jewish Law plays an incontrovertible role in establishing the ethical perimeters for every individual, and, finally, that every move 'beyond' this limit shall necessarily be qualified as a 'transgression'. Each of these assumptions is intrinsically associated with the notion of a 'limit': only *within* a specific limit does Jewish life acquire sense and dignity. On the contrary, the 'transgression' of this limit posits itself as a movement that goes 'beyond' a specific ethical and intellectual limit with the clear consequence of being excluded if not banished from the community. The risk of 'transgression', in turn, threatens the institution of the Jewish intellectual elite both from a practical and hermeneutical point of view: namely, by acting out a deliberate 'transgression' of a specific commandment, by inadvertently transgressing a specific commandment, but also by proposing a radical interpretation of a commandment. Whereas the first two cases can be adjudicated quite easily by repressing the wrongdoers, in the first case, or educating them, in the latter, — the third case is the true danger to the Rabbinic elite: a radical interpretation that not only causes but also justifies 'transgression'. It is then not surprising if the perimeter of a correct interpretation has usually been guarded when not fenced twice: on a semantic and on an ethical level.

2. THE SEMANTIC BOUNDARY OF 'LITERAL SENSE' IN RABBINIC LITERATURE

The first way for imposing a limit to any radical — erratic, if not errant — interpretation of the law undoubtedly is the notion of 'literal sense'. In Jewish hermeneutics, the 'literal sense' is commonly designated with the Hebrew term *peshat* (simple, plain), exactly because it represents the most 'simple unity' of meaning.[5] Different from other hermeneutical practices privileging metaphorical, allegorical, and mystical interpretations over the merely 'literal sense', the Rabbinic notion of *peshat* usually represents the fundamental boundaries of the epistemological universe of meaning. As far as hermeneutics can involve the examination of the same Biblical verse in additional perspectives — as anticipated: metaphorical (derash), mythical (remez), and mystical (sod) —, the notion of 'literal sense' is the inalienable, basic minimal unit of meaning. Jewish commentators usually refrain from quantifying this minimal dimension of meaning and disagree on a clear denomination of it but are adamant in assuming that at least *each word* of Scripture — regardless of its morphological, grammatical, or syntactic function — has a perpetual 'literal sense' based on the theological premise that the Holy Writ *must* be fully significant in its every minimal detail.[6] What is this 'literal sense' exactly?

---

5   The evolution in Rabbinic literature of the notions of 'simple meaning' (peshat) and 'exegetical meaning' (derash) is reconstructed in David Weiss Halivni, *Peshat and Derash: Plain and Applied Meaning in Rabbinic Exegesis* (Oxford: Oxford University Press, 1991).

6   The abstract noun for 'exegesis according to the literal sense' is generally the Hebrew term *pashtut* or, more rarely, *pashtanut*. Both these terms denote the 'plain meaning' in terms of 'simplicity' in either literal or derogative sense. Upon closer linguistic

The term *peshat* itself exhibits a complex semantics, usually connoting at least three partially overlapping meanings: first, 'literal sense' as opposed to any metaphorical or symbolic reading; second, a 'straightforward sense' as suggested by reasonable, contextual exegesis, and therefore resonating with a 'philological sense'; third, the 'correct sense' of a verse as opposed to any metaphorical understanding that diverts from the 'straightforward sense'. Regardless of these specific differences, it should suffice to point out that the fundamental role of *peshat* corresponds to the intrinsic quality of a Biblical expression from which to derive any supplementary legal knowledge. This general understanding of *peshat* is clearly maintained by a Rabbinic dictum, reported in Hebrew in the Babylonian Talmud and disseminated in almost all later Talmudic commentary, with a descriptive and functional purpose: '[A] [Biblical] verse does not escape from its plain [meaning]' (ein miqra yotze mi-yedey pshuto).[7]

And yet, this apparently self-evident meaning of the term *peshat* is complicated further by some Medieval Bible commentators, especially by Rabbi Samuel ben Meir, the Rashbam, who was also the grandson of the famous French-Jewish interpreter Rabbi Shlomo Itzhaqi, better known as Rashi. In his seminal commentary on the book of Genesis, Rashbam makes a notable observation about the nature of the *peshat*:

> [O]ur Rabbi Shlomoh, my mother's father, the illuminator of the eyes of the exile [me'ir 'eyney golah], who wrote commentaries on the Law, the Prophets, and the Writing, paid attention to expound the plain meaning of the Bible [le-farsh peshuto shel Miqra], and I, Shmuel, son of Rabbi Meir Rashi's son-in-law, have argued with him, and he admitted to me that if he had the opportunity, he would have to do additional commentaries, since plain meanings [ha-peshutot] are established as new meanings [ha-metchadeshim] each day.[8]

---

    examination, *pashtut* is the abstract noun derived from the Hebrew adjective *pashut* (simple), while *pashtanut* is an abstract noun derived from the Hebrew noun *pashtan* (literal exegete). In this sense, *pashtanut* is probably a more correct, albeit more rare expression. For a recent definition of *peshat* specifically with respect to Jewish Law, see Mordechai Z. Cohen, 'A Talmudist's Halakhic Hermeneutics: A New Understanding of Maimonides' Principle of *Peshat* Primacy', *Jewish Studies: An Internet Journal*, 10 (2012), pp. 257–359 <https://jewish-faculty.biu.ac.il/files/jewish-faculty/shared/JSIJ4/cohen.pdf> [accessed 10 April 2022].

7   Babylonian Talmud, Tractate Shabbat, fol. 63a (my translation, F.D.B.).

8   Rabbi Shlomo ben Meir (Rashbam), commentary on Genesis 37. 21 (my translation, F.D.B.). The rabbis employ the intensive-reflective form of the Hebrew verb *chadash*

Notably, the Rashbam suggests that the *peshat* evolves in time without losing its fundamental 'originary' connotations, so to say. The assumption that 'plain meanings' (ha-peshutot) are constantly 'innovated' (ha-metchadeshim) is not self-evident. It rather reflects a complex dialectics between time and meaning, since time passes 'every day' and allows for 'establishing new meanings' that, on the other hand, are still believed to belong to the same 'plain' one from which they have originated. This dynamic does not really suggest that there is a sort of 'Hegelian' progression of meaning in time but rather that *peshat* does not denote a static, monadic unit of sense but is rather immersed in time itself. The implicit presupposition is that Jewish tradition allows for each 'newly established' meaning to dwell within the perimeter from which a Biblical never escapes, as eloquently maintained in the Talmud.

Accordingly, the perimeter of Jewish hermeneutics is solidly posited: whatever interpretation one can make of a Biblical verse, its plain meaning shall never be neglected — exactly because it is the most simple component of meaning. This does not imply that literal meaning is not yet meaning and requires, say, a more spiritual attitude to substantiate it but rather that literal meaning is a kind of semantic substance that cannot ever be deserted even by the most daring interpreter. The Hebrew phraseology is devoid of any moral or linguistic obligation; the negative form ('does not escape') rather describes a matter of fact, as if the Rabbinic dictum were merely stating a truism: a Biblical verse never loses its plain meaning, regardless of what kind of hermeneutical process it undergoes. The occasion for introducing this hermeneutical principle is also of great interest. The starting point is the Biblical prescription not to carry anything outside the home on Shabbat (Exodus 16. 29; Numbers 15. 32–36) as well as the prescription to be found in the Mishnah — the earlier Hebrew law book the Talmud comments on — that explicitly prohibits anyone exiting their house on Shabbat 'with a sword, bow, shield, lance, or spear'.[9] The Talmud here objects as follows: everyone

---

    as a technical expression 'to be established as a new interpretation'. Cf. Marcus Jastrow, *A Dictionary of the Targumim, the Talmud Babli, and the Yerushalmi, and the Midrashic Literature*, 2 vols. (London: Luazac, 1903), I, p. 427.

9   Mishnah, Tractate Shabbat 6. 4 (my translation, F.D.B.).

is allowed to bring, carry, or wear anything that does not qualify as a 'tool' but rather qualifies as an 'ornament', since it is a common part of his/ her outfit. Therefore, the Talmud asks whether these very objects — sword, bow, shield, lance, or spear — shall be considered either 'supplementary' (and thus prohibited) or 'ornamental' (and thus admitted). The discussion is held in Aramaic and goes as follow:

> Abaye said to Rav Dimi and others say Rav Awia [said to him] and others say Rav Joseph [said] to Rav Dimi and others say [Rav Dimi said] to Rav Awia and others say Abaye [said to] Rav Joseph: what is Rabbi Eliezer's reason [ta'am] for saying that [sword, bow, shield, lance, or spear] are ornaments for him? Since it is written: 'gird thy sword upon thy thigh, O mighty one, thy glory and thy majesty' [Ps 45:4]. Rav Kahana said to Mar bar Rav Huna: is [this] written in the words of Scripture? He said to him: a [Biblical] verse does not escape from its plain [meaning] [pshuto]. Rav Kahana said to him: by the time I was eighteen years old I had studied [hawah gimarna] the whole Shas [= the Talmud] yet I did not know that a [Biblical] verse [outside the Pentateuch] does not leave its plain [meaning] until today. What does he inform us? That a man should study [de-ligmar] and subsequently understand [li-sbor] [by his own reason].[10]

This Talmudic passage shows the complex dialectics between literal and non-literal sense as well as the tension between knowledge acquired in the traditional study of the Talmud and knowledge acquired through the use of reason. Both these epistemological and intellectual boundaries intersect and overlap implicitly, since they prescribe a quite rigorous discipline of mind. The passage states that it is possible to interpret not only the Pentateuch but also Scripture in general beyond its 'plain meaning' (peshat) only under several conditions: preserving the fundamental sense of a Biblical verse and appreciating the traditional study that precedes— both in time and acumen — someone's individual abilities. A solid economics of knowledge is then established in this way: Scripture is the focal point of knowledge and its 'plain meaning' is its unalienable fundamental meaning that one should study first in the traditional way — in a Rabbinic seminar together with one's own

---

10 Babylonian Talmud, Tractate Shabbat, fol. 63a (my translation, F.D.B.).

fellows — and only later understand on one's own, on the basis of one's intellect and competence.[11]

3. THE ETHICAL BOUNDARY OF 'LITERAL SENSE' IN RABBINIC LITERATURE AND ITS EXCEPTIONS

The second way of imposing a limit to any radical interpretation of the law is more complex and depends on the former one. It presupposes that there is an inalienable 'sense' in a Biblical verse and therefore assumes, by implication, that there is a 'plain' — or strict — sense for any Biblical commandment. Accordingly, a commandment does not need to be exhaustive, especially on account of a broader sense for 'justice'. In other terms, the observation of a commandment might also require a specific 'sense for justice': a sort of peculiar 'touch'. This supplementary sense undoubtedly is 'mercy' that the Rabbis here introduced with a double purpose: extending the observation of the law 'beyond' its strict, literal sense and yet preserving this 'exceptional' interpretation of the law from becoming heretical. Besides, there would be a subtle connection between 'exodus' and 'exceptionality'.[12] The name for this legal institution in the Jewish hermeneutics is called, in Hebrew, *lifnim mi-shurat ha-din*: literally, 'within the line of the law' — which might correspond to the idiomatic expression 'beyond the letter of the law'.

This principle recurs in some passages from the Babylonian Talmud and is generally specified with the help of some examples. It usually admits someone's liability of observing a commandment 'beyond' the strict expectations prescribed by the letter of the law — without compromising its 'literal sense' and, on the contrary, producing a supplementary positive effect in the individual who is addressed by the law itself.

For instance, a Talmudic passage treats the case of a poor woman who asked a rabbi to negotiate for her a coin that eventually turned out to be fake:

---

11   See my article: Federico Dal Bo, "'A Sage Understands of His Knowledge" (mHag 2:1): Degrees and Hierarchy of Knowledge in Abraham Abulafia', *Mediaevalia. Textos e estudos*, 36 (2017), pp. 61–73 <http://dx.doi.org/10.21747/21836884/med36a3>.

12   It might not be surprising that Hebrew phraseology betrays a specific lexical familiarity between 'exiting (in exile)' and 'escaping (the ordinary)'. Indeed, the Hebrew idiom for 'being an exception' literally says: 'leaving the general condition' (la-tze't min ha-klal).

> Along came [a woman] who showed a *dinar* to Rabbi Hiyya and [he] said to her that it was excellent. Then she came back and said to him: I have shown it [to others] and they said to me it was evil and no one would take it from me. [Rav Hiyya] said to Rav: alas, exchange [it with a good one] and write down in my register as a bad one.[13]

When later asked about the reason why he exchanged a false coin with a genuine one, Rav Hiyya admits that it was for the sake of the woman whom he himself had mistakenly assured that her coin was not fake. According to the Talmudic law of transactions, Rav Hiyya would not have been prescribed to do anything specific when the woman came back complaining that she was falsely informed about her coin, and yet, he had been persuaded by a deeper sense for humanity and justice to assume responsibility for his previous misjudgment. Therefore, he means to help the — quite likely poor — woman, providing her a genuine coin in exchange.

How shall this act of generosity be evaluated according to a formal, juridical point of view? Does it belong to or rather escape the strict commandment of the law? Is it consistent with or eccentric to the Biblical prescriptions?

At first, one should note how difficult it is to render the Hebrew expression *lifnim mi-shurat ha-din* either literally as 'within the line of the law' or idiomatically as 'beyond the letter of the law'. Yet this difficulty hardly is of a merely linguistic nature — it rather involves implicit theological expectations. On the one hand, the exact use of the preposition *li-fnim* (within) in order to designate someone's liability of acting in an exceptional way clearly prescribes, in a Jewish perspective, the exact legal perimeter that circumscribes any moral initiative by a single individual. In other terms, there might be no call for exceptionality: the legal boundary of a commandment can be 'passed by' but not really 'transgressed', as long as there is a specific and actual benefit for a third party. This would hardly be qualified as leniency with respect to specific legal boundaries — rather as practical sense

---

13   Babylonian Talmud, Tractate Baba Qamma, fol. 99b (my translation, F.D.B.). On this passage and similar sources, see also: Federico Dal Bo, 'Economic Speculation and the Sacred', 'Market Prices', 'Market Intervention and the Common Good', and 'Market Intervention and the Common Good', in *Judaism and the Economy: A Sourcebook*, ed. by Michael Satlow (Abingdon: Routledge, 2018), pp. 46–47, 48, 53–54, 69–70.

with respect to a plastic treatment of a stiff regulation of life. On the other hand, the idiomatic rendering of the sentence as 'beyond the letter of the law' exactly mobilizes a number of presuppositions that are alien to Jewish theological assumptions and especially implies an inner conflict between what 'the letter' requires to be done and what 'the spirit' suggests ought to be done.

The economy of this dilemma has usually been represented in the stereotypical opposition between a 'legalistic' attitude that would be intrinsically 'greedy' and a 'moral' generosity of the 'spirit' at least potentially antinomic.[14] With respect to this, it is obvious that Rav Hiyya has not transgressed against any law while exchanging a fake coin with a genuine one. He has rather 'supplemented' the Talmudic law of negotiation by introducing some additional variables, such as: sympathy, good heart, generosity — or, shortly, 'morality'. And yet this act of generosity has a particular placement 'within' the Talmudic system of negotiation: it is not required by the strict law and yet it is still coherent, congruent with the legal case at stake — the wrong evaluation of a coin. Rav Hiyya has then taken responsibility for his mistake and committed an act of generosity 'within' the system of negotiation — he exchanged the fake coin with a genuine one — without contesting it. In other terms, the principle *lifnim mi-shurat ha-din* encourages moral acts that might be 'extraordinary' with respect to a stringent interpretation of the law but that shall take place 'within' a very specific perimeter: normativity.

4. TRANSGRESSING BOUNDARIES

Orthodox Judaism has then posited semantic and moral boundaries to the interpreter's freedom with a specific aim: circumscribing the per-

---

14 The opposition between a 'spiritual' and 'carnal' sense of Scripture is traditionally established by the literature on Augustine but dates back to a specific reception of the Pauline polemics with respect to Jewish Law. Only recently has modern scholarship offered a more complex insight into Paul's attitude. See the classic works: E. P. Sanders, *Paul and Palestinian Judaism* (Philadelphia, PA: Fortress, 1977) and Daniel Boyarin, *A Radical Jew: Paul and the Politics of Identity* (Berkeley: University of California Press, 1994). Cf. also Federico Dal Bo, 'Paul's Definition of "Circumcision of the Heart": A Transcultural Reading of Romans 2:28–29', in *Torah: Functions, Meanings, and Diverse Manifestations in Early Judaism and Christianity*, ed. by William M. Schniedewind, Jason M. Zurawski, and Gabriele Boccaccini (Atlanta, GA: SBL, 2021), pp. 397–410.

imeter of interpretation and placing Scripture — and, by implication, the Talmud — necessarily at its centre. Both the inalienable nature of the 'literal sense' (peshat) and the moral reasons for interpreting 'beyond the letter of the law' (lifnim mi-shurat ha-din) establish a limit that none shall be allowed to transgress against — or only at the cost of becoming a heretic.

The connection between trespassing a boundary and becoming heretical is not incidental. There is indeed a famous passage that describes Elisha ben Abbuya — an ambiguous early figure of a Jewish heretic — who transgresses both the perimeter of the Shabbat and, by implication, any other moral boundary:

> Our Rabbis taught a deed about Acher [= Elisha ben Abbuya] who was riding on a horse on Shabbat. Rabbi Meir was walking behind him to learn Scripture from his mouth. [Acher] said to him: Meir, turn to your back, since I have already measured by the hooves of my horse that thus far extends the Sabbath domain. [Rabbi Meir] said to him: So you too, return yourself. [Acher] said to him: And haven't I already told you that I've already heard from beyond the veil [of heaven]: 'Return [shuvu], you rebellious children' [Jeremia 3. 22] — except Acher?[15]

A superficial reading of this passage would probably emphasize the wicked nature of Elisha ben Abbuya who is transgressing the boundaries of the Shabbat and refuses any conversion. Yet a closer reading of the text should appreciate how topography and morality are carefully conflated. At first, one should note how Elisha was doubly transgressing the Shabbat: both by riding a horse, which is obviously subject to the prescription of Sabbatical rest (Deuteronomy 5. 14), and by riding it beyond the Talmudically established perimeter of two thousand cubits (equalling 830 meters) past the city limits.[16] This double transgression is then supplemented by Elisha's impossibility of 'returning' — both physically and morally — to his own place. In other terms,

---

15 Babylonian Talmud, Tractate Chagigah, fol. 15a (my translation, F.D.B.). For a more detailed reading of this passage, see Federico Dal Bo, '"My Mother Tongue Is a Foreign Language". On Edmond Jabès's Writing in Exile', in *Untying the Mother Tongue: On Language, Affect, and the Unconscious*, ed. by Antonio Castore and Federico Dal Bo (Berlin: ICI Berlin Press, forthcoming).

16 Talmud of the Land of Israel, Tractate Shabbat, 1. 1, fol. 2c (my translation, F.D.B.).

Elisha's transgression is virtually destined to turn into an everlasting 'trespassing' — a sort of erratic movement beyond any physical, ritual, and moral boundary. The Talmud reacted to Elisha's rejection of the Rabbinic boundaries to life and ethics in quite an eloquent way: his name was erased from the records of the Rabbinic annuals and stigmatically replaced with the sobriquet *acher*, 'the other one' — making it obvious that there is no alternative 'outside' the perimeter of Jewish Law that wouldn't entail the loss if one's identity and becoming someone else entirely. There is almost no need to emphasize the intrinsic violence of this *damnatio memoriae*, although the exclusion of Elisha ben Abbuya from the legitimate Rabbinic establishment has never implied the removal of some of his teachings — as if someone's rulings on the law could acquire an independent existence.[17] The Talmud somehow acknowledges that teaching and personality are not necessarily connected or, at least, that they can be disconnected when it is necessary.

5. DECONSTRUCTING BOUNDARIES:
FROM 'LITERAL SENSE' AND BEYOND

This precaution towards teaching and personality also reverberates in two modern texts: *Uprightness of the Heart*, printed in 1737 in Amsterdam by the Italian Kabbalist Rafael Immanuel Chay ben Abraham Ricchi and *The Guide for the Perplexed of the Time* — written by the Jewish-Galician philosopher Nachman Krochmal (1785-1840) and published posthumously by Leopold Zunz only in 1851. Both these texts reflect, in different ways, a concern to preserve the perimeter of 'literal sense', and yet also the awareness that this might result in a limitation of hermeneutic abilities.

In his work *Uprightness of the Heart*, Ricchi offers a Kabbalistic interpretation of Biblical and Talmudic passages. At a certain point, he elaborates on the subdivision of Jewish hermeneutics and suggests

---

17 On Elisha ben Abbuya and some specific gender issues: Federico Dal Bo, 'Legal and Transgressive Sex, Heresy, and Hermeneutics in the Talmud: The Cases of Bruriah, Rabbi Meir, Elisha ben Abuya and the Prostitute', in *Jewish Law and Academic Discipline. Contributions from Europe*, ed. by Elisha Ancselovits and George R. Wilkes, Jewish Law Association Studies, 26 (Liverpool: Deborah Charles, 2016), pp. 128–51.

that Oral Law could by principle entertain a different relationship with the 'literal sense' of Scripture:

> Oral Law was not was not suitable to writing because it simply directs the [Biblical] verse out of its [literal] meaning [motziah et ha-miqra mi-yedey peshuto] and while directing it out of the [literal] meaning, it is possible to interpret via allusion [derekh remez] various mutually conflicting interpretations that are not in the [literal] meaning, since a [Biblical] verse hasn't but one single literal meaning [she-ein le-miqra ela peshat echad] and if there is also another interpretation this is similar to the former one and so all of them need to be built on the same fundament [yesod] of the literal meaning of the [Biblical] passage.[18]

These hermeneutical precautions also resonate in the later *Guide for the Perplexed of the Time* that Krochmal wrote moving from similar premises but emphasizing the need to contain free hermeneutics even more strictly.

Krochmal's *Guide of the Perplexed of the Time* was clearly inspired in form and content by Maimonides's almost homonymous medieval Judeo-Arabic tractate *Guide for the Perplexed*, written with a clear purpose: promoting the true understanding of the real spirit of Jewish Law. Not all that differently from his prestigious predecessor, Krochmal intends to justify the centrality of Jewish Law in the multimillenary life of Israel and, especially, to describe Israel's supernal gift as its ability to seek God in the most proper way. This actually involves a correct appreciation of the limitations that are imposed on the interpretation of Jewish Law. Not surprisingly, Krochmal refers to the Rabbinic notion of 'literal sense' in a quite traditional way but he also indulges in some additional remarks — that might also have a different impact on Jewish hermeneutics. The passage is complex but worth mentioning in full:

> [A] great general [rule] was laid down for all of our predecessors, may all their memories be for a blessing: 'a [Biblical] verse

---

18 Rafael Immanuel Chay ben Abraham Ricchi, *Yoshev Levav* (Amsterdam 1742), p. 29a (Beit 2, Cheder 2, Chapter 1, §9) (my translation, F.D.B.). The Hebrew term *remez* (clue, gesture, hint, intimation) usually designates an allegorical or symbolic interpretation.

does not depart [iotze] from its plain meaning'[19] and 'you interpret an interpretation',[20] that is to say: the Sages can make the [Biblical] verse escape [le-hotzi'a et ha-miqra] to some specific end and desired benefit so it will be alluded [romez] or guided [more] to either on [the basis of] a law that has either been received, studied, fixed, and determined in the Oral Law, or on [the basis] of some ethical [principle], knowledge, and conception of a virtue [...] Despite this possibility, there is no one who can make it escape absolutely from it literal sense, that is to say: to make it escape from its first and natural understanding [muvan ha-rishon we-ha-tiv'i] of the words and utterances, from the ways how it is used in an expression [be-lashon], or from its connection with what is before or after it, or from what it is told about it or the close meaning from the Holy Writings.[21]

On the one hand, Krochmal attributes to the Rabbinic elite the ability to interpret Scripture in order to derive from it a series of legal, ritual, and moral commandments. On the other hand, Krochmal encapsulates the Rabbis' ability of interpreting Scripture within traditionally convenient boundaries — namely within the perimeter of the 'literal sense'. The economy of his argumentation seems at first very traditional. Krochmal appears to refer to the conventional appreciation both of the Rabbinic elite and the limitations it imposed. As far as the Rabbis are entitled to interpret Scripture and to derive — potentially new — senses from it, they are nevertheless bound to the imperative of respecting the semantic integrity of the text. The 'literal sense' is indeed the inviolable perimeter of meaning and it necessarily prescribes an intrinsic limitation to Rabbinic interpretation.

Yet the reasons for such a limitation are not made explicit. Krochmal is quite laconic: 'there is no one who can ...' (ein mi she-yekhol). Therefore it is difficult to understand whether someone's inability to transgress this limitation — this 'boundary' — should be considered moral, linguistic, or ontological. If there is neither a linguistically nor an ontologically established necessity for preserving these boundaries,

---

19 Babylonian Talmud, Tractate Shabbat, fol. 63a (my translation, F.D.B.).
20 This is another Rabbinic principle disseminated in Jewish literature.
21 Nachman Krochmal, *More Nevuchim ha-Zeman*, ed. by Leopold Zunz (Lviv: Joseph Schneider, 1851), p. 206 (Chapter 14: 'Ha-Aggadah') <https://books.google.de/books?id=GtUFcSlkpKUC&pg> [accessed 9 April 2022] (my translation, F.D.B.).

then this inability can only be moral. As a result, the respect of these boundaries is somehow fragile, arbitrary, and fundamentally depends on some specific circumstances — if it's not intrinsically 'plastic' and 'malleable'. The claim that the 'literal sense' would be an inalienable limitation to interpretation is apparently put into danger by Krochmal himself — who plays with the Rabbis' ancient phraseology and offers me the occasion to move away from the traditional notion of 'interpretation' towards a radical one.

The aforementioned ancient Hebrew dictum: 'a [Biblical] verse does not escape from its plain [meaning]' is founded on the idiomatic use of the verb *yatza* — which basically means 'to exit' and that also has a number of extremely important semantic variations: 'to leave', 'to depart', and 'to make an exodus'. This semantic difference is particularly evident while contrasting the basic verbal form with the causative verbal form: namely, *la-tz'et* (to exit) with *le-hotzi'a* (to make exit). Yet the principle that a Biblical verse cannot 'escape' its 'literal sense' assumes then a different connotation, when the verb 'to exit' (la-tze't) is hermeneutically changed into a causative form (le-hotzi'a) with multiple meanings: 'to make exit', specifically in Krochmal's sense as 'to make a [Biblical] verse escape' (le-hotzi'a) — and especially as 'to make an exodus' (le-hotzi'a). This apparently innocuous Hebrew verb 'to exit' would then have a tremendous theological-political potential — especially when it is interpreted in the Biblical perspective of the Exodus. In light of the 'plasticity' of the Hebrew language, one could extract the verb 'to escape' from the original Hebrew dictum, submit it to a morphological manipulation, and re-install it into the core of the Talmudic hermeneutical principle — with this final result: 'the Sages have the capacity *to make a [Biblical] verse effect an exodus*' (she-yesh iekholut be-yad ha-chachamim *le-hotzi'a et ha-miqra*). When carefully examined, Krochmal's words — *le-hotzi'a et ha-miqra* — evidently are a careful rephrasing of the original Talmudic dictum: 'a [Biblical] verse does not escape from its plain [meaning]'.[22] Yet the familiarity between the basic and the causative form of the verb as well as the familiarity between 'causing something to exit' and 'making it effect an exodus' — expressed with the same verbal causative form *le-hotzi'a*

---

22   Babylonian Talmud, Tractate Shabbat, fol. 63a (my translation. F.D.B.).

— might suggest a different reading of Krochmal's principle. It is clear, on the surface, that Krochmal intends to say that the Rabbis possess the ability to 'extract' a specific meaning from the Biblical verse, which in turn has to be subject to the hermeneutical principle that interpreting a text cannot infringe on the 'literal sense' of the verse. Besides, this 'impossibility', as already remarked, is not an 'inability' but rather a sort of moral imperative. 'No one may …' should then be understood more correctly as 'no one shall …' Krochmal's principle to 'direct a [Biblical] verse' (le-hotizi'a et ha-miqra) without 'escaping from the literal sense' (yotze mi-peshtuto) would ultimately have to be rephrased more deeply as the moral command not to 'provoke an exodus' from the 'literal sense': 'no one may *make a [Biblical] verse effect an exodus* from its plain meaning …' (ein mi she-iekhol le-hotzi'au le-gamre mi-peshuto). Therefore, both the Talmudic dictum about the 'literal sense' and Krochmal's strictly associated moral imperative would then sound more sinister — as a desperate precaution against a primordial, atavistic Jewish fear: claiming a divine prerogative.

This divine prerogative would be, in the present case, God's ability to 'make Israel effect an exodus' from the Land of Egypt — from slavery, idolatry, and spiritual lowness. Accordingly, it would be disrespectful if the Talmudic interpreters claimed for themselves the ability to impose 'an exodus' on Scripture. This precaution against the Rabbis' ability 'to provoke an exodus' would yet be ambivalent. On the one hand, it would surely be consistent with Krochmal's pious inclination not to make a claim about something that is inherently divine. The ability of inducing Scripture 'to effect an exodus' could practically be fulfilled by the Rabbis who, in turn, should consequently be subjected to a punishment — just like David had been punished for taking a census, which was a divine prerogative (1 Chronicles 21). On the other hand, Krochmal's precautions would reveal the double nature of Rabbinic hermeneutics, hidden in the double meaning of the Hebrew verb *le-hotzi'a*: either 'to make a [Biblical] verse escape' or 'to make a [Biblical] verse effect an exodus'.

One could object that the production of several semantic variants from the same verbal root would be the linguistic effect deriving from the morphology of the Semitic verb — fundamentally based on the permutation of a common, usually triliteral verbal root with a complex system of prefixes and suffixes. Consequently, one could then undermine the 'family likeness' between the acts of 'exiting', 'leaving', 'departing', and 'effecting an exodus' — by assuming that this is only a linguistic effect deriving from the manipulation of the same Hebrew root. As far as this remark is linguistically correct or rather exactly *because* this remark is linguistically correct, it does not rule out the theological-political implications of Krochmal's words and especially his claims that the Rabbinic elite is entitled to interpret Scripture but constrained by the 'literal sense'. Whoever objects to this manipulation of the Talmudic principle would undoubtedly be right from a linguistic point of view but would fail from a hermeneutical point of view — they would fail to appreciate the intimately metaphysical nature of Jewish hermeneutics and, by implication, the conflation of moral, linguistic, and theological facts. This typically Jewish manipulation of the text would have a clear impact on the hermeneutical principle that the 'literal sense' is unalienable or 'natural', as Krochmal maintained. Accordingly, a Biblical verse cannot 'escape' its plain, literal meaning, because this would be just like delivering the text to an infinite errancy: the verse would not just 'exit' the realm of its semantic possibilities but also be cast away outside its own 'literal meaning', as if it was forced to leave its semantic territory for a foreign country, like an 'exodus'.

Yet this manipulation of the Rabbinic dictum would differ in principle from any morphological permutation of a common verbal root. Rabbinic hermeneutics differs from modern linguistics especially because it does not simply 'describe' a linguistic phenomenon but projects it unto a 'theological-political' background. Strictly speaking, linguistics may accept the notion that language as a human product may be arbitrary — in the Saussurean sense of the 'arbitrariness of the sign' — but Rabbinic hermeneutics cannot accept that. Hebrew is the matrix of Scripture, and therefore any linguistic phenomenon always points to a deeper meaning. And yet, when correctly employed, the conjugation of the Hebrew verb 'to exit' into its variants — 'escaping', 'leaving', 'departing', 'effecting an exodus', and so on — would help unmask the theological-political tensions underlying and supporting the Orthodox Jewish assumption that Scripture ought to be 'the centre' of Jewish life. The perimeter established by the notion of 'literal sense' would hardly be a mere semantic-linguistic event

— it would rather supplement and support the 'moral persuasion' that specific commandments shall not merely be interpreted strictly according to the law (mi-shurat ha-din) and yet, at the same time, that they will not be 'excessive' or transgress the perimeter of the legal system (lifnim mi-shurat ha-din). Both morals and hermeneutics would appear to oppose any 'drift' — whether exilic, erratic, or errant movement that would eventually divert from the orientation of traditional Orthodox life and eventually from the 'axis' of a correct, well-tempered, and straight-forward line. I use the metaphor of 'drift' with the clear purpose to emphasize the phonocentric economy of this presupposition: the 'drift' (kulindeitai) is a Platonic metaphor used to describe, in negative terms, the destiny of a written text that 'rolls away' from the proper meaning, since nobody can vouch for it.[23] The Rabbis would fear neither someone's excessive teachings nor someone's excessive personality. On the one hand, any radical, untempered, or excessive interpretation of the law could conversely be neutralized, tempered, and harmonized by the congregation of interpreters of the law. On the other hand, any radical, rebel, and heretical personality could conversely be educated, reprimanded, or even banished from the congregation of interpreters of the law. Again, teaching and personality could equally be tempered, controlled, and harmonized. The idiomatic expression 'to bring someone back to his senses' would exactly describe this hermeneutical and pedagogical mission: bringing them back to the correct appreciation of the authentic 'taste' (ta'am) or 'reason' of the commandments.

Yet Krochmal's words appear to unsettle the harmony of this legal system — especially because they acknowledge that the hermeneutical principle 'not to direct Scripture' beyond its 'literal sense' actually is ambiguous and designates both a simply exegetical and a theological-political assumption. When interpreted in simple, if not 'exoteric' terms, the principle to 'make a [Biblical] verse exit' — and yet still fall within the perimeter of the 'literal sense' — would provide only

---

23 The *locus classicus* obviously is Plato's *Phaedrus*, trans. by Alexander Nehamas and Paul Woodruff, in Plato, *Complete Works*, ed. by John M. Cooper and D. S. Hutchinson (Indianapolis, IN: Hackett, 1997), pp. 506–56 (p. 552) (275e). On this, see the famous analysis in Jacques Derrida, 'Plato's Pharmacy', in Derrida, *Dissemination*, trans. by Barbara Johnson (London: Athlone Press, 1981), pp. 67–186 (p. 144).

a semantic and exegetical precaution: as mentioned above, the 'literal sense' is the most simple unit of meaning that has to be preserved in order to provide a coherent legal or narrative interpretation of the text. Yet when interpreted in view of its theological-political potentialities, the principle 'not to make a [Biblical] verse exit' from its 'literal sense' would rather sound like a moral imperative not to claim divine prerogatives — even if one is able and eligible to do so. There would then be two different levels of meanings in Krochmal's principle — just like Maimonides's *Guide of the Perplexed* can be read either in an exoteric or esoteric way.

Yet a question arises: how would Scripture be provoked to an exodus? What then is the relationship between Scripture and spatiality?

6. JUDAISM: A JURIDICAL 'WAY OF LIFE' AND ITS THEOLOGICAL-POLITICAL IMPLICATIONS

There is an intimate relationship between law and spatiality in Judaism. Besides, the ordinary notion of 'law' is not juridical, in the first place, rather spatial: the 'Jewish law' is called *halakhah* — which is obviously connected to the Hebrew verb *la-lekhet*, 'to go'. The use of this etymology in Rabbinic commentaries is so common that one could surely conclude that the act of keeping the Jewish commandment would not be a spiritual or metaphysical attachment to God in the first place — rather a 'way of life', in its most proper sense: a set of ethnically specific customs by which to live. Therefore, the very essence of 'being' Jewish (Yiddishkeit) would fundamentally consist in adhering to a Jewish life and accepting the divine law in the first place — but only secondarily would it consist in adopting a set of given specific juridical rules, called after several legal names: 'commandments' (mitzwot), 'laws' (choqim), and 'statutes' (mispatim).

One of the most famous examples for this overlapping of spatiality and spiritualit is the Rabbinic commentary on a laconic verse from the short Book of Ruth that describes two daughters-in-law, Ruth and Orpa, going back to the land of Yehudah together with Noemi, after the death of their husbands. The Bible simply states: 'and they went (watalachnah) on the way to return (la-shuv) to the land of Moria' (Ruth 1. 7).

The Rabbis transformed these few words in the narrative epitome to the act of conversion through an adherence to Jewish Law. The occasion was provided by the abundance of spatial expressions: 'going', 'on the way', and 'to go back'. According to the hermeneutic principle that no word is superfluous in Scripture, the Rabbis interpreted this redundant phraseology as an allegorical hint suggesting a deeper transformation: not simply the spatial movement from the land of Moab to the land of Yehuda — rather the spiritual commitment of accepting to leave the incestuous land of idolatry (Moab) for the land of God (Yehuda). This act of 'returning' to Israel could easily be interpreted by the Rabbis as an act of 'conversion' (teshuvah) — as clearly designated by the infinitive form *la-shuv*: 'to return'. It was especially the etymological familiarity between the act of 'going' with the notion of 'Jewish law' that enabled the Rabbis to elaborate on this stringent Biblical verse and to assume that the 'spatial movement' back to Israel was profoundly analogous with a 'conversion' — as if spatiality were the 'letter' for a 'spiritual' transformation. Accordingly, a pre-Talmudic narrative commentary on the Bible — the famous *Midrash Rabbah* — elaborates as follows:

> '[A]nd they went on the way to return to the land of Judah' [Ruth 1. 7]: Rav Yehudah said [in the name of] Rabbi Yohanan: they transgressed the letter of the law [shurat ha-din] and went to the Festival. Another interpretation [...] 'and they went' [wa-talachnah] [...] they were busy with the laws of proselytes [ba-halakhot gerim].[24]

This Rabbinic commentary notably indulges the connection between law and spatiality both in a negative and a positive way. In the — specified and possibly idiosyncratic — opinion of Rabbi Yehudah, the feminine verb *wa-talachnah* (and they went) would designate a 'transgression' of the 'strict letter of the law' (mi-shurat ha-din), as if the women's act of 'moving' here consisted in an act of 'trespassing' the 'line' between licit and illicit behavior. According to another anonymous — unspecific and therefore probably mostly accepted — opinion, the verse would on the contrary designate a positive spiritual development: the almost mimetic phonetic similarity between the feminine

---

24 Midrash Rabbah, Ruth Rabbah 2. 12 on Ruth 1. 7 (my translation, F.D.B.).

verb *wa-talachnah* (and they went) and the feminine noun *halakhah* (Jewish law) would then be taken very seriously as a clear sign for conflating spatiality and spirituality — with a clear consequence: in the moment in which these two women actually accepted to 'enter' the Land of God, they entered the 'perimeter' of the law by adopting its correspondent 'way of life'.

Yet this exegesis was hardly a simple opportunity for showing an aptitude for interpreting Scripture. The careful mobilization both of spatiality and spirituality was aiming at a much more dramatic opportunity: justifying the imperfect lineage of the future king David in front of 'the letter of the law'. There were indeed two conflicting matters of fact: on the one hand, the absolute prohibition for Israel to associate itself sexually or maritally with the house of Moab (Deuteronomy 23. 3–6); on the other hand, the genealogy of David clearly stemmed from Ruth — his great-grandmother (Ruth 4. 17). There was then a precise theological-political necessity behind the effort of conflating spatiality and spirituality: showing that the juridically otherwise imperfect lineage from Ruth to David had already been amended by an act of conversion — coinciding with the ingression 'within' the perimeter of Jewish Law, when 'they went on the way to return to the land of Yehudah' (Ruth 1. 7). The Rabbis' insistence on overlapping spatiality and spirituality then obeys the theological-political purpose of fixing a specific geographical and theological point that would exert a centripetal force of attraction: the Land of Israel — as source for law, morality, and institutions.

The notion of 'exodus' obviously involves an 'exit', especially because it implies that the present — geographic, moral, ritual, or metaphysical — condition is not the apt, proper one. In this sense, 'exiting' involves a search for its own 'properness' that tellingly lies 'beyond' the actual perimeter of reality. The central event in the Hebrew Bible indeed is the 'exodus' from the Land of Egypt exactly because this exit from a foreign land, where the Jews had suffered slavery for four-hundred years, would emblematically designate a fundamental transformation into their geographical, moral, ritual, and metaphysical coordinates. Leaving Egypt consisted, at once, in 'ascending' to the Land of Israel, adopting its 'customs', keeping its 'rituals', and eventually being metaphysically united with its God. Therefore, the 'exit from

Egypt' (yetzi'at Mitzraiyym) is celebrated in the Hebrew Bible as the most important event that precedes the donation of Scripture and the edification of the State of Israel.

Interestingly enough, the overlap of spatiality and spirituality is exemplified by a formidable Greek word: 'exodus'. This term only reproduces both phonetically and morphologically the Greek concept of *exodos* that generically designates a 'departure' from a place but mostly represents the epitome for every departure: the exit from the Land of Egypt. And yet the Greek term *exodos* seems to multiply the number of associations that superimpose spatiality and spirituality — both due to its components and due to its use. On the one hand, as it is obvious, the Greek term *exodos* translates the Hebrew notion of *yetzi'at Mitzraiyym* and makes it the obvious centre of the narration in the homonymous Greek Biblical book; the Book of Exodus indeed designates much more emphatically God's redeeming action into the world than the slightly opaque Hebrew tile: *Shemot* (Names) — from the first word of the text. On the other hand, the Greek term *exodus* amplifies the theological-political potentialities that are inherent to the Hebrew notion of *yetzi'at Mitzraiyym* especially due to its formidable morphology: *exodos* does not simply designate a 'departure' from a location but also the 'way-out' from it — by necessarily suggesting that any 'departure' (exodos) is a movement taken in a 'way' (hodos) that takes 'out from' (ex-) another place. In other terms, the word *exodos* seems to offer almost paradigmatically what the Rabbis had analytically found in the short verse from the Book of Ruth: 'and they went on the way to return ...' (Ruth 1. 7). In this respect, the Greek term *exodos* would designate both the act of 'exiting' and the 'means' for exiting: a 'departure' through a 'way', a 'path' (hodos) that is both *ex-hodos* (way-out) and *meth-hodos* (way-through).

It is within this very complex context that it is necessary to ask, then, what it is 'to effect an exodus' — and specifically 'to make a [Biblical] verse effect an exodus' from its 'literal sense': only in this way can Krochmal's opportunely modified principle say something decisive and important on the notion of 'errancy'.

7. ABRAHAM'S DOUBLE CALLING AND ABRAHAM'S DOUBLE 'EXODUS'

The dynamics of 'exodus' — happily summarized in the almost homonymous Greek term *exodos* that represents the morphological and semantical model for this concept in any modern language — appears to be at work as long as the action of 'leaving' (la-tze't) is inherently projected to a final destination. This obviously is at first a formal — neither temporal nor spatial — presupposition. The event of 'exodus' is taking place as soon as God — the main actor in history — decides to 'extract' human beings from their ordinary environment and to address them to a specific goal or task. The latter, in turn, can be left vague, slightly unexpressed or undetermined. So is, for instance, the first promise that God makes to Moses, announcing the Jews' imminent redemption from slavery, their being led out of the Land of Egypt and 'to the land that [He] swore with uplifted hand to give to Abraham, to Isaac, and to Jacob' (Exodus 6. 8). The *exit* from the Land of Egypt indeed is the main event in the history of the people of Israel. More specifically, it posits itself as the ultimate *exception* in the face of the *ordinary* existence of slavery: an *event* of salvation within an *existence* crystallized in a tragedy that had been going on for four hundred years. The calling is indeed the truest exception — whereas the final destination paradoxically is less important, as if it were a sort of empirical detail, and additional information with respect to the metaphysical event that is taking place and is eventually providing a supernal salvation. It is for these reasons that the ultimate goal — reaching the Land of Israel — is mentioned only by way of a circumlocution, just exactly as a circumlocution mentions to Abraham the ultimate goal of his 'exit' from the Land of Ur towards an almost undistinguishable 'land that I will tell you about' (Genesis 12. 1).

Both these two kinds of 'exit' have the same goal: reaching an indefinite land that will eventually coincide with Israel. Yet Abraham's calling is more peculiar: Abraham is called out from the most paradigmatic land of the Middle East, Babylon, the land of idolatry, of dispersion of languages, and the land from which the most authoritative text in Rabbinic Judaism — the Babylonian Talmud — will issue and represent the 'exilic centre' of the future Jewish life. There is obviously no historical or historiographical connection between Abraham's initial residence and the instalment of the most important Rabbinic seminaries, several centuries later, in the land of Babylon. Yet this connection is surely theological or, better put, can more easily be sustained by claiming that both Oral and Written Scripture are not really subject to the category of time: '[T]here is no before or after in Scripture' (ein muqdam u-me'uchar ba-Torah).[25]

This principle — originated in the early Hebrew commentary on the Book of Exodus and then disseminated throughout the entire Rabbinic literature — raises the notion of 'exception' to a metaphysical level: when theologically relevant, a Scriptural congruence shall not be easily, profanely, or secularly be overlooked as if it were a simple 'coincidence', but rather as Scriptural evidence for a specific 'metaphysical causality'. If Abraham was called out from Babylon, then Babylon should somehow resonate with the deepest reason for his calling. And yet this similarity might be extended further and connected to a supplementary similarity — between Abraham being called out from the Land of Ur (Genesis 12. 1) and his being called to sacrifice his son Isaac (Genesis 22. 2):

> Go from your country, your people and your father's household to the land that I will show you (Genesis 12. 1)

> And He said, Take please your son, your only son, whom you dearly love, Isaac, and go into the land of Moriah; and offer him there for a burnt offering upon one of the mountains which I will tell you of (Genesis 22. 2)

The linguistic similarity between the first and the second call — such as the use of the same exhortation to leave and to address to an undetermined land — seems then to provide a reason for assessing a continuity between Abraham's exit from Babylon and his willingness to sacrifice his son. This continuity is both geographical and theological: on the one hand, Abraham will eventually be moving even further away from Babylon, towards Mount Moria; on the other hand, he will eventually be obeying God again, with no practical detail about what is going

---

25   Sifrey Ba-Midbar 64. 1 (my translation, F.D.B.). Cf. also Talmud of the Land of Israel, Tractate Sheqalim, 6. 1, fol. 49d.

to happen. One might then conclude that if Abraham was eventually asked to sacrifice his son Isaac on Mount Moria far away from Babylon, then Babylon must somehow reveal the deepest reason for this atrocious command.

According to the principle that everything in Scripture is simultaneous and immanent at the same textual level, Abraham is apparently called out to abide by two different 'exodus': a geographical one from the land of Babylon and a theological one from the law. Just as Abraham was ordered to leave Babylon— which will be the future 'exilic' land of Jewish Law and the Babylonian Talmud —, so is he ordered to bring forth his 'exodus' up to the extreme consequence: sacrificing his son. Besides, the 'metaphysical necessity' shall not be mistaken for the obvious assumption that sacrificing one's own son is a serious transgression of Scripture but rather needs to be understood in Kabbalistic terms — as a transgressive act that is meant to bring balance to the system of *sefirot*. In a famous passage from the Zohar, the binding of Isaac is theocentrically interpreted as a divine self-testing by which God will teach Himself about the necessity of freedom and constraint, mercy and judgement, opting for a 'golden middle way':

> However, the blessed Holy One always deals strictly with the religious in all that they do, because He knows they will not stray right or left. So He tests them, not for His own sake, since He knows their impulse and the strength of their faith, but rather for their sake, to elevate them. As He did with Abraham.[26]

With respect to this, it is then finally apparent what an exodus from the law is: a tenebrous 'path' that inverts the 'moral ways' of the *halakhah* because it departs from the 'exilic centre' of Babylon in order to install a sort of 'non-exilic centre' that Rabbinic tradition identified exactly with Mount Moria — the elevation on which the Temple of Jerusalem would eventually be erected. Abraham's movement out from the Land of Ur is then allegorically an 'exit' from a future land of exile, Babylon, that will eventually be the cradle for the most formidable Jewish law book of all times — the Babylonian Talmud — the prestige of which

---

26 *Zohar* 1. 140a. For the translation, see: *The Zohar*, II, p. 276.

would almost surpass the unparalleled one of Scripture.[27] It is indeed this product of 'exile' that fundamentally opposes Abraham's 'literal' obedience to God's unsound order to sacrifice his own son. It is indeed this singularly decentralized centre for Jewish Law that will ultimately oppose the order to sacrifice someone's son for the sake of the national glory of Israel and propose, on the contrary, its sublimation in rites and customs. When interpreted in this sense, Abraham's 'exodus' out from the Land of Ur is then a simultaneously geographical and ethical 'exit' that appears to substantiate the actual risk that is inherently connected to the Rabbis' ability 'to make Scripture effect an exodus', as claimed by Krochmal. When Scripture is brought out in an 'exodus', its movement would then depart from the solid terrain of an 'exilic law' — just like the Talmud is — and radicalize the event of Abraham's being called to sacrifice his own son by producing a notable inversion of the notion of 'literal sense'. In Rabbinic terms 'literal sense' means the 'plain sense' of a commandment according to its most basic moral components: as a result, there cannot 'literally' be any command to sacrifice one's son, since this is clearly forbidden in many places by the 'letter' of Scripture (Leviticus 20. 2–5): therefore, the absurd seeming order 'to offer him there for a burnt offering' (Genesis 22. 2) *must* necessarily mean something different like — by some small grammatical manipulations — 'to bring him up there' in order to sacrifice the proper animal: 'a ram caught by its horns' (Genesis 22. 13) that has always been there.

And yet this 'literal sense' that has always been there had almost been neglected, just like a 'purloined letter' — in every sense of the expression. Only those who have been brought outside the safe perimeter of the 'literal sense' and delivered to an 'exodus' out from Babylon — out from the 'exilic law' — would be able to react, to argue, and to comment on an impossible order: to sacrifice one's own son, despite all literal opposition to such an order in Scripture.

---

27 On the notion of literary perfection and the rivalry between Scripture and the Talmud — or, more correctly, the Mishnah — see Federico Dal Bo, *Deconstructing the Talmud: The Absolute Book* (Abingdon: Routledge, 2019), pp. 130–32.

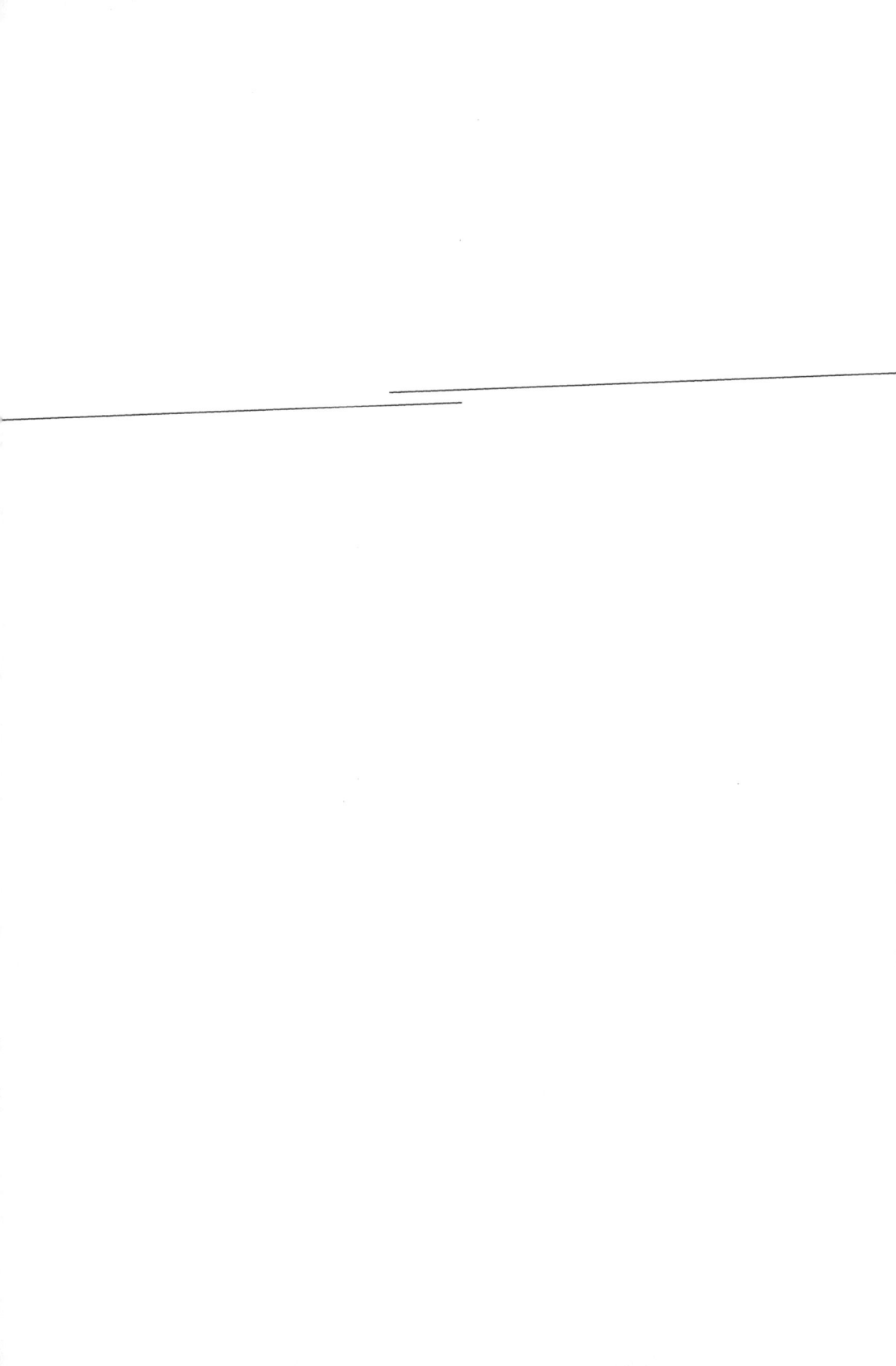

References

BIBLIOGRAPHY

Abbas, Ackbar, *Poor Theory and New Chinese Cinema: Jia Zhangke's 'Still Life'*, public lecture, Critical Theory Institute, University of California, Irvine, 3 December 2008 <http://www.humanities.uci.edu/critical/pdf/AbbasPoorTheoryStillLife.pdf> [accessed 5 May 2016]

Abbas, Ackbar, and D. Goldberg, 'Poor Theory: An Open-Source Manifesto' (2019), published on the platform 'Foundry', University of California Humanities Research Institute (UCHRI), <https://uchri.org/foundry/poor-theory/> [accessed 16 September 2021].

Abrams, Daniel, 'The Invention of the *Zohar* as a Book', in Abrams, *Kabbalistic Manuscripts and Textual Theory: Methodologies of Textual Scholarship and Editorial Practice in the Study of Jewish Mysticism* (Los Angeles, CA: Cherub Press, 2010), pp. 224–428

Ad Hoc Committee on the Future of Scholarly Publishing, 'The Future of Scholarly Publishing', *Profession 2002* (New York: MLA, 2002), pp. 172–86 <https://www.mla.org/Resources/Guidelines-and-Data/Reports-and-Professional-Guidelines/Publishing-and-Scholarship/The-Future-of-Scholarly-Publishing> [accessed 21 April 2022]

Agamben, Giorgio, 'Bartleby, or On Contingency', in Agamben, *Potentialities: Collected Essays in Philosophy*, ed. & trans. by Daniel Heller-Roazen (Stanford, CA: Stanford University Press, 1999), pp. 243–71 <https://doi.org/10.1515/9780804764070-017>

—— *The Time That Remains: A Commentary on the Letter to the Romans*, trans. by Patricia Dailey (Stanford, CA: Stanford University Press, 2005) <https://doi.org/10.1515/9781503619869>

Albers, Josef, *Interaction of Color* (New Haven, CT: Yale University Press, 2009)

Amaro, António Rafael, 'The Late Construction of Portugal Welfare State: The Failure of the Social Corporativist State (1933–74)', *Memoria y civilización*, 21 (2018), pp. 437–54

Anwar Khumaini, 'Dulu Mbah Petruk, sekarang Mbah Emar', *Merdeka.com*, 20 May 2012 <http://www.merdeka.com/peristiwa/dulu-mbah-petruk-sekarang-mbah-semar.html> [accessed 4 July 2021]

Anzaldúa, Gloria, 'La Prieta', in *The Gloria Anzaldúa Reader*, ed. by Ana-Louise Keating (Durham, NC: Duke University Press, 2009), pp. 38–50 <https://doi.org/10.1215/9780822391272-010>

Arendt, Hannah, *The Origins of Totalitarianism* (New York: Harcourt, Brace & World, 1968)

Aristotle, *The Complete Works of Aristotle*, ed. by Jonathan Barnes, 2 vols (Princeton, NJ: Princeton University Press, 1984)
—— *Nicomachean Ethics*, trans. by H. Rackham, Loeb Classical Library, 73 (Cambridge, MA: Harvard University Press, 1926) <https://doi.org/10.4159/DLCL.aristotle-nicomachean_ethics.1926>
—— *Nicomachean Ethics*, trans. by W. D. Ross, revised by J. O. Umson, in *The Complete Works of Aristotle*, II, pp. 1729–1867
—— *Parts of Animals*, trans. by W. Ogle, in *The Complete Works of Aristotle*, I, pp. 994–1086 <https://doi.org/10.2307/j.ctt5vjv4w.27>
—— *Rhetoric*, trans. by W. Rhys Roberts, in *The Complete Works of Aristotle*, II, pp. 2152–2269
Armes, Roy, *Patterns of Realism: A Study of Italian Neo-Realist Cinema* (South Brunswick, NJ: A. S. Barnes, 1971)
Azoulay, Ariella, *The Civil Contract of Photography* (New York: Zone Books, 2008)
Bachelard, Gaston, *The Psychoanalysis of Fire*, trans. by Alan Ross (London: Routledge and Kegan Paul, 1964)
Badiou, Alain, *Saint Paul: The Foundations of Universalism*, trans. by Ray Brassier (Stanford, CA: Stanford University Press, 2003
Badmington, Neil, 'Theorizing Posthumanism', *Cultural Critique*, 53 (Winter 2003), pp. 10–27 <https://doi.org/10.1353/cul.2003.0017>
Baer, Drake, 'Billionaire VC Peter Thiel Says Silicon Valley's "Obsession" with Disruption Is Totally Misguided', Business Insider, 18 September 2014 <https://www.businessinsider.com/peter-thiel-disruption-is-stupid-2014-9> [accessed 15 June 2022]
Bakhtin, Mikhail, *Rabelais and his World*, trans. by Helene Iswolsky (Bloomington: Indiana University Press, 1984)
Barotsi, Rosa, 'Contemporary European Cinema, Time, and the Everyday' (unpublished doctoral thesis, University of Cambridge, 2014)
Barthes, Roland, 'Photos-chocs', in Barthes, *Mythologies* (Paris: Seuil, 2005), pp. 98–100
—— 'Shock Photos', in Barthes, *The Eiffel Tower and Other Mythologies*, trans. Richard Howard (Berkeley: University of California Press, 1997), pp. 71–73
Baumann, Zygmunt, *Modernity and Ambivalence* (Cambridge: Cambridge University Press, 1991)
Becker, A. L., 'Text-Building, Epistemology, and Aesthetics in Javanese Shadow Theatre', *Dispositio*, 5.13–14 (1980), pp. 137–68
Beckett, Samuel, *Worstward Ho* (New York: Grove, 1983)
Bekaert, Geert, 'Le réel du discours. Eupalinos ou l'architect', trans. by David McKay, *OASE*, 75 (2008), pp. 227–39
Benjamin, Walter, 'Die Farbe vom Kinde aus betrachtet', in Benjamin, *Gesammelte Schriften*, VI: *Fragmente vermischten Inhalts. Autobiographische Schriften* (1985), pp. 110–12

—— *Gesammelte Schriften*, ed. by Rolf Tiedemann and Hermann Schweppenhäuser, 7 vols (Frankfurt a.M.: Suhrkamp, 1972–91)
—— 'Kleine Geschichte der Photographie', in Benjamin, *Gesammelte Schriften*, II: *Aufsätze, Essays, Vorträge* (1977), pp. 368–85
—— *Origin of the German 'Trauerspiel'*, trans. by Howard Eiland (Cambridge, MA: Harvard University Press, 2019) <https://doi.org/10.4159/9780674916357>
—— 'Phantasie', in Benjamin, *Gesammelte Schriften*, VI: *Fragmente vermischten Inhalts. Autobiographische Schriften* (1985), pp. 114–17
Bennington, Geoffrey, *Scatter 1: The Politics of Politics in Foucault, Heidegger, and Derrida* (New York: Fordham University Press, 2016) <https://doi.org/10.5422/fordham/9780823270521.001.0001>
Bennis, Warren, and Burt Nanus, *Leaders: The Strategies for Taking Charge* (New York: Harper & Row, 1985)
Bennis, Warren, and Philip Slater, 'Democracy Is Inevitable', *Harvard Business Review*, 42.2 (March–April 1964), pp. 51–59
Bergson, Henri, *Laughter: An Essay on the Meaning of the Comic*, trans. by Cloudesley Brereton (New York: Macmillan, 1911) <https://doi.org/10.1037/13772-000>
—— *The Two Sources of Morality and Religion*, trans. by R. Ashley Audra and Cloudesley Brereton with W. Horsfall Carter (Notre Dame, IN: University of Notre Dame Press, 1977)
Berkovits, Eliezer, *Not in Heaven: The Nature and Function of Halakha* (New York: Ktav Publishing House, 1983)
Berlant, Lauren, *Cruel Optimism* (Durham, NC: Duke University Press, 2011) <https://doi.org/10.1215/9780822394716>
Blanchot, Maurice, 'Speaking Is Not Seeing', in Blanchot, *The Infinite Conversation*, trans. by Susan Hanson (Minneapolis: University of Minnesota Press, 1993), pp. 25–32
Bojanić, Petar, and Damiano Cantone, eds, *Un matrimonio sfortunato. Derrida e l'architettura* (= *Aut aut*, 368 (2015))
Boltanski, Luc, and Ève Chiapello, *The New Spirit of Capitalism*, trans. by Gregory Elliott (London: Verso, 2005)
Bordeleau, Erik, 'Soulful Sedentarity: Tsai Ming-Liang at Home at the Museum', *Studies in European Cinema*, 10.2–3 (2013), pp. 179–94
Boyarin, Daniel, *A Radical Jew: Paul and the Politics of Identity* (Berkeley: University of California Press, 1994)
Braidotti, Rosi, *Nomadic Theory: The Portable Rosi Braidotti* (New York: Columbia University Press, 2012)
—— *The Posthuman* (Cambridge: Polity, 2013)
Brandon, James R., ed., *On Thrones of Gold: Three Javanese Shadow Plays* (Honolulu: University of Hawaii Press, 1993)
Brehm, Alfred Elmut, *Brehms Thierleben. Allgemeine Kunde des Thierreichs. Große Ausgabe*, 2nd, rev. and enlarged edn, 10 vols (Leipzig: Bibliographisches Institut, 1876–79) <https://doi.org/10.5962/bhl.title.1067>

Brooks, Mary Elizabeth, *A King for Portugal: The Madrigal Conspiracy 1594–95* (Madison: University of Wisconsin Press, 1964)

Brown, William, 'Melancholia: The Long, Slow Cinema of Lav Diaz', in *Slow Cinema*, ed. by Tiago de Luca and Nuno Barradas Jorge (Edinburgh: Edinburgh University Press, 2016), pp. 112–22 <https://doi.org/10.1515/9780748696031-013>

Brunette, Peter, *The Films of Michelangelo Antonioni* (Cambridge: Cambridge University Press, 1998) <https://doi.org/10.1017/CBO9780511624346>

Butler, Judith, and Gayatri Chakravorty Spivak, *Who Sings the Nation-State? Language, Politics, Belonging* (Calcutta: Seagull Books, 2007)

Butters, Ronald R., John M. Clum, and Michael Moon, eds, *Displacing Homophobia* (Durham, NC: Duke University Press, 1990)

Calvo, Emilio Rivas, and Carlos D'Abreu, 'Alacazarquivir. El enigma (o el rescate del cuerpo d'el rey don Sebastian)', *Praça Velha, Revista Cultural da Cidade da Guarda*, 21 (July 2007), pp. 39–59

Cammelli, Michele, *Canguilhem philosophe. Le Sujet et l'erreur*, preface by Etienne Balibar (Paris: PUF, 2022)

Cartier-Bresson, Henri, *The Decisive Moment: Photographs by Henri Cartier-Bresson* (New York: Simon & Schuster, 1952)

—— *Images à la sauvette* (Paris: Verve, 1952)

Chow, Rey, *The Protestant Ethnic and the Spirit of Capitalism* (New York: Columbia University Press, 2002)

Christensen, Clayton M., and Joseph L. Bower, 'Disruptive Technologies: Catching the Wave', *Harvard Business Review*, 73.1 (January–February 1995), pp. 43–53 <https://hbr.org/1995/01/disruptive-technologies-catching-the-wave> [accessed 4 May 2022]

Christensen, Clayton M., Michael E. Raynor, and Rory McDonald, 'What Is Disruptive Innovation?', *Harvard Business Review*, 93.12 (December 2015), pp. 44–53 <https://hbr.org/2015/12/what-is-disruptive-innovation> [accessed 10 May 2022]

Clark, Marshall, 'Shadow Boxing: Indonesian Writers and the Ramayana in the New Order', *Indonesia*, 72 (2001), pp. 159–87

—— '"Smells of Something like Postmodernism": Emha Ainun Nadjib's Rewriting of the Mahabharata', in *Clearing a Space: Postcolonial Readings of Modern Indonesian Literature*, ed. by Keith Foulcher and Tony Day (Leiden: KITLV Press, 2002), pp. 273–92

Cohen, Brianne, and Alexander Streitberger, eds, *The Photofilmic: Entangled Images in Contemporary Art and Visual Culture*, Lieven Gevaert Series, 21 (Leuven: Leuven University Press, 2016)

Cohen, Mordechai Z., 'A Talmudist's Halakhic Hermeneutics: A New Understanding of Maimonides' Principle of *Peshat* Primacy', *Jewish Studies: An Internet Journal*, 10 (2012), pp. 257–359 <https://jewish-faculty.biu.ac.il/files/jewish-faculty/shared/JSIJ4/cohen.pdf> [accessed 10 April 2022]

Cooper, Melinda, *Family Values: Between Neoliberalism and the New Social Conservativism* (New York: Zone Books, 2017) <https://doi.org/10.2307/j.ctt1qft0n6>
Critchley, Simon, *On Humour* (London: Routledge, 2002)
Cutting, James E., Jordan E. DeLong, and Christine E. Nothelfer, 'Attention and the Evolution of Hollywood Film', *Psychological Science*, 21.3 (2010), pp. 432–39
Dal Bo, Federico, *Deconstructing the Talmud: The Absolute Book* (Abingdon: Routledge, 2019) <https://doi.org/10.4324/9781315459899>
—— 'Economic Speculation and the Sacred', 'Market Prices', 'Market Intervention and the Common Good', 'Market Intervention and the Common Good', in *Judaism and the Economy: A Sourcebook*, ed. by Michael Satlow (Abingdon: Routledge, 2018), pp. 46–47, 48, 53–54, 69–70 <https://doi.org/10.4324/9781351137065>
—— *Emanation and Philosophy of Language: An Introduction to Joseph ben Abraham Giqatilla* (Los Angeles, CA: Cherub Press, 2019)
—— 'Legal and Transgressive Sex, Heresy, and Hermeneutics in the Talmud: The Cases of Bruriah, Rabbi Meir, Elisha ben Abuya and the Prostitute', in *Jewish Law and Academic Discipline. Contributions from Europe*, ed. by Elisha Ancselovits and George R. Wilkes, Jewish Law Association Studies, 26 (Liverpool: Deborah Charles, 2016), pp. 128–51
—— *Massekhet Keritot: Text, Translation, and Commentary*, A Feminist Commentary on the Babylonian Talmud, v.7 (Tübingen: Mohr Siebeck, 2013)
—— 'La mística de los palacios divinos en siglo XIII. Los *heikhalot bereshit* y *heikhalot pekudei* en el *Zóhar*', in *Kabbala judía y mística carmelitana. Encuentros en Sefarad*, ed. by Sancho Fermin (Avila: Grupo Editorial Forte & CITeS – Universidad de la Mistica, 2020), pp. 169–93
—— '"My Mother Tongue Is a Foreign Language". On Edmond Jabès's Writing in Exile', in *Untying the Mother Tongue: On Language, Affect, and the Unconscious*, ed. by Antonio Castore and Federico Dal Bo (Berlin: ICI Berlin Press, forthcoming)
—— 'Paul's Definition of "Circumcision of the Heart": A Transcultural Reading of Romans 2:28–29', in *Torah: Functions, Meanings, and Diverse Manifestations in Early Judaism and Christianity*, ed. by William M. Schniedewind, Jason M. Zurawski, and Gabriele Boccaccini (Atlanta, GA: SBL, 2021), pp. 397–410 <https://doi.org/10.2307/j.ctv2cw0sj7.24>
—— '"A Sage Understands of His Knowledge" (mHag 2:1): Degrees and Hierarchy of Knowledge in Abraham Abulafia', *Mediaevalia. Textos e estudos*, 36 (2017), pp. 61–73 <https://doi.org/10.21747/21836884/med36a3>
Dale, Karen, and Gibson Burrell, 'Disturbing Structure. Reading the Ruins', in *Culture and Organization*, 2 (2011), pp. 107–21
De Abreu, Maria José, 'Still Passing: Crisis, Youth and the Political Economy of Fog in Limbo', *Scapegoat: Landscape, Architecture, Political Economy*, 8 (May 2015), special issue *Weather*, pp. 60-70

De Matos, Marta, 'Estado-providência em Portugal e as políticas sociais: Avaliação da implementação das cantinas sociais' (unpublished doctoral dissertation, ISCTE — Instituto Universitário de Lisboa, 2014) <http://hdl.handle.net/10071/9008.> [accessed 8 December 2021]

Deleuze, Gilles, 'Anti-Œdipe et Mille Plateaux. Cours Vincennes: Sur la musique' (8 March 1977), transcription, *WebDeleuze*, ed. by Richard Pinhas and Benoit Maurer <https://www.webdeleuze.com/textes/183> [accessed 14 September 2019]

Deleuze, Gilles, and Félix Guattari, *A Thousand Plateaus: Capitalism and Schizophrenia*, trans. by Brian Massumi (Minneapolis: University of Minneapolis Press, 1987)

—— *Mille plateaux. Capitalisme et schizophrénie* (Paris: Minuit, 1980)

Demoris, Emmanuelle, *Camera con vista* (Marseille: Shellac Sud, 2012)

Demos, T. J., *The Migrant Image: The Art and Politics of Documentary during Global Crisis* (Durham, NC: Duke University Press, 2013) <https://doi.org/10.1215/9780822395751>

Derrida, Jacques, *Dissemination*, trans. by Barbara Johnson (London: Athlone Press, 1981) <https://doi.org/10.7208/chicago/9780226816340.001.0001>

—— 'Khôra', trans. by Ian McLeod, in Derrida, *On the Name*, ed. by Thomas Dutoit (Stanford, CA: Stanford University Press, 1995), pp. 89–127

—— 'Plato's Pharmacy', in Derrida, *Dissemination*, pp. 67–186

Derrida, Jacques, and Peter Eisenman, *Chora L Works*, ed. by Jeffrey Kipnis and Thomas Leeser (New York: Monacelli, 1997)

Descartes, René, *Discours de la méthode*, in *Œuvres philosophiques*, I (1963): 1618–1637, pp. 567–650

—— *Discourse on Method*, in Descartes, *Philosophical Writings*, I (1985), pp. 111–50

—— *Meditations on First Philosophy*, in Descartes, *Philosophical Writings*, II (1984), pp. 1–60

—— 'Objections and Replies', in Descartes, *Philosophical Writings*, II, pp. 63–397

—— *Œuvres philosophiques*, ed. by Ferdinand Alquié, 3 vols (Paris: Garnier, 1963–73)

—— *Les Passions de l'âme*, in Descartes, *Œuvres philosophiques*, III (1973): 1643–1650, pp. 941–1103

—— *The Philosophical Writings of Descartes*, trans. by John Cottingham, Robert Stoothoff, Dugald Murdoch, 3 vols (Cambridge: Cambridge University Press, 1984–1991) <https://doi.org/10.1017/CBO9781107340824>

Deuber-Mankowsky, Astrid, and Christoph F. E. Holzhey, eds, *Situiertes Wissen und regionale Epistemologie. Zur Aktualität Georges Canguilhems und Donna J. Haraways* (Vienna: Turia + Kant, 2013) <https://doi.org/10.37050/ci-07>

Doane, Mary Ann, *The Emergence of Cinematic Time: Modernity, Contingency, the Archive* (Cambridge, MA: Harvard University Press, 2002) <https://doi.org/10.4159/9780674263024>

Emha Ainun Nadjib, *Gerakan Punakawan Atawa Arus Bawah* (Yogyakarta: Yayasan Bentang Budaya, 1994)

Emmelhainz, Irmgard, and the Otolith Group (Kodwo Eshun and Anjalika Sagar), 'A Trialogue on Nervus Rerum', October, 129 (Summer 2009), pp. 129–32 <https://doi.org/10.1162/octo.2009.129.1.129>

Fernando Pessoa, *Mensagem*, ed. by Fernando Cabral Martins (Lisbon: Planeta DeAgostini, 2006)

Fidelis, Malgorzata, *Women, Communism, and Industrialization in Postwar Poland* (Cambridge: Cambridge University Press, 2014)

Filger, Sheldon, 'Donald Trump, Presidential Politics and the Art of Disruptive Innovation', *Huffpost*, blog, 23 September 2015 <https://www.huffpost.com/entry/donald-trump-presidential_b_8183138> [accessed April 27 2022]

Florida, Nancy K., 'Reading the Unread in Traditional Javanese Literature', *Indonesia*, 44 (October 1987), pp. 1–15 <https://doi.org/10.2307/3351218>

Foucault, Michel, 'Different Spaces', trans. by Robert Hurley, in *Foucault, Essential Works of Foucault, 1954-1984*, ed. by Paul Rabinow, 3 vols (New York: New Press, 1998–2001), II: *Aesthetics, Method, and Epistemology*, ed. by James D. Faubion (1998), pp. 175–85

Fraser, Nancy, 'Rethinking the Public Sphere: A Contribution to the Critique of Actually Existing Democracy', *Social Text*, 25/26 (1990), pp. 56–80

Freedberg, David, and Vittorio Gallese, 'Motion, Emotion and Empathy in Esthetic Experience', *Trends in Cognitive Sciences*, 11/5 (May 2007), pp. 197–203 <https://doi.org/10.1016/j.tics.2007.02.003>

Freud, Sigmund, *The Pelican Freud Library*, trans. by James Strachey, rev. and ed. by Angela Richards, 15 vols (Harmondsworth: Penguin, 1973–86), III (1976): *Jokes and their Relation to the Unconscious*

Freund, Gisèle, *La Photographie en France au dix-neuvième siècle. Essai de sociologie et d'esthétique* (Paris: La Maison des Amis des Livres/A. Monnier, 1936)

Fudge, Erica, *Brutal Reasoning: Animals, Rationality, and Humanity in Early Modern England* (Ithaca, NY: Cornell University Press, 2006) <https://doi.org/10.7591/9781501727191>

Furth, Charlotte, *A Flourishing Yin: Gender in China's Medical History, 960–1665* (Berkeley: University of California Press, 1999)

Geertz, Clifford, *The Religion of Java* (London: The Free Press, 1960)

Geertz, Hildred, 'Latah in Java: A Theoretical Paradox', *Indonesia*, 5 (April 1968), pp. 93–104 <https://doi.org/10.2307/3350765>

Germano, William, *Getting It Published: A Guide for Scholars and Anyone Else Serious about Serious Books* (Chicago: University of Chicago Press, 2001)

Glissant, Édouard, 'For Opacity', in Glissant, *Poetics of Relation*, pp. 189–94

―― *Poetics of Relation*, trans. by Betsy Wing (Ann Arbor: University of Michigan Press, 1997) <https://doi.org/10.3998/mpub.10257>

Goethe, Johann Wolfgang von, *Entwurf einer Farbenlehre*, in Goethe, *Sämtliche Werke nach Epochen seines Schaffens. Münchner Ausgabe*, ed. by Karl Richter and others (Munich: Hanser, 1986–99), x: *Die Farbenlehre*, ed. by Peter Schmidt (1989), pp. 17–273

―― *Italian Journey*, trans. by W. H. Auden and Elisabeth Mayer (New York: Pantheon, 1962)

Gordon, Mordechai, *Humor, Laughter, and Human Flourishing: A Philosophical Exploration of the Laughing Animal* (Cham: Springer, 2014) <https://doi.org/10.1007/978-3-319-00834-9>

Gorfinkel, Elena, 'Weariness, Waiting: Endurance and Art Cinema's Tired Bodies', *Discourse*, 34.2–3 (Spring/Fall 2012), pp. 311–47 <https://doi.org/10.13110/discourse.34.2-3.0311>

Goto, Yumi, 'Rinko Kawauchi's Illuminance', *Time.com*, 11 April 2011 <http://time.com/3776240/rinko-kawauchis-illuminance/> [accessed February 20, 2015]

Greenblatt, Stephen, 'Call for Action on Problems in Scholarly Book Publishing: A Special Letter from Stephen Greenblatt', 28 May 2002 <https://www.mla.org/Resources/Guidelines-and-Data/Reports-and-Professional-Guidelines/Publishing-and-Scholarship/Call-for-Action-on-Problems-in-Scholarly-Book-Publishing/A-Special-Letter-from-Stephen-Greenblatt> [accessed 20 April 2022]

Grosz, Elizabeth, 'The Future of Space: Toward an Architecture of Invention', in Grosz, *Architecture from the Outside: Essays on Virtual and Real Space*, foreword by Peter Eisenman (Cambridge, MA: MIT Press, 2001), pp. 109–30

Gržinić, Marina, 'Shifting The Borders of The Other: An Interview With Trinh T. Minh-ha', *Telepolis*, 12 August 1998 <http://www.heise.de/tp/artikel/3/3265/1.html> [accessed 5 May 2016]

Gumbrecht, Hans Ulrich, *Our Broad Present: Time and Contemporary Culture*, trans. by Henry Erik Butler (New York: Columbia University Press, 2014) <https://doi.org/10.7312/gumb16360>

Habermas, Jürgen, *The Structural Transformation of the Public Sphere: An Inquiry into a Category of Bourgeois Society* (Cambridge: Massachussetts: MIT Press, 1991)

Hacker, Andrea, 'In Defense of the Edited Book', *A Hacker's View*, blog, 3 December 2013 <http://www.andreahacker.com/in-defense-of-the-edited-book/> [accessed 2 May 2022]

Hardt, Michael, and Antonio Negri, *The Commonewealth* (Cambridge, MA: Harvard University Press, 2009)

Havel, Václav, *Open Letters: Selected Writings 1965–1990*, ed. by Paul Wilson (New York: Knopf, 1991)

―― 'Power of the Powerless', trans. by Paul Wilson, *International Journal of Politics*, 15.3–4 (Fall/Winter 1985–86), pp. 23–96

Heidegger, Martin, 'Plato's Doctrine of Truth', in *Philosophy of the Twentieth Century: An Anthology*, ed. by William Barrett and Henry D. Aiken, 4 vols (New York: Random House, 1962), III: pp. 251–70
Henderson, Brian, 'Toward a Non-Bourgeois Camera Style', *Film Quarterly*, 24.2 (1970), pp. 2–14
Hersenhorn, David, and Paul McLeary, 'Ukraine's "Iron General" is a Hero, But He's No Star', *Politico*, 8 April 2022 <https://www.politico.com/news/2022/04/08/ukraines-iron-general-zaluzhnyy-00023901> [accessed 9 May 2022].
Hobbes, Thomas, *The Elements of Law, Natural and Politic*, ed. by Ferdinand Tönnies (Cambridge: Cambridge University Press, 1928)
―― *Leviathan*, ed. by Noel Malcolm, 3 vols (Oxford: Clarendon, 2012) <https://doi.org/10.1093/oseo/instance.00025178>
Holzhey, Christoph F. E., 'Weathering Ambivalences: Between Language and Physics', in *Weathering: Ecologies of Exposure*, ed. by Christoph F. E. Holzhey and Arnd Wedemeyer, Cultural Inquiry, 17 (Berlin: ICI Berlin Press, 2020), pp. 3–40 <https://doi.org/10.37050/ci-17>
Huang Di Nei Jing Su Wen: An Annotated Translation of Huang Di's Inner Classic — Basic Questions, ed. by Paul U. Unschuld, 2 vols (Berkeley: University of California Press, 2011)
The I Ching; or, Book of Changes, trans. by Cary F. Baynes, foreword by C. G. Jung, Bollingen Series, 19 (New York: Pantheon Books, 1950)
I Ging. Das Buch der Wandlungen, trans. by Richard Wilhelm, 2 vols (Jena: Eugen Diederichs, 1924)
Ibrahim Ghaffar, 'Embah Setia Menunggu Merapi', *Dewan Masyarakat*, July 2006, pp. 54–55
Inandiak, Elizabeth D., *Merapi Omahku* (Yogyakarta: Babad Alas Elizabeth D. Inandiak/Heri Dono, 2010)
Irigaray, Luce, *Speculum of the Other Woman*, trans. by Gillian C. Gill (Ithaca, NY: Cornell University Press, 1985)
Ishida, Tetsuro, 'An Interview with Kawauchi Rinko: An Obsession with Time and Memory', in Rinko Kawauchi, *Illuminance, Ametsuchi, Seeing Shadow* (Kyoto: Seigensha, 2012), pp. 125-128
Janion, Maria, *Niesamowita Słowiańszczyzna* (Kraków: Wydawnictwo Literackie, 2006)
Jastrow, Marcus, *A Dictionary of the Targumim, the Talmud Babli, and the Yerushalmi, and the Midrashic Literature*, 2 vols. (London: Luazac, 1903)
Joubert, Laurent, *Treatise on Laughter*, trans. and annotated by Gregory David de Rocher (Tuscaloosa: University of Alabama Press, 1980)
Kafka, Franz, 'Der Bau', in Kafka, *Beim Bau der Chinesischen Mauer. Ungedruckte Erzählungen und Prosa aus dem Nachlaß*, ed. by Max Brod and Hans-Joachim Schoeps (Berlin: Kiepenheuer, 1931), pp. 77–133
―― 'Der Bau', *Witiko. Zeitschrift für Kunst und Dichtung*, 1 (1928), pp. 89–104
―― 'Before the Law', in Kafka, *The Complete Stories*, pp. 4–5

—— 'The Burrow', trans. by Willa and Edwin Muir, in Kafka, *The Complete Stories*, pp. 325–59
—— *The Complete Stories*, ed. by Nahum N. Glatzer (New York: Schocken, 1971)
—— 'Fragments from Notebooks and Loose Pages', in Kafka, *Dearest Father: Stories and Other Writings* (New York: Schocken Books, 1954)
—— 'The Great Wall of China', in Kafka, *The Complete Stories*, pp. 235–47
—— *Letters to Milena*, trans. and intro. by Philip Boehm (New York: Schocken, 1990)
—— 'Unpublished Works 1922–1924', in *The Kafka Project*, ed. by Mario Nervi (1999–2007) <http://www.kafka.org/index.php?ichentlief> [accessed 5 July 2021]
Kant, Immanuel, *Critique of Judgment*, trans. and introduction by Werner S. Pluhar (Indianapolis, IN: Hackett, 1987)
Karatani, Kojin, *Architecture as Metaphor: Language, Number, Money*, ed. by Michael Speaks, trans. by Sabu Kohso (Cambridge, MA: MIT Press, 1995)
Kawauchi, Rinko, *AILA* (Tokyo: Little More, 2004)
—— *Ametsuchi* (New York: Aperture, 2013)
—— *Approaching Whiteness* (Tokyo: Goliga, 2013)
—— *Cui Cui* (Tokyo: Foil; Arles; Actes Sud; Paris: Fondation Cartier pour l'art contemporain, 2005)
—— *The Eyes, the Ears: Photographs and Words* (Tokyo: Foil, 2005)
—— *Hanabi* (Tokyo: Ritorumoa, 2001)
—— *Hanako* (Tokyo: Ritoru Moa, 2001)
—— *The River Embraced Me* (Tokyo: torch press, 2016)
—— *Semear* (Tokyo: FOIL, 2007)
—— *Sheets* (Berlin: Kominek Books, 2013)
Kawauchi, Rinko, and Masakazu Takei, *Utatane* (Tokyo: Ritorumoa, 2001)
Kawauchi, Rinko, and Terri Weifenbach, *Gift* (Tokyo: Amana, 2014)
Keeler, Ward, *Javanese Shadow Play, Javanese Selves* (Princeton, NJ: Princeton University Press, 1987)
Kelsky, Karen L., 'Should I Do an Edited Collection?', *The Professor Is In*, 24 July 2012 <https://theprofessorisin.com/2012/07/24/should-i-do-an-edited-collection/> [accessed 7 May 2022]
Kirchmayr, Raoul, 'L'arte dell'*espacement*', *Aut aut*, 368 (2015), pp. 62-87
Kondratowicz, Ewa, *Szminka na sztandarze. Kobiety Solidarnosci 1980–1989* (Warsaw: Wydawnictwo Sic!, 2001)
Krochmal, Nachman, *More Nevuchim ha-Zeman*, ed. by Leopold Zunz (Lviv: Joseph Schneider, 1851) <https://books.google.de/books?id=GtUFcSlkpKUC&pg> [accessed 9 April 2022]
Kundera, Milan, 'The Tragedy of Central Europe', *New York Review of Books*, 31.7 (26 April 1984), pp. 33-38
La Mettrie, Julien Offray de, *Machine Man and Other Writings*, ed. and trans. by Ann Thomson (Cambridge: Cambridge University Press, 1996)

Landgraf, Edgar, 'Self-Forming Selves: Autonomy and Artistic Creativity in Goethe and Moritz', *Goethe Yearbook*, 11 (2002), pp. 159–76

Laqueur, Thomas, *Making Sex: Body and Gender from the Greeks to Freud* (Cambridge, MA: Harvard University Press, 1990)

Lauwaert, Maaike, 'Helden van de tegenzin', *Tubelight*, 66 (January 2010) <https://www.tubelight.nl/helden-van-de-tegenzin/> [accessed 16 September 2021], English trans. as 'Heroes of Reluctance: On Hesitation as an Active Act', author's website <http://maaikelauwaert.com/articles/joseph-vogl/> [accessed 16 September 2021]

Lebner, Ashley, 'After the Medium: Rereading Stories on a String and the War of Canudos', *Journal of American Academy of Religion*, 89.4 (December 2021), pp. 1290–1333 <https://doi.org/10.1093/jaarel/lfab097>

Lepore, Jill, 'The Disruption Machine: What the Gospel of Innovation Gets Wrong', *The New Yorker*, 23 June 2014 <https://www.newyorker.com/magazine/2014/06/23/the-disruption-machine> [accessed 10 May 2022].

Leria, Manuel, and Ortíz de Saracho, 'El acta de entrega del cuerpo del rey don Sebastián', *Transfretana*, 7 (2001), pp. 135–44

Levine, Robert, *Vale of Tears: Revisiting the Canudos Massacre in Northeastern Brazil, 1893–1897* (Berkeley: University of California Press, 1995)

Lopes, Maria Antónia, 'Os pobres e a assistencia publica', in *História de Portugal*, ed. by José Mattoso, 8 vols (Lisbon: Circulo de Leitores, 1993–94), v: *O liberalismo* (1993), pp. 500–15

Love, Heather, *Norms, Deviance, and the Queer Ordinary?*, lecture, ICI Berlin, 22 June 2015, video recording, mp4, 47:09 <http://doi.org/10.25620/e150622>

Lysloff, René, 'A Wrinkle in Time: The Shadow Puppet Theatre of Banyumas (West Central Java)', *Asian Theatre Journal*, 10.1 (1993), pp. 49–80

MacDougall, David, *Transcultural Cinema* (Princeton, NJ: Princeton University Press, 1998)

März, Moses, '"Embracing Opacity:" Interview with Ntone Edjabe (Chimurenga Magazine)', *AfricAvenir International — African Renaissance, Development, International Collaboration and Peace*, interview conducted on 14 July 2011 <http://www.africavenir.org/nc/news-details/article/embracing-opacity-interview-with-ntone-edjabe-chimurenga-magazine.html> [accessed 5 May 2016]

Majewska, Ewa, 'The Utopia of "Solidarity" Between Public Sphere and Counterpublics: Institutions of the Common Revisited', *Utopian Studies*, 2.29 (2018), pp. 229–47

Mangkunegara VII, *On the Wayang Kulit (Purwa) and its Symbolic and Mystical Elements*, trans. by Claire Holt (Southeast Asia Program, Dept. of Far Eastern Studies, Cornell University, 1957)

Margulies, Ivone, 'Exemplary Bodies: Reenactment in *Love in the City*, *Sons, and Close Up*', in *Rites of Realism: Essays on Corporeal Cinema*, ed. by

Ivone Margulies (Durham, NC: Duke University Press, 2003), pp. 217–44 <https://doi.org/10.1215/9780822384618-014>

—— *Nothing Happens: Chantal Akerman's Hyperrealist Everyday* (Durham, NC: Duke University Press, 1996) <https://doi.org/10.1215/9780822399254>

Matt, Daniel C., ed., *The Zohar*, trans. and commentary by Daniel C. Matt and others, Prizker Edition, vols. 12 (Stanford, CA: Stanford University Press, 2003–2017), XII (2017): *Zoharic Compositions*, trans. by Nathan Wolski and Joel Hecker

Matynia, Elżbieta, 'The Lost Treasures of Solidarity', *Social Research*, 68. 4 (2001), pp. 917–36

McCraw, Thomas, *Prophet of Innovation: Joseph Schumpeter and Creative Destruction* (Cambridge, MA: Harvard University Press, 2007)

McPherson, James, 'From the President: A Crisis in Scholarly Publishing', *Perspectives on History*, 41.7 (October 2003) <https://www.historians.org/publications-and-directories/perspectives-on-history/october-2003-x43317> [accessed 3 May 2022]

Melville, Herman, 'Bartleby, the Scrivener', in Melville, *The Piazza Tales, and Other Prose Pieces, 1839–1860*, ed. by Harrison Hayford, Alma A. MacDougall, G. Thomas Tanselle, and others (Evanston, IL: Northwestern University Press, 1987), pp. 13–45 <https://doi.org/10.1093/oseo/instance.00209193>

Mendes, Luis, 'Gentrificação túristica em Lisboa: Neoliberalismo, financeirização e urbanismo austeritário em tempos de pós-crise capitalista 2008–2009', *Cadernos Metrópole*, 39 (2017), pp. 479–512

Mendes, Luis, and André Carmo, 'State-Led Gentrification in an Era of Neoliberal Urbanism: Examining the New Urban Lease Regime in Portugal', paper presented at the conference *Contested Cities: From Contested Cities to Global Urban Justice — Critical Dialogues*, Madrid, 4–7 July 2016, and available at the conference website <http://contested-cities.net/working-papers/2016/state-led-gentrification-in-an-era-of-neoliberal-urbanism-examining-the-new-urban-lease-regime-in-portugal/> [accessed 6 December 2021].

Merchant, Brian, 'Life and Death in Apple's Forbidden City', *Guardian*, 18 June 2017 <https://www.theguardian.com/technology/2017/jun/18/foxconn-life-death-forbidden-city-longhua-suicide-apple-iphone-brian-merchant-one-device-extract> [accessed 20 September 2017]

—— *The One Device: The Secret History of the iPhone* (New York: Little, Brown and Company, 2017)

Minh-ha, Trinh T., *When the Moon Waxes Red: Representation, Gender and Cultural Politics* (London: Routledge, 1991)

Mitchell, W. J. T., 'Idolatry: Nietzsche, Blake and Poussin', in *Things: Religion and the Question of Materiality*, ed. by Dick Houtman and Birgit Meyer (New York: Fordham University Press, 2012), pp. 112–26

Mitroupolous, Angela, 'Oikopolitics, and Storms', *The Global South*, 3.1 (2009), pp. 66–82

Moore, David C., 'Is the Post- in Postcolonial the Post- in Post-Soviet? Toward a Global Postcolonial Critique', *PMLA*, 116.1 (2001), pp. 111–28

Morreall, John, *Comic Relief: A Comprehensive Philosophy of Humor* (Chichester: Wiley-Blackwell, 2009) <https://doi.org/10.1002/9781444307795>

—— 'A New Theory of Laughter', *Philosophical Studies*, 42.2 (September 1982), pp. 243–54 <https://doi.org/10.1007/BF00374037>

Morris, Rosalind C., *In the Place of Origins: Modernity and its Mediums in Thailand* (Durham, NC: Duke University Press, 2000)

Mrázek, Jan, *Phenomenology of a Puppet Theatre: Contemplations on the Art of Javanese Wayang Kulit* (Leiden: KITLV Press, 2005)

Muehlebach, Andrea, '*Complexio Oppositorum*: Notes on the Left in Neoliberal Italy', *Public Culture*, 21.3 (2009), pp. 495–515

Negt, Oskar, and Alexander Kluge, *Public Sphere and Experience: Toward an Analysis of the Bourgeois and Proletarian Public Sphere*, trans. by Peter Labanyi, Jamie Owen Daniel, and Assenka Oksiloff (Minneapolis: University of Minnesota Press, 1993)

Newitt, Malyn, *Portugal's Third Empire: Portugal in Africa in the Last Hundred Years* (London: C. Hurst, 1981)

Nietzsche, Friedrich, 'The Twilight of the Idols', in *The Works of Nietzsche*, trans. by Thomas Common (London: T. Fisher Unwin, 1899)

O'Conell, Mark, 'The Stunning Success of "Fail Better": How Samuel Beckett Became Silicon Valley's Life Coach', *Slate*, 29 January 2014 <https://slate.com/culture/2014/01/samuel-becketts-quote-fail-better-becomes-the-mantra-of-silicon-valley.html> [accessed 31 May 2022]

OED Online (Oxford: Oxford University Press, 2020) <http://www.oed.com>

Offe, Claus, 'Capitalism by Democratic Design? Democratic Theory Facing the Triple Transition in East Central Europe', *Social Research*, 71.3 (2004), pp. 501–28

Ost, David, *The Defeat of Solidarity: Anger and Politics in Postcommunist Europe* (Ithaca, NY: Cornell University Press, 2005) <https://doi.org/10.7591/9781501729270>

Pasolini, Pier Paolo, *Empirismo eretico* (Milan: Garzanti Libri, 2000)

Pateman, Carole, *The Disorder of Women: Feminism and Political Theory* (Cambridge: Polity Press, 1989)

Pausacker, Helen, 'Presidents as Punakawan: Portrayal of National Leaders as Clown-Servants in Central Javanese Wayang', *Journal of Southeast Asian Studies*, 35.2 (2004), pp. 213–33

Peck, Jamie, 'Austerity Urbanism: American Cities Under Extreme Economy', *City*, 16.6 (2012), pp. 626–56

Pemberton, John, *On the Subject of 'Java'* (Ithaca, NY: Cornell University Press, 1994) <https://doi.org/10.7591/9781501729362>

Penn, Shana, *Solidarity's Secret: The Women Who Defeated Communism in Poland* (Ann Arbor: University of Michigan Press, 2006) <https://doi.org/10.3998/mpub.17617>

Pereira, Pedro Teotónio, *A Batalha do Futuro* (Lisbon: Livraria Clássica, 1937)

Pessoa, Fernando, *Sobre Portugal. Introdução ao problema nacional*, ed. by Maria Isabel Rocheta and Maria Paula Morão (Lisbon: Aticá, 1978)

Pinter, Frances, and Laura White, 'Development of Book Publishing Business Models and Financing', in *Academic and Professional Publishing*, ed. by Robert Campbell, Ed Pentz, and Ian Borthwick (Oxford: Chandos, 2012), pp. 171–93

Plato, *Phaedrus*, trans. by Alexander Nehamas and Paul Woodruff, in Plato, *Complete Works*, ed. by John M. Cooper and D. S. Hutchinson (Indianapolis, IN: Hackett, 1997), pp. 506–56

—— *The Republic*, trans. by G. M. A. Grube, rev. by C. D. C. Grube, in Plato, *Complete Works*, ed. by John M. Cooper (Indianapolis, IN: Hackett, 1997), pp. 971–1223

'The Poetry and Brief Life of a Foxconn Worker: Xu Lizhi (1990–2014)', *Nao* blog on Libcom.org <http://libcom.org/blog/xulizhi-foxconn-suicide-poetry> [accessed 4 August 2017]

Powell, Helen, *Stop the Clocks!: Time and Narrative in Cinema* (London: I. B. Tauris, 2012) <https://doi.org/10.5040/9780755693863>

Pramoedya Ananta Toer, *Exile: Pramoedya Ananta Toer in Conversation with Andre Vltchek and Rossie Indira* (Chicago: Haymarket Books, 2006)

Preciado, Paul B., *Manifiesto contra-sexual. Prácticas subversivas de identidad sexual*, trans. by Julio Díaz and Carolina Meloni (Madrid: Opera Prima, 2002)

'Principles and Strategies for the Reform of Scholarly Communication 1', American Library Association, 1 September 2006 <https://www.ala.org/acrl/publications/whitepapers/principlesstrategies> [accessed 15 April 2022]

Purdy, Daniel L., *On the Ruins of Babel: Architectural Metaphor in German Thought* (Ithaca, NY: Cornell University Press, 2011) <https://doi.org/10.7591/cornell/9780801476761.001.0001>

'Q. Who First Originated the Term VUCA (Volatility, Uncertainty, Complexity and Ambiguity)?', website of the U.S. Army Heritage and Education Center at the U.S. Army War College, 22 November 2021 <https://usawc.libanswers.com/faq/84869> [accessed 23 January 2022]

Rabasa, José, *Tell Me the Story of How I Conquered You: Elsewheres and Ethnosuicide in the Colonial Mesoamerican World* (Austin: University of Texas Press, 2011) <https://doi.org/10.7560/728752>

Ramachandran, V. S., 'The Neurology and Evolution of Humor, Laughter, and Smiling: The False Alarm Theory', *Medical Hypotheses*, 51.4 (October

1998), pp. 351–54 <https://doi.org/10.1016/S0306-9877(98)90061-5>
Rancière, Jacques, *Disagreement: Politics and Philosophy*, trans. by Julie Rose (Minneapolis: University of Minnesota Press, 2004)
—— *The Hatred of Democracy*, trans. by Steve Corcoran (London: Verso, 2014)
—— *The Philosopher and his Poor*, ed. and intro. by Andrew Parker, trans. by John Drury, Corinne Oster, and Andrew Parker (Durham, NC: Duke University Press, 2003) <https://doi.org/10.1215/9780822385707>
Rautzenberg, Markus, 'Die Empfindung eines Objekts als Beobachtung ausgeben. Das Haiku als "Sprachfotografie" bei Roland Barthes und Andrej Tarkowskij', *Kodikas/Code. Ars Semeiotica*, 37.3–4 (2014), pp. 349–60
—— 'Was ist postmetaphysische Präsenztheorie?', in Rautzenberg, *Die Gegenwendigkeit der Störung. Aspekte einer postmetaphysischen Präsenztheorie* (Zürich: Diaphanes, 2009), pp. 21–45
Renger-Patzsch, Albert, *Die Welt ist schön* (Munich: Einhorn-Verlag, 1928)
Riabczuk, Mykoła, *Ukraina. Syndrom postkolonialny* (Warszawa: Kolegium Europy Wschodniej im. Jana Nowaka-Jeziorańskiego, 2014)
Ricchi, Rafael Immanuel Chay ben Abraham, *Yoshev Levav* (Amsterdam 1742)
Rimawan Prasetiyo, 'Pesan Terakhir Mbah Maridjan dan Kisahnya Tepat Ramalkan Letusan Merapi Gara-gara Burung', *Tribunwow*, 28 July 2017, <https://wow.tribunnews.com/2017/07/28/pesan-terakhir-mbah-maridjan-dan-kisahnya-tepat-ramalkan-letusan-merapi-gara-gara-burung> [accessed 4 July 2021]
Ronell, Avital, *Stupidity* (Champaign: University of Illinois Press, 2002)
Rosas, Fernando, *Salazar e o poder. A arte de saber durar* (Lisbon: Tinta da China, 2013)
Rosenfield, Leonora, *From Beast-Machine to Man-Machine* (New York: Octagon Books, 1968)
Salt, Barry, *Moving Into Pictures: More on Film History, Style, and Analysis* (London: Starword, 2006)
Sanders, E. P., *Paul and Palestinian Judaism* (Philadelphia, PA: Fortress, 1977)
Scholette, Gregory, *The Dark Matter: Art and Politics in the Age of Enterprise Culture* (London: Pluto Press, 2013)
Schumpeter, Joseph A., *Capitalism, Socialism, and Democracy* (New York: Harper & Brothers, 1942)
Scorsese, Martin, and Nicholas Pileggi, *Goodfellas* (London: Faber & Faber, 1990)
Serres, Michel, *Le Tiers-Instruit* (Paris: François Bourin, 1991)
—— *The Troubadour of Knowledge*, trans. by Sheila Faria Glaser and William Paulson (Ann Arbor: University of Michigan Press, 1997) <https://doi.org/10.3998/mpub.9722>
Shaftesbury, Anthony Ashley Cooper, Third Earl of, 'An Essay on the Freedom of Wit and Humour — A Letter to a Friend' [1709] <http:

//www.earlymoderntexts.com/assets/pdfs/shaftesbury1709a_1.pdf> [accessed 1 October 2019]

Sholis, Brian, 'Interview with Hans Gremmen, Designer of Rinko Kawauchi's *Ametsuchi*', publisher's website <http://www.aperture.org/blog/interview-with-hans-gremmen/> [accessed 10 March 2015]

Siegel, James, *Solo in the New Order: Language and Hierarchy in an Indonesian City* (Princeton, NJ: Princeton University Press, 1986) <https://doi.org/10.1515/9780691228341>

Simmel, Georg, 'The Ruin', in *Georg Simmel, 1858–1918: A Collection of Essays, with Translations and a Bibliography*, ed. by Kurt H. Wolff (Cleveland: Ohio State University Press, 1959), pp. 259–66

Sindhunata, *Semar Mencari Raga* (Yogyakarta: Kanisius, 1996)

Spencer, Herbert, 'On the Physiology of Laughter' [1860], in Spencer, *Essays on Education and Kindred Subjects* (London: Dent, 1911), pp. 298–309

Spivak, Gayatri Chakravorty, 'Can the Subaltern Speak?', in *Marxism and the Interpretation of Culture*, ed. by Cary Nelson and Lawrence Grossberg (Chicago: University of Illinois Press, 1988), pp. 271–313

—— *A Critique of Postcolonial Reason* (Cambridge, MA: Harvard University Press, 1999) <https://doi.org/10.2307/j.ctvjsf541>

Sri Mulyono, *Apa dan Siapa Semar* (Jakarta: CV Haji Masagung, 1989)

Staniszkis, Jadwiga, *Poland's Self-Limiting Revolution*, trans. by Jan Gross (Princeton: Princeton University Press, 1984)

Steiner, George, *After Babel: Aspects of Language and Translation* (Oxford: Oxford University Press, 1975)

Stolze Lima, Tânia, 'O dois e seu múltiplo: reflexões sobre o perspectivismo emu ma cosmologia tupi', *Mana*, 2.2 (1996), pp. 21–47

Sumastuti Sumukti, 'An Analysis of Semar Through Selected Javanese Shadow Play Stories' (unpublished doctoral thesis, University of Hawaii, 1990)

Talcott, Samuel, *Georges Canguilhem and the Problem of Error* (Cham: Palgrave Macmillan, 2019) <https://doi.org/10.1007/978-3-030-00779-9>

Townsend, Robert B., 'History and the Future of Scholarly Publishing', *Perspectives on History*, 41.7 (October 2003) <https://www.historians.org/publications-and-directories/perspectives-on-history/october-2003/history-and-the-future-of-scholarly-publishing> [accessed 3 May 2022]

Tristuti Rachmadi Suryasaputra, 'My Life as a Shadow Master under Suharto', in *Beginning to Remember: The Past in the Indonesian Present*, ed. by Mary S. Zurbuchen (Singapore: Singapore University Press, 2005), pp. 38–46

Uehlinger, Christoph, *Weltreich und 'eine Rede'. Eine neue Deutung der sogenannten Turmbauerzählung (Gen 11,1–9)* (Göttingen: Vandenhoeck & Ruprecht, 1990)

Valéry, Paul, *Eupalinos, or The Architect*, in *Collected Works of Paul Valéry*, ed. by Jackson Mathews, 15 vols (Princeton, NJ: Princeton University Press, 1956–75), IV: *Dialogues*, trans. by William McCausland Stewart (1956), pp. 65–150

Vitruvius, *Ten Books on Architecture*, trans. by Ingrid D. Rowland, commentary by Thomas Noble Howe, Ingrid D. Rowland, and Michael J. Dewar (Cambridge: Cambridge University Press, 1999) <https://doi.org/10.1017/CBO9780511840951>

Viveiros de Castro, Eduardo, 'Cannibal Metaphysics: Amerindian Perspectivism', *Radical Philosophy*, 182 (November–December 2013), pp. 17–28

Wahlberg, Malin, *Documentary Time: Film and Phenomenology* (Minneapolis: University of Minnesota Press, 2008)

Wallerstein, Immanuel, *European Universalism: The Rhetoric of Power* (New York: New Press, 2006)

—— 'Semi-Peripheral Countries and the Contemporary World Crisis', *Theory and Society*, 3.4 (Winter 1976), pp. 461–83 <https://doi.org/10.1007/BF00161293>

Warner, Michael, ed., *Fear of a Queer Planet: Queer Politics and Social Theory* (Minneapolis: University of Minnesota Press, 1993)

Waters, Lindsay, *Enemies of Promise: Publishing, Perishing, and the Eclipse of Scholarship* (Chicago, IL: Prickly Paradigm Press, 2004)

Weber, Max, *The Protestant Ethic and the Spirit of Capitalism*, trans. by Talcott Parsons, foreword by R. H. Tawney (London: Allen & Unwin, 1930)

Weber, Samuel, *Theatricality as Medium* (New York: Fordham University Press, 2004) <https://doi.org/10.5422/fso/9780823224159.001.0001>

Webster, Peter, *The Edited Collection: Pasts, Present, and Futures* (Cambridge: Cambridge University Press, 2020) <https://doi.org/10.1017/9781108683647>

Webster, Peter, Pat Thomson, and Mark Carrigan, 'Edited Collections May Still Have Much to Offer Academics in the Humanities and Social Sciences', *LSE Impact Blog*, London School of Economics, 23 July 2013 <https://blogs.lse.ac.uk/impactofsocialsciences/2013/07/23/in-defence-of-edited-collections/> [accessed 2 May 2022]

Weigand, Hermann J., 'Franz Kafka's "The Burrow" ("Der Bau"): An Analytical Essay', *PMLA*, 87.2 (1972), pp. 152–66

Weiss Halivni, David, *Peshat and Derash: Plain and Applied Meaning in Rabbinic Exegesis* (Oxford: Oxford University Press, 1991)

Wielgosz, Przemysław, 'Od zacofania i spowrotem. Wprowadzenie do ekonomii politycznej peryferyjnego miasta przemysłowego', in *Futuryzm miast przemysłowych*, ed. by Martin Kaltwasser, Ewa Majewska, and Kuba Szreder (Kraków: Korporacja ha! Art, 2007), pp. 241–53

Wigley, Mark, 'The Art to Listen to Architecture', in *Eisenman/Krier: Two Ideologies*, ed. by Cynthia C. Davidson (New York: Monacelli, 2004), pp. 119–31

Wynter, Sylvia, 'Unsettling the Coloniality of Being/Power/Truth/Freedom: Towards the Human, after Man, its Overrepresentation — An Argument', *CR: The New Centennial Review*, 3.3 (2003), pp. 257–337

Xiang, Zairong, 'Oracle from 2018: Transdualism, or the A/History of Yin-Yang', *Heichi Magazine*, 23 December 2021 <http://www.heichimagazine.org/en/articles/1067/oracle-from-2018-zairong-xiang-transdualism-or-the-a-history-of-yin-yang> [accessed 29 March 2022]

Zöllner, Frank, 'L'uomo vitruviano di Leonardo da Vinci, Rudolf Wittkower e l'*Angelus Novus* di Walter Benjamin', *Raccolta viciana*, 26 (1995), pp. 329–58

Zuromskis, Catherine, *Snapshot Photography: The Lives of Images* (Cambridge, MA: MIT Press, 2013)

FILMOGRAPHY

Eat, dir. by Andy Warhol (1963)

Enthus Susmono, *Dewa Ruci* [The Resplendent God], Contemporary Wayang Archive, Singapore <http://cwa-web.org/en/DewaRuci> [accessed 4 July 2021]

Goodfellas, dir. by Martin Scorsese (Warner Bros. Pictures, 1990)

Jules et Jim, dir. by François Truffaut (Cinédis, 1962)

'讓貞子生活在我們抗日的這片沃土上，她的心再冰冷也會融化' (Let Sadako live on our fertile land of anti-Japanese struggle and even her frozen heart can be melted), online meme video, YouTube, n.d., <https://youtu.be/2gxptjlYRjE> [accessed 29 March 2022]

Mafrouza — Oh la nuit!, dir. by Emmanuelle Demoris (Les Films de la Villa, 2007)

Mafrouza/Coeur, dir. by Emmanuelle Demoris (Les Films de la Villa, 2010)

La main du papillon, dir. by Emmanuelle Demoris (Les Films de la Villa, 2010)

Makhdoumin / A Maid for Each, dir. by Maher Abi Samra (Icarus Films, 2016)

Nervus Rerum, dir. by The Otolith Group (2008)

Paraboles, dir. by Emmanuelle Demoris (Les Films de la Villa, 2010)

Paris nous appartient, dir. by Jacques Rivette (Diaphana, 1961)

Que faire?, dir. by Emmanuelle Demoris (Les Films de la Villa, 2010)

Ring, dir. by Hideo Nakata (Ringu/Rasen Production Committee, 1998)

Sleep, dir. by Andy Warhol (1963)

Super Pumped, created by Brian Koppelman and David Levien (Showtime, 2022–)

'Duka Bencana Merapi. Mbah Maridjan meninggal sujud', news clip video, YouTube <https://www.youtube.com/watch?v=UVGKtatChK8> [accessed 1 July 2015; video no longer available]

WeCrashed, created by Drew Crevello and Lee Eisenberg (Apple TV+, 2022–)

Week-end, dir. by Jean-Luc Godard (Athos Films, 1967)

Notes on the Contributors

Rosa Barotsi is a Marie Curie fellow based at the Università Cattolica des Sacro Cuore in Milan. She is a film scholar trained at the University of Cambridge, where she received her PhD in 2014, and was a postdoctoral fellow at the ICI Berlin, where she developed a project on Slow Cinema and debt. Along with Saima Akhtar and Clio Nicastro, she co-founded the ongoing research project 'In Front of the Factory' in 2016. Her research and publications focus on the intersections between film, gender, and work, with an emphasis on Italian and Greek cinema. She is currently developing a project on women filmmakers in Italy in the period 1965–2015.

James Burton is senior lecturer in Cultural Studies and Cultural History at Goldsmiths, University of London. He is a former research fellow of the Humboldt Foundation and the ICI Berlin. He publishes in the fields of cultural theory, philosophy, media, and literature, with particular interests in process philosophy, ecology, and speculative fiction. He is the author of *The Philosophy of Science Fiction: Henri Bergson and the Fabulations of Philip K. Dick* (2015), and co-editor with Erich Hörl of *General Ecology* (2017). Recent articles include 'Manimism: Worrying about the Relationship between Rationality and Animism', *New Formations*, 104–05 (2021) and 'Astronoetic Voyaging: Speculation, Media and Futurity', in *The Future of Media* (2022).

Antonio Castore holds a PhD in comparative literature from the University of Turin, where he also lectured on Italian poetry and translation studies. Former research fellow at the Folger Shakespeare Library, Washington D.C., and the ICI Berlin, he is the author of a new Italian translation and critical edition of Shakespeare's *The Comedy of Errors* and *Pericles, Prince of Tyre* (in *Tutte le opere*, ed. by F. Marenco (2015–18)). He has authored two monographs: *Il dialogo spezzato. Forme dell'incomprensione in letteratura* (2011) and *Grottesco e riscrittura* (2012). His research spans from literary theory to the interconnections between literature and linguistics, philosophy, and architecture, with a special interest in literary and artistic experiences that question aesthetic and cultural 'borders'.

Federico Dal Bo is research assistant at the collaborative research centre 'Material Text Cultures' at Heidelberg University. He holds a PhD in Translation Studies from the University of Bologna (2005) and a PhD in Jewish Studies from the Freie Universität Berlin (2009). He is the author of several monographs, among them *La lingua malata. Linguaggio e violenza nella filosofia contemporanea* (2008), *Emanation and Philosophy of Language: An Introduction to Joseph ben Abraham Giqatilla* (2019), *Deconstructing the Talmud: The Absolute Book* (2019), *Il linguaggio della violenza. Estremismo e ideologia nella filosofia contemporenea* (new edition, 2020), and *The Lexical Field of the Substantives of 'Word' in Ancient Hebrew: From the Bible to the Mishnah* (2021). His work focuses on Talmud, Kabbalah, Jewish hermeneutics, and translation studies, with a particular interest in deconstruction and its application to religious texts. www.federicodalbo.eu

Christoph F. E. Holzhey is the founding director of the ICI Berlin Institute for Cultural Inquiry, which he has led since 2007. He received a PhD in theoretical physics (1993) and another one in German literature (2001). He has run several projects at the ICI Berlin and (co-)edited several volumes, including *Tension/Spannung* (2010), *Multistable Figures* (2014), *De/Constituting Wholes* (2017), *Re-* (2019), and *Weathering* (2020).

Maria José de Abreu is assistant professor of anthropology at Columbia University and the author of numerous articles as well as the monograph *The Charismatic Gymnasium: Breath, Media, and Religious Revivalism in Contemporary Brazil* (2021). She received her PhD from the University of Amsterdam and has been a postdoctoral fellow at the Forum Transregionale Studien, the ICI Berlin, and the international research centre 'Re:Work — Work and Human Lifecylcle in Global History' at the Humboldt-Universität zu Berlin. Her work engages with a range of anthropological, philosophical, and literary debates about religion, temporality, movement, personhood, the human senses and their technological extensions, with a special focus on logics of the political in current neoliberal governance, media, and right-wing populism.

Preciosa de Joya's work focuses on Southeast Asian philosophy and intellectual history. She has a degree in philosophy from Ateneo de Manila University (MA on Walter Benjamin, 2006) and Southeast Asian Studies from the National University of Singapore (PhD thesis 'In Search of Filipino Philosophy', 2013). She is currently a lecturer at the Singapore University of Social Sciences after having taught at Ateneo de Manila for a number of years.

Ewa Majewska is a feminist philosopher of culture. She received her PhD from the University of Warsaw and has taught at the University of Warsaw, the Jagiellonian University in Cracow, and the Academy of Art in Szczecin. She has been a postdoctoral fellow at the Institute of Human Sciences (IWM) in Vienna (2013–14) and at the ICI Berlin (2014–16, 2019–20). She has published many articles in, among others, *e-flux*, *Signs*, *Third Text*, and *Jacobin*, as well as numerous books, among them *Feminist Antifascism: Counterpublics of the Common* (2021). She recently contributed to *Unchaining Solidarity: On Mutual Aid and Anarchism with Catherine Malabou* (2021).

Clara Masnatta received a PhD from Harvard University and the Humboldt-Universität zu Berlin. She is an independent curator, scholar, and author based in Berlin and Buenos Aires. She is the author of *Gisèle Freund: Photography on the Stage* (2022, forthcoming) and has contributed to *'Disassembled Images': Allan Sekula and Contemporary Art* (2019); *La cámara como método. La fotografía moderna de Grete Stern y Horacio Coppola* (2021); *About Raymond Williams* (2010); and the publication for Rinko Kawauchi's retrospective at the Kunst Haus Wien in 2015. She curated the exhibition *Gisèle Freund: Exposición-Espectáculo* at the Museo Sívori in Buenos Aires, in cooperation with the IMEC, Institut Français, and INA in France. Masnatta was a fellow at the ICI Berlin (2014–16, affiliated 2016–18). She was a guest curator at the Museum of Modern Art of Buenos Aires (2014–17) and is currently associated with the Museo Evita — Instituto Nacional de Investigaciones Históricas Eva Perón.

Arnd Wedemeyer earned his PhD from the Humanities Center at Johns Hopkins University, and taught at Princeton and Duke University before joining the ICI Berlin, as fellow, then as senior researcher, and finally as the founding editor of ICI Berlin Press. His research focuses on continental philosophy, comparative literature, and art and cultural history. He has published on Kant, Kafka, Jacob Taubes and Carl Schmitt, Jorge Luis Borges and Mynona, Joseph Beuys and Catherine Malabou. He has co-edited *Re-: An Errant Glossary* (2018), Claude Lefort, *Dante's Modernity: An Introduction to the 'Monarchia'. With an Essay by Judith Revel* (2020), and *Weathering: Ecologies of Exposure* (2020).

Zairong Xiang is the author of *Queer Ancient Ways: A Decolonial Exploration* (2018) and assistant professor of comparative literature and associate director of art at Duke Kunshan University. He was chief curator of the 'minor cosmopolitan weekend' at Berlin's Haus der Kulturen der Welt and edited its catalogue *minor cosmopolitan: Thinking Art, Politics, and the Universe Together Otherwise* (2020). His research intersects feminisms and queer theories, literary and visual studies, philosophical and religious inquiries in their decolonial variants in Spanish, English, Chinese, French, and Nahuatl. A member of the Hyperimage Group, he co-curated the 2021 Guangzhou Image Triennial. His current projects deal with the concepts of 'transdualism' and 'shanzhai/counterfeit' in the Global South, especially Latin America and China. www.xiangzairong.com

Index

Abbas, Ackbar 87 n. 35, 88 n. 37, 89
Abbuya, Elisha ben 216, 217
Agamben, Giorgio 2 n. 3, 68 n. 43, 179, 180
Akerman, Chantal 85
Albers, Josef 145
Althusser, Louis 171, 179
Amaro, António 137 n. 23, 140
Antonioni, Michelangelo 83, 84
Arendt, Hannah 135
Aristotle 21, 52, 54 n. 9, 57, 63, 67, 189, 193
Azoulay, Ariella 156
Bachelard, Gaston 43, 44 n. 64
Bakhtin, Mikhail 21, 22, 40
Bandarra, Gonçalo Anes 117, 118 n. 6
Barthes, Roland 88, 148, 149, 152, 156
Baudrillard, Jean 148
Beattie, James 53
Becker, A. L. 19, 21, 34
Beckett, Samuel 1
Bekaert, Geert 103 n. 18, 104
Benjamin, Walter 82, 100, 142 n. 3, 145 n. 11
Bennis, Warren 12, 14
Bergson, Henri 49, 59, 62–66, 69 n. 43, 73, 95
Berkovits, Rabbi Eliezer 204, 205
Berlant, Lauren 2
Berro, Rania 88
Bikont, Anna 195
Blanchot, Maurice 39, 40, 43
Boltanski, Luc 13, 14
Bordeleau, Erik 172

Brehm, Alfred Elmut 93 n. 1
Brod, Max 94 n. 3, 112
Brown, William 92
Bujak, Zbigniew 181
Butler, Judith 152 n. 24, 180
Canguilhem, Georges 10
Cartier-Bresson, Henri 143, 145
Chiapello, Ève 13, 14
Chow, Rey 171
Christensen, Clayton 11, 14
Clark, Marshall 28, 29
Coelho, Pedro Passos 130
Conselheiro, António 117 n. 5
Cooper, Melinda 136 n. 21, 137
Cutting, James 81
Deleuze, Gilles 10, 11 n. 25, 172, 178, 183, 196–198
Demoris, Emmanuelle 16, 76–80, 87–91
Demos, T. J. 79, 80 n. 11
Derrida, Jacques 37, 40, 42, 98, 101 n. 16, 223 n. 23
Descartes, René 43, 52, 58, 62, 108–111
Diaz, Lav 92
Doane, Mary Ann 82
Dodziuk, Anna 195
Duda-Gwiazda, Joanna 195
Durkheim, Émile 14
Dymant, Dora 112
D'Orey, Inês 17, 113, 114, 117 n. 5, 119, 121, 134, 140
Edelman, Lee 163
Edjade, Ntone 80
Eisenman, Peter 95 n. 5, 98 n. 10
Emha Ainun Nadjib 28
Eshun, Kodwo 79

Ferraz, Artur Ivens 138
Ferro, António 138
Fidelis, Małgorzata 195, 196
Foucault, Michel 184, 185 n. 21
Fraser, Nancy 178, 192, 193
Freedberg, David 148
Freud, Sigmund 53, 54, 55 n. 13, 56, 64 n. 32, 191
Fudge, Erica 57
Furth, Charlotte 166
Geertz, Hildred 33
Genet, Jean 79
Germano, William 5 n. 13, 6, 7
Giorno, John 84
Glissant, Édouard 11 n. 25, 29 n. 25, 78–80, 177, 178, 183
Godard, Jean-Luc 84–86
Goenawan Mohamad 29
Goethe, Johann Wolfgang von 110, 111, 153
Gremmen, Hans 143, 144
Grosz, Elizabeth 95
Gruault, Jean 76
Guattari, Felix 11 n. 25
Guattari, Félix 178, 183, 196–198
Gumbrecht, Hans Ulrich 152, 153
Habermas, Jürgen 178, 189, 191–194
Haraway, Donna J. 10 n. 24, 177
Hardt, Michael 180
Havel, Václav 178–181, 199
Heidegger, Martin 36, 37, 39
Henderson, Brian 84, 85 n. 29
Hobbes, Thomas 51, 52, 54, 60, 62, 67
Huillet, Danièle 84
Husserl, Edmund 150
Inandiak, Elizabeth 45, 46
Indiana, Robert 84
Irigaray, Luce 191, 191 n. 39

Itzhaqi, Rabbi Shlomo 'Rashi' 210
Janion, Maria 182
Joubert, Laurent 57, 58, 62
Kafka, Franz 16, 93–112
Kant, Immanuel 53, 56, 57 n. 18
Karatani, Kojin 107, 108
Kawauchi, Rinko 17, 141–158
Keeler, Ward 26, 32
Kluge, Alexander 178, 181, 191, 192
Kondratowicz, Ewa 194 n. 49, 195
Krochmal, Nachman 217–224, 227, 231
Krzywonos, Henryka 194
Kula, Witold 185
Kundera, Milan 187
La Bruyère, Louis-Claude Chéron de 65
La Mettrie, Julien Offray de 58
Labiche, Eugène Marin 65
Labuda, Barbara 195
Laqueur, Thomas 166
Lévi-Strauss, Claude 68
Lima, Tânia Stolze 68
Liotta, Ray 72
Love, Heather 78 n. 7
Luczywo, Helena 195
Luxemburg, Rosa 177
Lysloff, René 21
MacDougall, David 81–83
Malowist, Marian 185
Margulies, Ivone 83 n. 22, 84, 85
Maridjan 44–47
Martin, Lesley A. 144
Marx, Karl 192
Matoso, José 119
Matynia, Elżbieta 191
Meir, Rabbi Samuel ben 'Rashbam' 210, 211
Melville, Herman 2 n. 2

INDEX

Minh-ha, Trinh T. 90, 91 n. 44
Mitchell, W. J. T. 188
Molière 65–67
Morreall, John 51 n. 1, 52 n. 2, 53, 69, 70
Muehlebach, Andrea 120, 132
Mulyono, Sri 30
Nano Riantiarno 28
Nanus, Burt 12, 14
Negri, Antonio 180
Negt, Oskar 178, 181, 191, 192
Nietzsche, Friedrich 35, 38, 188 n. 32
Offe, Claus 185
Ost, David 199, 199 n. 58
Otolith Group 79
Pasley, Malcolm 112
Pasolini, Pier Paolo 88
Paul 68, 215 n. 14
Pausacker, Helen 27, 28, 28 n. 23
Peck, Jamie 134
Pemberton, John 27, 30 n. 28
Penn, Shana 194 n. 49, 195
Pereira, Pedro Teotónio 136, 137
Pesci, Joe 72
Pessoa, Fernando 79, 118 n. 6, 119
Pieńkowska, Alina 194
Plater, Emilia 195
Plato 15, 35–39, 54 n. 9, 62, 89 n. 40, 98 n. 10, 223 n. 23
Powell, Helen 82
Pramoedya, Ananta Toer 26
Preciado, Paul Beatriz 166
Purdy, Daniel 108 n. 39, n. 40, 109, 110
Rabasa, José 172, 173
Racine, Jean 65
Rancière, Jacques 178, 180, 189–191, 198

Rautzenberg, Markus 148 n. 15, 150
Regulska, Elzbieta 195
Renger-Patzsch, Albert 144 n. 9
Riabczuk, Mykoła 182
Ricchi, Rafael Immanuel Chay ben Abraham 217, 218 n. 18
Rivette, Jacques 76
Rosas, Fernando 135
Rossellini, Roberto 83
Rousseau, Jean-Jacques 190
Sagar, Anjalika 79
Salazar, António de Oliveira 16, 130, 131, 135–139
Salt, Barry 81
Scholette, Gregory 191
Schopenhauer, Arthur 53
Schumpeter, Joseph 11, 12
Scorsese, Martin 72 n. 47
Sebastian, King of Portugal 17, 115–119, 132–134
Serres, Michel 10
Shaftesbury, Anthony Ashley Cooper, Third Earl of 53, 55
Siegel, James 33, 34
Silva, Cavaco 122 n. 13
Simmel, Georg 16, 100, 101, 104, 106
Sindhunata 28, 29
Socrates 34, 35, 38, 54, 104
Sowa, Janek 199
Spencer, Herbert 53, 55, 56, 58, 62
Spivak, Gayatri Chakravorty 173, 180, 185, 187
Staniszewska, Grażyna 195
Staniszkis, Jadwiga 193–195
Stengers, Isabelle 172
Straub, Jean-Marie 84
Suharto 25, 25 n. 12, 27, 28

Sumastuti Sumukti 30
Szczesna, Joanna 195
Tomisawa, Haruko 157
Tristuti Rachmadi Suryasaputra 23, 25
Truffaut, Francois 76
Tschumi, Bernard 98 n. 10
Valéry, Paul 16, 100, 102–104
Vitruvius 105–107
Viveiros de Castro, Eduardo 68
Vogl, Joseph 89
Walentynowicz, Anna 181, 189, 194
Wallerstein, Immanuel 185–187
Warhol, Andy 84–86
Weber, Max 12, 14
Weber, Samuel 35, 36, 38, 39 n. 54
Webster, Peter 7–9
Weifenbach, Terri 143
Weigand, Hermann J. 93 n. 1, 112
Wigley, Mark 105
Wilde, Oscar 163
Wojciechowicz, Joanna 195
Wujec, Ludwika 195
Wynter, Sylvia 61
Xu, Lizhi 174, 175
Zavattini, Cesare 83, 84, 86
Zunz, Leopold 217, 219 n. 21
Zuromskis, Catherine 155
Žižek, Slavoj 171, 179

Cultural Inquiry

EDITED BY CHRISTOPH F. E. HOLZHEY
AND MANUELE GRAGNOLATI

VOL. 1   TENSION/SPANNUNG
Edited by Christoph F. E. Holzhey

VOL. 2   METAMORPHOSING DANTE
Appropriations, Manipulations, and Rewritings
in the Twentieth and Twenty-First Centuries
Edited by Manuele Gragnolati, Fabio Camilletti,
and Fabian Lampart

VOL. 3   PHANTASMATA
Techniken des Unheimlichen
Edited by Fabio Camilletti, Martin Doll, and Rupert Gaderer

VOL. 4   Boris Groys / Vittorio Hösle
DIE VERNUNFT AN DIE MACHT
Edited by Luca Di Blasi and Marc Jongen

VOL. 5   Sara Fortuna
WITTGENSTEINS PHILOSOPHIE DES KIPPBILDS
Aspektwechsel, Ethik, Sprache

VOL. 6   THE SCANDAL OF SELF-CONTRADICTION
Pasolini's Multistable Subjectivities, Geographies, Traditions
Edited by Luca Di Blasi, Manuele Gragnolati,
and Christoph F. E. Holzhey

VOL. 7   SITUIERTES WISSEN
UND REGIONALE EPISTEMOLOGIE
Zur Aktualität Georges Canguilhems und Donna J. Haraways
Edited by Astrid Deuber-Mankowsky
and Christoph F. E. Holzhey

VOL. 8   MULTISTABLE FIGURES
On the Critical Potentials of Ir/Reversible Aspect-Seeing
Edited by Christoph F. E. Holzhey

VOL. 9   Wendy Brown / Rainer Forst
THE POWER OF TOLERANCE
Edited by Luca Di Blasi and Christoph F. E. Holzhey

Vol. 10   DENKWEISEN DES SPIELS
Medienphilosophische Annäherungen
Edited by Astrid Deuber-Mankowsky and Reinhold Görling

Vol. 11   DE/CONSTITUTING WHOLES
Towards Partiality Without Parts
Edited by Manuele Gragnolati and Christoph F. E. Holzhey

Vol. 12   CONATUS UND LEBENSNOT
Schlüsselbegriffe der Medienanthropologie
Edited by Astrid Deuber-Mankowsky and Anna Tuschling

Vol. 13   AURA UND EXPERIMENT
Naturwissenschaft und Technik bei Walter Benjamin
Edited by Kyung-Ho Cha

Vol. 14   Luca Di Blasi
DEZENTRIERUNGEN
Beiträge zur Religion der Philosophie im 20. Jahrhundert

Vol. 15   RE-
An Errant Glossary
Edited by Christoph F. E. Holzhey and Arnd Wedemeyer

Vol. 16   Claude Lefort
DANTE'S MODERNITY
An Introduction to the Monarchia
With an Essay by Judith Revel
Translated from the French by Jennifer Rushworth
Edited by Christiane Frey, Manuele Gragnolati,
Christoph F. E. Holzhey, and Arnd Wedemeyer

Vol. 17   WEATHERING
Ecologies of Exposure
Edited by Christoph F. E. Holzhey and Arnd Wedemeyer

Vol. 18   Manuele Gragnolati and Francesca Southerden
POSSIBILITIES OF LYRIC
Reading Petrarch in Dialogue

Vol. 19   THE WORK OF WORLD LITERATURE
Edited by Francesco Giusti and Benjamin Lewis Robinson

Vol. 20   MATERIALISM AND POLITICS
Edited by Bernardo Bianchi, Emilie Filion-Donato,
Marlon Miguel, and Ayşe Yuva

Vol. 21   OVER AND OVER AND OVER AGAIN
          Reenactment Strategies in Contemporary Arts and Theory
          Edited by Cristina Baldacci, Clio Nicastro,
          and Arianna Sforzini

Vol. 22   QUEERES KINO / QUEERE ÄSTHETIKEN
          ALS DOKUMENTATIONEN DES PREKÄREN
          Edited by Astrid Deuber-Mankowsky
          and Philipp Hanke

Vol. 23   OPENNESS IN MEDIEVAL EUROPE
          Edited by Manuele Gragnolati
          and Almut Suerbaum

Vol. 24   ERRANS
          Going Astray, Being Adrift, Coming to Nothing
          Edited by Christoph F. E. Holzhey
          and Arnd Wedemeyer

Vol. 25   THE CASE FOR REDUCTION
          Edited by Christoph F. E. Holzhey
          and Jakob Schillinger